The Foreign Language Teacher's

IN

SPANISH VERSIONS 2 AND 3

Mario Toglia
Patricia A. Lennon

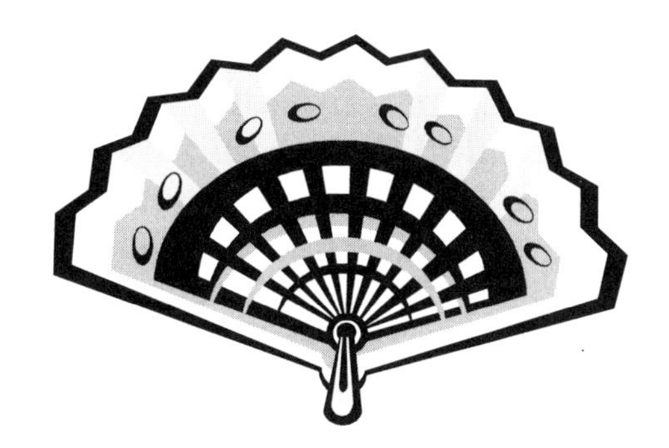

Language Consultants:
John Christianson
Maria Puccio

Graphics:
John Christianson

ISBN 1-879279-34-7

Proficiency Press Company
18 Lucille Avenue, Elmont, NY 11003
1 888 744 8363

Cover design by B. Soll Design, Inc.

BOOKS BY PROFICIENCY PRESS

The Teacher's Handbook: Aiming for Proficiency in French
Teacher's Handbook: Aiming for Proficiency in German
Teacher's Handbook: Aiming for Proficiency in Italian
Teacher Handbook: Aiming for Proficiency in Spanish
Portfolio Assessment Tasks for the Beginning Level (All Languages)
Authentic Assessment for the Intermediate Level in Spanish
Authentic Assessment for the Intermediate Level in French
C'est Ton Tour, Aiming for Proficiency in French
Du Bist Dran, Aiming for Proficiency in German
Te Toca a Ti, Aiming for Proficiency in Spanish
Te Toca a Ti, Audio Cassette in Spanish
Tocca a Te, Aiming for Proficiency in Italian
It's Your Turn to Speak English (ESL)
Hallo! Hier Bin Ich!
¡Hola Soy Yo!
Ciao! Sono Io!
Salut! C'est Moi!
Suivez-Moi, Aiming for Proficiency in French
Seguimi, Aiming for Proficiency in Italian
Sígueme, Aiming for Proficiency in Spanish
The Intermediate Student Activity Book
Internet Tasks for Second Language Students (All Languages)
The Teacher's Guide for the NYS Foreign Language Proficiency Exam
The Writing Tasks Guide for the Updated NYS Regents Exam In LOTE

Printed in the USA

ABOUT THE AUTHORS

Mr. Mario Toglia (BS in French, Fordham University School of Education; MA in French, Brooklyn College) has taken graduate courses at the McGill University Ecole Française d'Eté in Montreal and Fordham University. Mr. Toglia was a teacher in the New York City school system for 35 years and taught French, Spanish and Italian at Shell Bank Junior High School in Brooklyn. He co-authored the Scope and Sequence Handbook for Foreign Language Teachers for NYC District 22 and has presented numerous workshops in communicative techniques. Mr. Toglia is an ESL instructor for the Sewanhaka Central High School District and teaches an enrichment program in Spanish for the Elmont UFSD on Long Island.

Ms. Patricia Lennon (BA in Spanish, Molloy College; MA in Spanish, St. John's University; "Teacher of the Year," Sewanhaka High School District; two AATSP scholarships; finalist as "Teacher of the Year for New York State"; Embassy of Spain Scholarship, Salamanca, Spain) Ms. Lennon is a teacher of Spanish, the Chairperson of Foreign Languages at Elmont Memorial High School and the Coordinator of Foreign Languages for the Sewanhaka Central High School District. She co-authored *Sewanhaka Central High School District's Curriculum Guides* for Spanish and co-authored Proficiency Press publications: *The Teacher's Handbook in Spanish, Te Toca A Ti, Portfolio Assessment for the Beginning Level, Sígueme, Authentic Assessment for the Intermediate Level*, and *It's Your Turn to Speak English*. She has created and taught a BOCES sponsored job related Spanish course for teachers and administrators. Ms. Lennon is a presenter of workshops on language proficiency, methodology and authentic assessment. She is an adjunct lecturer for Adelphi University and teaches the AP Course in Spanish Language. She is a member of the AATSP (past president of the Long Island Chapter and past newsletter editor), LILT and NYSAFLT. She is currently writing her doctoral thesis and plans to complete her doctoral program this year.

Mr. John G. Christianson has a Bachelor's Degree in Spanish from Hunter College, CUNY, a Masters Degree in Teaching of Spanish from Queens College, CUNY, and has completed his coursework for a Masters Degree in Educational Administration from Touro College. He has also studied at the Universidad Complutense de Madrid in Spain. He is currently working as a teacher of Spanish in Floral Park Memorial High School of the Sewanhaka Central High School District. He has presented workshops on the use of technology in the foreign language classroom, and communicative techniques for teaching foreign language. He has also co-authored laboratory manuals for third year Spanish, and for a pilot FLEX program for the Sewanhaka Central High School District. Mr. Christianson has co-authored The Writing Tasks Guide for the Updated NYS Regents Exam in LOTE. He is currently a member of NYSAFLT, LILT, AATSP and FLACS.

INTRODUCTION

The Foreign Language Teacher's Handbook
IN SPANISH VERSIONS 2 AND 3

The Foreign Language Teacher's Handbook: in Spanish Versions 2 and 3 is a novice level assessment guide written independently by teachers for their colleagues.

Since 1989, our growing team of world language teachers has dedicated itself to creating practical, easy-to-use communicative materials for the proficiency-driven classroom. Our aim is foreign language proficiency for every student in the class.

Each topically oriented chapter of ***The Foreign Language Teacher's Handbook in Spanish Versions 2 and 3*** includes two original proficiency style assessments for each of the thirteen topics. There are twenty-six tests in all.

The Foreign Language Teacher's Handbook series may be used to enhance a pre-existing program of instruction, or in conjunction with student texts: *C'est Ton Tour* (French), *Du Bist Dran* (German), *Toca a Te* (Italian) and *Te Toca a Ti* (Spanish).

Consistent with the National Standards, ***The Foreign Language Teacher's Handbook in Spanish*** **Versions 2 and 3** facilitates teaching by providing a more efficient focus on what is really needed for successful assessment of the student's foreign language proficiency.

ACKNOWLEDGMENTS

We are grateful to the following people for their assistance in the creation and publication of this book:

For his guidance: Walter Kleinmann

For his technical assistance: John Christianson,

For artwork: John Christianson

For their understanding and support, we give special thanks to our families.

FOREIGN LANGUAGE TEACHER'S HANDBOOK IN SPANISH
VERSIONS 2 AND 3

TABLE OF CONTENTS

WRITING TASK RUBRIC

	4	3	2	1
Objective/ Task	Fulfills the task, uses appropriate ideas and presents ideas in a logical sequence.	Fulfills the task by using mostly relevant ideas.	Fulfills the task but there are some irrelevancies.	Makes at least one statement, which fulfills the task.
Vocabulary	Uses a full range of level appropriate nouns, verbs and adjectives. Uses relevant words to expand the topic.	Uses a variety of relevant and appropriate vocabulary to address the task.	Uses vocabulary that is sometimes not appropriate or relevant to the task.	Uses limited vocabulary, which is often inappropriate for the task.
Structure	Demonstrates a high degree of control of structure. - subject verb agreement - noun/adjective agreement - correct word order -spelling Errors **do not** impede the comprehensibility of the passage.	Demonstrates some control of structure. - subject verb agreement - noun/adjective agreement - correct word order -spelling Errors **do not** impede the comprehensibility of the passage.	Demonstrates inaccuracies in the control of structure. - subject verb agreement - noun/adjective agreement - correct word order -spelling Errors **do** impede the comprehensibility of the passage.	Exhibits little control of structure. Errors hinder overall comprehensibility of passage.
Word Count Names of people and English products do not count. (K-Mart, Pepsi)	Utilizes 30 or more comprehensible words in the target language that develop the task. (20+) Chapters 1-5	Utilizes 25-29 comprehensible words in the target language that develop the task. (15-19) Chapters 1-5	Utilizes 20-24 comprehensible words in the target language that develop the task. (10-14) Chapters 1-5	Utilizes 15-19 comprehensible words in the target language that develop the task. (5-9) Chapters 1-5

***For compositions of 20 words, use the word count in parenthesis.**

Student Name ____ **Date** __________

Writing Tasks Checklist

Refer to the Writing Rubrics for an explanation of each category.

	4	3	2	1	0
Objective • Satisfies the task's objective • Uses appropriate ideas • Presents ideas in a logical sequence					
Vocabulary • Uses level appropriate nouns, verbs and adjectives • Uses a variety of relevant words					
Structure • Subject/verb agreement • Noun/adjective agreement • Correct word order • Spelling					
Word Count • Comprehensible • In target language • Appropriate for the task	**30+** **(20+)**	**25-29** **(15-19)**	**20-24** **(10-14)**	**15-19** **(5-9)**	**<15** **(<5)**

For compositions of 20 words use the word count in parenthesis.

Total Raw Score	
Final Task Score	

Conversion Chart

14 - 16 = 10
11 - 13 = 8
8 - 10 = 6
5 - 7 = 4
2 - 4 = 2
0 - 1 = 0

HANDBOOK 2

Thirteen Complete Proficiency Tests
by Topic

PERSONAL IDENTIFICATION

PERSONAL IDENTIFICATION 2

PERSONAL IDENTIFICATION 2

TEACHER'S SCRIPT FOR THE EXAM, PART II (Listening, 30%)

Part 2a Directions: For each question, you will hear some background information in English. Then you will hear a passage in Spanish twice, followed by a question in English. Listen carefully. After you have heard the question, read the question and the four suggested answers. Choose the best answer and write its number in the appropriate space on your answer sheet. (9%)

1. You are with your mother at the doctor's office. Your mother wants to correct an error that appeared on an insurance form. She is speaking to the secretary and she says:

   Perdón, señorita. La fecha de nacimiento de mi hijo no es el once de mayo. Su cumpleaños es el cinco de noviembre.

   What is incorrect on the insurance form? (4)

2. Your mother is talking to you about her friend. She says:

   Susana es una persona sincera. Ella es paciente, generosa y simpática. Es una buena amiga.

   What is your mother describing about her friend? (3)

3. Hector is telling you about his cousins. He says:

   Tengo tres primas y un primo. Mi prima Rosa tiene el pelo largo y es rubia. Mis primas Lucía y Patricia tienen el pelo corto. Ellas son morenas. Mi primo Alberto tiene el pelo corto también. El es pelirrojo.

   Which cousin has red hair? (1)

Part 2b Directions: For each question, you will hear some background information in English. Then you will hear a passage in Spanish twice, followed by a question in Spanish. Listen carefully. After you hear the question, read the question and the four suggested answers. Choose the best answer and write its number in the appropriate space on your answer sheet. (9%)

4. Pedro's brother got married last week. He is telling you about his sister-in-law. He says:

   La esposa de mi hermano se llama Luisa. Ella nació en la ciudad de Madrid, en España. Habla español, naturalmente. Habla inglés muy bien. Ella es profesora de inglés en Madrid.

   ¿Cuál es la nacionalidad de Luisa? (4)

5. Your pen pal from Puerto Rico is describing his sister. He says:

   Mi hermana es una muchacha muy bonita. Es morena. No es gorda.
   Es muy delgada. Estudia mucho y es muy inteligente .

   ¿Cómo es la hermana de tu amigo? (3)

6. While on vacation in Florida, you meet a Hispanic boy. He says:

   Yo soy puertorriqueño. Yo hablo inglés y español. Nací en San Juan, la capital de Puerto Rico. Ahora vivo en el estado de Nueva York. Me gusta mucho jugar al fútbol y al básquetbol.

   ¿De dónde es el muchacho? (2)

Part 2c Directions: For each question, you will hear some background information in English. Then you will hear a passage in Spanish twice, followed by a question in English. Listen carefully. After you have heard the question, read the question and look at the four pictures on your test. Choose the picture that best answers the question and write its number in the appropriate space on your answer sheet. (12%)

7. You are in the main office at school. You hear two people talking. This is the conversation.

   - Buenos días, señora?
   - Buenos días, señor.
   - Me llamo Señor Rivera. Yo soy el padre de Juanito. ¿Y Ud.?
   - Yo soy Señora Martinez. Soy la profesora de matemáticas de su hijo.

   Which two persons are having the conversation? (1)

8. You are in a department store in Lima, Peru. You saw someone steal a watch from a showcase. You are now describing the person you saw to the security guard. You say:

   La señora no es jóven. Es muy vieja. El pelo es gris y corto.
   Es gorda y muy alta.

   Which of the following might be the thief? (2)

9. Your friend talks to you about what he does during winter recess. He says:

   Me gustan mucho los deportes. En febrero, me gusta esquiar. Esquío muy bien.

   What does this person do during winter recess? (4)

10. You are helping Maria choose a gift for her mother in a bookstore. She says:

    A mi madre le gusta leer. No le gusta ni cocinar ni viajar. Odia mirar la televisión. Mi madre es muy atlética. Le gusta mucho jugar deportes.

    Which book might you suggest that Maria buy? (2)

Listening Comprehension answers:
For all chapters, the answers are indicated in parentheses following each question.

Reading Comprehension:

3a. (8%) 11. __2__ 12. __4__ 13. __3__ 14. __2__
3b. (12%) 15. __3__ 16. __3__ 17. __4__ 18. __1__

PERSONAL IDENTIFICATION 2

Nombre ______________________________ Fecha ____________________

EXAMINATION

Part 1 SPEAKING (30%)
Part 2 LISTENING (30%)

Part 2a Directions: For each question, you will hear some background information in English. Then you will hear a passage in Spanish twice, followed by a question in English. Listen carefully. After you have heard the question, read the question and the four suggested answers. Choose the best answer and write its number in the appropriate space on your answer sheet. (9%)

1. What is incorrect on the insurance form?
   1. an address
   2. a zip code
   3. a telephone number
   4. a birth date

2. What is your mother describing about her friend?
   1. things that she dislikes
   2. her physical traits
   3. her personality traits
   4. her favorite activities

3. Which cousin has red hair?
   1. Alberto
   2. Lucía
   3. Rosa
   4. Patricia

Part 2b Directions: For each question, you will hear some background information in English. Then you will hear a passage in Spanish twice, followed by a question in Spanish. Listen carefully. After you hear the question, read the question and the four suggested answers. Choose the best answer and write its number in the appropriate space on your answer sheet. (9%)

4. ¿Cuál es la nacionalidad de Luisa?
   1. norteamericana
   2. italiana
   3. alemana
   4. española

5. ¿Cómo es la hermana de tu amigo?
   1. rubia
   2. gorda
   3. muy flaca
   4. tonta

6. ¿De dónde es el muchacho?
   1. Italia
   2. Puerto Rico
   3. la ciudad de San Francisco
   4. el estado de Nuevo México

Part 2c Directions: For each question, you will hear some background information in English. Then you will hear a passage in Spanish twice, followed by a question in English. Listen carefully. After you have heard the question, read the question and look at the 4 pictures on your test. Choose the picture that best answers the question and write its number in the appropriate space on your answer sheet. (12%)

7. Which two persons are having the conversation?

8. Which of the following persons might be the thief?

9. What does this person do during winter recess?

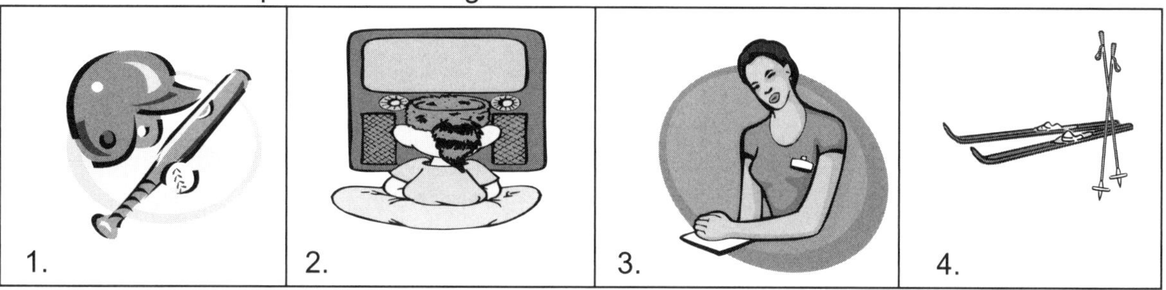

10. Which book might you suggest that Maria buy?

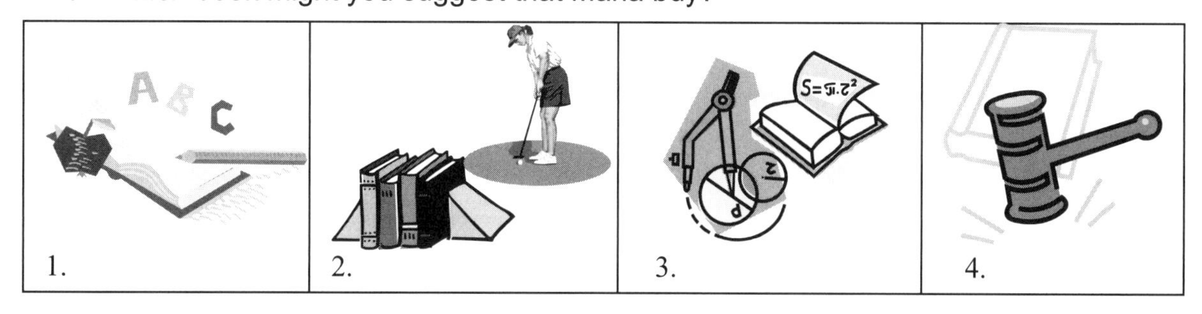

PERSONAL IDENTIFICATION 2

Part 3a Directions: Answer the question in English based on the reading selection in Spanish. Choose the best answer to each question. Base your choice on the content of the reading selection. Write the number of your answer in the appropriate space on your answer sheet. (8%)

REUNION DE LA FAMILIA MARTINEZ

Fecha: sábado, el 10 de marzo
Hora: desde las diez hasta las seis
Donde: El Parque Cinco Islas
San Juan
Teléfono: 453-7852

11. On what day of the week is this event?
1. Sunday
2. Saturday
3. Tuesday
4. Thursday

Yo estoy muy bien porque me gusta comer vegetales y frutas

12. What does this advertisement suggest you do?
1. visit a doctor
2. brush one's teeth every day
3. visit a farm
4. eat healthy

SOLICITUD DE EMPLEO

A. Nombre y Apellido *Juan Vargas*
B. Dirección *46 Calle San Martin*
C. Ciudad *Buenos Aires*
D. Fecha de nacimiento *el 5 de enero de 1980*
E. País de nacimiento *Argentina*
F. Intereses *la música latinoamericana, viajar, bailar*

13. Which item on this form do you fill out to say where you were born?
1. (B) 2. (C) 3. (E) 4. (F)

De: hotellima@aol.com
A: jmwt6@juno.com
Fecha: viernes, el 12 de junio de 2002 18:26:29 -0400
Objeto: dirección de tu primo

Querida Juanita,
Perú es un país magnífico. Me gustan mucho los monumentos incas. Mañana voy a San Pedro de Lloc, el pueblo donde vive tu primo Eduardo. Quiero visitarlo.
Por favor, ¿Cuál es la dirección de tu primo?
Saludos,
Valentina

14. What is Valentina requesting in this e-mail message ?
    1. money
    2. someone's address
    3. travel directions to a particular museum
    4. a homework assignment on Peru

Part 3b Directions: Answer the question in Spanish based on the reading selection in Spanish. Choose the best answer to each question. Base your choice on the content of the reading selection. Write the number of your answer in the appropriate space on your answer sheet (12%).

CENSO DE 1930

Apellido y nombre	Relación	Edad	Profesión
García Torres, Juan	padre	45	pianista
Ortiz Marcos, Marta	madre	43	ama de casa
García Ortiz, Teresa	hija	13	estudiante
García Ortiz, Oscar	hijo	11	estudiante
Giraldo Ortega, Bernardo	esposo	30	doctor
Ponce Gómez, Norma	esposa	26	secretaria

15. ¿Cuántos años tiene Bernardo?

    1. doce 2. veinte 3. treinta 4. trece

16. ¿Quién toca un instrumento musical en su profesión?
    1. Bernardo Giraldo Ortega
    2. Oscar García Ortiz
    3. Juan García Torres
    4. Norma Ponce Gómez

Anuncios de Amigos de Correspondencia

Me llamo Roberto. Vivo en Buenos Aires. Tengo catorce años. Mi clase favorita es la clase de cerámica. Me gusta visitar museos en mi ciudad.

Me llamo Carolina. Soy alemana y vivo en Berlin. Quiero una amiga española a quien le gusta leer novelas de detective. Tengo quince años.

Me llamo Arturo. Vivo en Caracas, la capital de Venezuela. Soy atlético y fuerte. Me gusta esquiar, nadar, jugar al volibol y al fútbol. Tengo dieciséis años.

Me llamo Juanita y vivo en Phoenix, Arizona. Quiero una amiga en México que hable inglés. A mi me gusta salir con amigas, viajar, comer comida mexicana. Odio lavar los platos y trabajar en casa. Tengo catorce años.

17. Según los anuncios, ¿quién vive en los Estados Unidos?
    1. Arturo
    2. Roberto
    3. Carolina
    4. Juanita

18. Según los anuncios, ¿a quién le gusta jugar a los deportes?
    1. Arturo
    2. Roberto
    3. Carolina
    4. Juanita

Part 4 Writing (20%)

Part 4 Directions: Choose two of the three writing tasks provided. Your answer to each of the two questions should be written entirely in Spanish and should contain a minimum of **30 words.**

Place names and brand names written in Spanish count as one word. Contractions are counted as one word. Salutations, closings and commonly used abbreviations are included in the word count. Numbers, unless written as words, and names of people do not count as words.

Be sure that you have satisfied the purpose of the task. The sentence structure and /or expressions used should be connected logically and demonstrate a wide range of vocabulary with minimal repetition.

4a. You are the editor-in-chief of the Spanish Club's newspaper. You want one of your club reporters to interview a famous Hispanic person from your community. Write a note to the reporter as to what questions you would like him/her to ask this famous person. You may wish to include questions asking:

- The person's age and birth date
- The place of birth
- The current address including zip code
- What activities this person like to do
- The telephone of his/her office

4b. You are looking for a pen-pal in a Spanish-speaking country. Write an introductory letter describing yourself. You may wish to include:

- Your name, age, birth date
- What you look like
- A description of your personality
- Your likes and dislikes

4c. You have a pen pal in a Spanish speaking country. You are on vacation and have gone to meet him/her. Write a letter to your Spanish teacher describing how you and your pen pal are similar and different. In your letter you may wish to compare:

- Your physical traits
- Your personality traits
- Your interests and preferences for leisure activities
- Your preferences for various celebrities
- What languages you speak

ANSWER SHEET

Nombre y Apellido ______________________________ Fecha ______________

Part I **Speaking** __________ (30%)
Part 2 **Listening (30%)**

2a.	2b.	2c.
1._____	4._____	7._____
2._____	5._____	8._____
3._____	6._____	9._____
		10._____

PART 3: READING (20%)

3a.(8%)	3b.(12%)
11._____	15._____
12._____	16._____
13._____	17._____
14._____	18._____

Part 4 **Writing (20%) 20 words** **Write 2 paragraphs** **4a , 4b or 4c**

1 ____

2 ____

FAMILY

FAMILY LIFE 2

FAMILY LIFE 2

TEACHER'S SCRIPT FOR THE EXAM, PART II (Listening, 30%)

Part 2a Directions: For each question, you will hear some background information in English. Then you will hear a passage in Spanish twice, followed by a question in English. Listen carefully. After you have heard the question, read the question and the four suggested answers. Choose the best answer and write its number in the appropriate space on your answer sheet. (9%)

1. Pablo is describing his brother to you. He says:

   Ricardo es mi hermano mayor. El tiene veinte y siete años. El es alto y moreno. El es amable y simpático. Es profesor de matemáticas y trabaja en un colegio. El también es muy generoso.

   Which comment best describes Pablo's brother? (2)

2. You are in a paint store in Puerto Rico. An elderly man is speaking to the sales clerk. He says:

   Carlos es el esposo de mi hija. Carlos es músico. El toca la guitarra, el piano y también el saxofón. Es un buen esposo. Mañana él va a Miami para un concierto de jazz. .

   What does this man's son-in-law do for a living? (1)

3. Your classmate Alberto is telling you about his favorite relative. He says:

   El hermano de mi madre es mi pariente favorito. Mi Tío Pepe es una persona muy simpática . El es muy generoso con toda la familia. El agosto pasado mi tío Pepe, mi primo Ernesto y yo viajamos a Florida donde visitamos Disney World.

   Who is Alberto's favorite relative? (4)

Part 2b Directions: For each question, you will hear some background information in English. Then you will hear a passage in Spanish twice, followed by a question in Spanish. Listen carefully. After you have heard the question, read the question and the four suggested answers. Choose the best answer and write its number in the appropriate space on your answer sheet (9%).

4. Your friend Maria is calling you from her grandmother's house. She says to you:

   Mi madre está en el hospital con el nuevo bebé. El niño se llama Roberto. El es muy pequeño y adorable.

   ¿De quién habla María? (3)

5. You are in a department store in your neighborhood. You bump into your friend Margarita in the children's department. She is buying a baby rattle. She says to you:

   Tengo un nuevo primo. Se llama Bernardo. El domingo mi familia va a asistir al bautizo de mi nuevo primo. Mi hermana Rosa es la madrina y mi hermano Oscar es el padrino.

   ¿Quién es la madrina del bebé? (3)

6. Your friend Juanita is telling you about her daily routine. She says:

   Todos los días me despierto a las siete de la mañana. Luego me ducho y me visto. Antes de salir de casa, como la comida que mi abuela prepara. Llego a la escuela a las ocho y cuarto.

   ¿ A qué hora se levanta Juanita todos los días? (2)

Part 2c Directions: For each question, you will hear some background information in English. Then you will hear a passage in Spanish twice, followed by a question in English. Listen carefully. After you have heard the question, read the question and look at the four pictures on your test. Choose the picture that best answers the question and write its number in the appropriate space on your answer sheet. (12%)

7. You are at a graduation party. Laura is telling you about her sister Carmen. She says:

   Carmen tiene diecinueve años. Ella es muy estudiosa. En septiembre ella va a asistir a una universidad en el estado de Massachusetts. Ella quiere una bicicleta para viajar en el pueblo y mi padre le va a comprar una bicicleta nueva.

   What will Carmen need to travel for college? (4)

8. Felipe is telling you how his family helps out at home. He says:

   En mi familia mi madre prepara la comida. Mi hermana pone la mesa. Mi padre lava los platos. ¿Y yo? Yo saco la basura.

   What chore does Felipe do at home? (3)

9. You are arriving at your Spanish pen pal's home tomorrow on the noon train. You want to know who will pick you up at the station. Your friend tells you it will be one of her grandparents and the family pet. She describes both to you:

   Mi abuelo es un hombre alto y delgado. El tiene sesenta años. El tiene el pelo corto y gris. El perro es grande. Es blanco y negro también .

   Who is coming to pick you up? (2)

10. Your grandmother is showing you old photographs from her family album. She is describing one photograph to you. She says:

    Esta es mi foto favorita. En la foto mi mamá tiene tres años. Ella está con su madre y las dos abuelas. Se celebra el Día de las Madres.

    Which picture is being described? (3)

Listening Comprehension Answers:
For all chapters, the answers are indicated in parentheses following each question. (See questions 1-10 on the previous pages.)

Reading Comprehension answers:

3a. (8%) 11. __3__ 12. __4__ 13. __4__ 14. __2__

3b. (12%) 15. __1__ 16. __3__ 17. __4__ 18. __1__

FAMILY LIFE 2

Nombre ______________________________ Fecha ____________________

EXAMINATION

Part 1 SPEAKING (30%)
Part 2 LISTENING (30%)

Part 2a Directions: For each question, you will hear some background information in English. Then you will hear a passage in Spanish twice, followed by a question in English. Listen carefully. After you have heard the question, read the question and the four suggested answers. Choose the best answer and write its number in the appropriate space on your answer sheet. (9%)

1. Which comment best describes Pablo's brother?
    1. He works in a bank.
    2. He is very generous.
    3. He is short.
    4. He is thirty-five years old.

2. What does this man's son-in-law do for a living?
    1. He is a musician
    2. He is a university professor
    3. He is a house painter
    4. He is a pilot.

3. Who is Alberto's favorite relative?
    1. his nephew
    2. his mother
    3. his brother
    4. his uncle

Part 2b Directions: For each question, you will hear some background information in English. Then you will hear a passage in Spanish twice, followed by a question in Spanish. Listen carefully. After you have heard the question, read the question and the four suggested answers. Choose the best answer and write its number in the appropriate space on your answer sheet (9%).

4. ¿ De quién habla Maria ?
    1. de su amigo
    2. de su primo
    3. de su hermano
    4. de su doctor

5. ¿Quién es la madrina del bebé?
    1. Margarita
    2. Bernardo
    3. Rosa
    4. Oscar

6. ¿A qué hora se levanta Juanita todos los días?
    1. a las seis
    2. a las siete
    3. a las ocho y media
    4. a las diez y cuarto

Part 2c Directions: For each question, you will hear some background information in English. Then you will hear a passage in Spanish twice, followed by a question in English. Listen carefully. After you have heard the question, read the question and look at the four pictures on your test. Choose the picture that best answers the question and write its number in the appropriate space on your answer sheet. (12%)

7. What will Carmen need to travel for college?

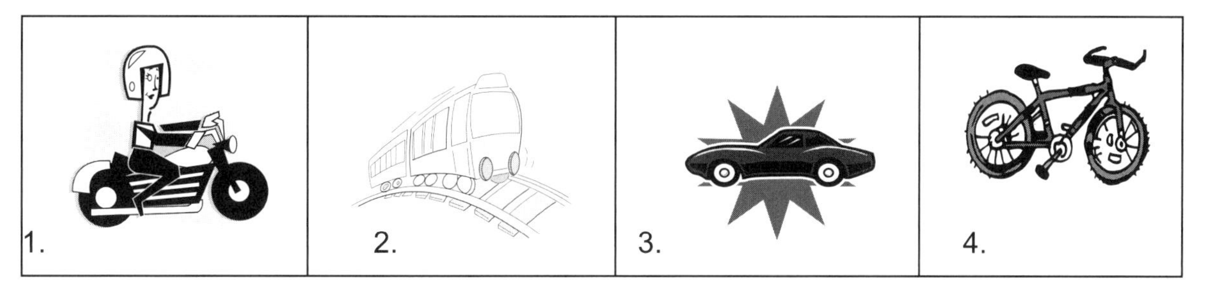

8. What chore does Felipe do?

9. Who is coming to pick you up?

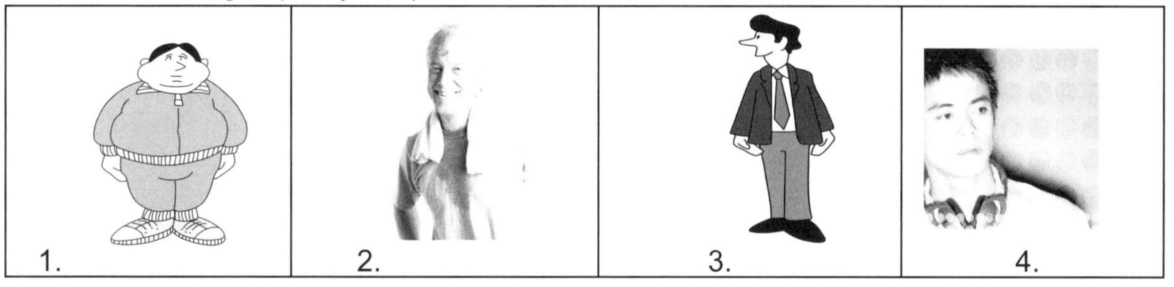

10. Which picture is being described?

Part 3a Directions: Answer the question in English based on the reading selection in Spanish. Choose the best answer to each question. Base your choice on the content of the reading selection. Write the number of your answer in the appropriate space on your answer sheet. (8%)

Las gemelas Olsen son muy famosas. Mary-Kate y Ashley tienen dieciséis años. Ellas son actrices y viven en California con sus padres. Las hermanas tienen el pelo rubio y los ojos azules. Ellas son delgadas y elegantes. Les gusta hacer actividades similares. Les gusta mirar la televisión, nadar y salir con los amigos.

Las dos muchachas prefieren la comida mexicana, especialmente los burritos. Ellas llevan la misma ropa pero en colores diferentes. Mary-Kate prefiere el amarillo, el azul y el blanco. Ashley prefiere los colores violeta, rosado y rojo.

11. According to the magazine article, how old are Mary-Kate and Ashley?
    1. 12 years old
    2. 18 years old
    3. 16 years old
    4. 17 years old

12. Which color is **NOT** one of Mary-Kate´s favorites?
    1. yellow
    2. blue
    3. white
    4. red

UNA ABUELA CONTENTA TE INVITA A UNA FIESTA DE CUMPLEAÑOS

Es la quinceañera de mi única nieta María Beatriz

Cuándo? El viernes, catorce de marzo
de las seis hasta las once
Dónde? En el Hotel San Luis Rey
Calle Hernán Cortés, 100
Guadalajara
Llámame (la abuela feliz) Dorotea Morales
775-8913

13. What is being celebrated?
    1. a national holiday
    2. a retirement
    3. a religious feast
    4. a birthday

14. What is the date of this event?
    1. August 11th
    2. March 14th
    3. September 15th
    4. January 6th

Part 3b Directions: Answer the question in Spanish based on the reading selection in Spanish. Choose the best answer to each question. Base your choice on the content of the reading selection. Write the number of your answer in the appropriate space on your answer sheet. (12%)

El Dentista del Año

El Doctor Vicente Tomaselli fue nombrado "Dentista Argentino del Año". El doctor Tomaselli nació en Italia en 1948. Hace veinte y seis años que él vive en Argentina. El vive ahora en Buenos Aires con su esposa alemana Heidi. Ellos tienen dos hijas y tres hijos. Una hija, Cecilia de Vargas, es también dentista y trabaja con su padre en su clínica dental en el centro.

El Doctor Tomaselli trabaja también en la Universidad de Medicina Dental como profesor de Higiene Oral. Su esposa dice que él es muy inteligente y simpático. El doctor es también atlético. Al doctor le gusta jugar al fútbol y al golf.

15. ¿Qué hace el doctor ?

1. Le gusta jugar a los deportes.
2. Le gusta tocar un instrumento musical.
3. Le gusta dormir.
4. Le gusta cocinar.

16. ¿Cuál es la nacionalidad de la esposa del doctor?

1. española
2. inglesa
3. alemana
4. italiana

CARLOS - m - CARMEN

DAVID - m - JULIA JUAN - m - RAQUEL

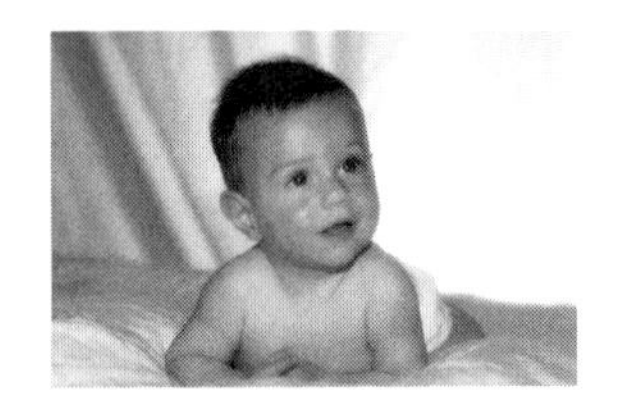

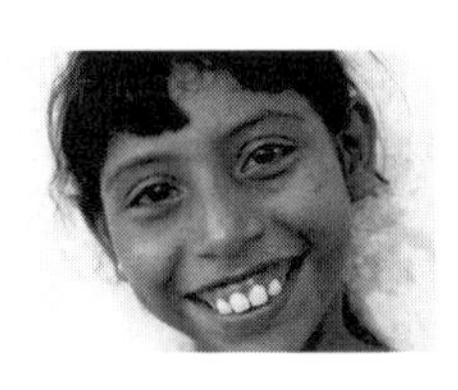

EDUARDO ELISA HECTOR HILDA

17. Según el árbol de familia, ¿quién es el padre de Julia ?
    1.Juan
    2. Carlos
    3. Eduardo
    4. David

18. Según el árbol de familia, ¿quiénes son primas?
    1. Hilda y Elisa
    2. Raquel y Julia
    3. Carmen y Julia
    4. Eduardo y Elisa

Part 4 Writing (20%)

Part 4 Directions: Choose two of the following writing tasks below. Your answer to each of the two questions should be written entirely in Spanish and should contain a minimum of **30 words.**

Place names and brand names written in Spanish count as one word. Contractions are counted as one word. Salutations, closings and commonly used abbreviations are included in the word count. Numbers, unless written as words, and names of people do not count as words.

Be sure that you have satisfied the purpose of the task. The sentence structure and /or expressions used should be connected logically and demonstrate a wide range of vocabulary with minimal repetition.

4a. You are going to appear on a family game show on TV. Write a letter to the director of the program and mention which five members of your family would like to appear. You may wish to include:

- The names of each person and their relationship to you.
- A description of each person's physical traits
- A description of each person's personality.
- What each person likes to do for a living
- What each person likes to do in his or her spare time.

4b. You have a pen pal in Spain. In Spanish, write a note to you pen pal describing what your family does on the weekend. You may wish to include:

- What activities your family does.
- What chores each member of your family does.
- When they do these activities or chores.
- Whether they like or dislike doing these activities.

4c. Your local newspaper is having a contest for Father of the Year. You want to nominate your father as "Father of the Year". Write a letter nominating him. You may wish to include:

- His name
- His occupation
- His physical characteristics
- Qualities about his personality
- Why he should be "Father of the Year."

ANSWER SHEET

Nombre y Apellido ______________________________ Fecha ______________

Part I **Speaking** __________ (30%)
Part 2 **Listening (30%)**

2a.	2b.	2c.
1._____	4._____	7._____
2._____	5._____	8._____
3._____	6._____	9._____
		10._____

PART 3: READING (20%)

3a.(8%)	3b.(12%)
11._____	15._____
12._____	16._____
13._____	17._____
14._____	18._____

Part 4 **Writing (20%) 20 words** **Write 2 paragraphs** **4a , 4b or 4c**

1____

2____

House and Home

HOUSE AND HOME 2

HOUSE AND HOME 2

TEACHER'S SCRIPT FOR THE EXAM, PART II (Listening, 30%)

Part 2a Directions: For each question, you will hear some background information in English. Then you will hear a passage in Spanish twice, followed by a question in English. Listen carefully. After you have heard the question, read the question and the four suggested answers. Choose the best answer and write its number in the appropriate space on your answer sheet (9%).

1. Teresa tells you where she sleeps when she visits her cousins in Colombia.

   Cuando visito a mis primos en Colombia, prefiero dormir en el sótano. Duermo en el sofá-cama. En el sótano hay un estereo, un televisor, una videocasetera, una computadora y un teléfono. Hay también una nevera pequeña.

   Where does Teresa choose to sleep? (3)

2. You are in a hospital with your mother. You meet a neighbor coming out of the elevator. She gives you the following news.

   ¡Buenas noticias! Mi hija única María tiene gemelos. Ahora soy la abuela de un muchacho y una muchacha. Soy muy feliz. Pero hay un problema. Mi hija y su esposo viven en un apartamento pequeño. No hay comedor y hay sólo un dormitorio.

   What do you expect Maria and her husband to eventually do ? (1)

3. Pedro is looking for his hand-held electronic game in the dining room. He asks his mother if she has seen it. She says:

   Sí, estaba en la mesa, pero tu hermana lo tiene ahora. Ella y su amiga Luisa quieren jugar con el juego electrónico. Ellas están en el jardín, jugando con el juego.

   In order to get his game, what will Pedro do next? (3)

Part 2b Directions: For each question, you will hear some background information in English. Then you will hear a passage in Spanish twice, followed by a question in Spanish. Listen carefully. After you have heard the question, read the question and the four suggested answers. Choose the best answer and write it on your answer sheet (9%).

4. You and your friends are talking about what your families do on the weekend. You say:

   La madre de mi padre es italiana. Cuando mi familia visita a nuestra abuela los domingos, ella hace una pizza deliciosa en el horno para nosotros. Hmm...es muy buena.
   ¿Que hace la abuela los domingos? (2)

5. It is Monday morning. Your mother is very busy and has asked you to call her office. You are speaking to her boss. You say:

   Mi madre no puede salir de la casa porque mi hermano menor no está bien. El tiene que guardar cama. Pero no es un problema. Mi madre tiene una computadora en la sala y ella puede trabajar desde aquí...en casa.

   ¿Quién está enfermo? (3)

6. You are visiting your pen pal in Puerto Rico. She is showing you around her house. She says:

   Esta habitación es mi favorita. Es muy moderna y grande. El lavaplatos es nuevo. La estufa y el horno son también nuevos, pero prefiero usar el microondas. Puedo cocinar un rosbif en sólo treinta minutos.

   ¿Cuál es su habitación favorita? (3)

Part 2c Directions: For each question, you will hear some background information in English. Then you will hear a passage in Spanish twice, followed by a question in English. Listen carefully. After you have heard the question, read the question and look at the 4 pictures on your test. Choose the picture that best answers the question and write its number in the appropriate space on your answer sheet. (12%)

7. It is twelve o´clock noon and you telephone your aunt on her cell phone. She tells you about her daily routine. She says:

   Voy de compras desde las ocho hasta las diez. Limpio la casa desde las diez hasta las once. Trabajo en el jardín desde las once hasta mediodía. Ahora estoy en la bañera. Sí, me baño todos los días a mediodía. Es la única hora que tengo para mí misma.

   ¿From where is your aunt speaking to you on her cell phone ? (3)

8. Your friend Cecilia is showing you her room. She says:

   En mi habitación todo es muy moderno. El teléfono es nuevo. La computadora y el escritorio son también nuevos. Todos los muebles son modernos, excepto la cama. Me gusta mucho esta cama porque es de mi bisabuela. Tiene más de cien años. La cama es vieja, pero es mi mueble favorito.

   What item in Cecilia's room used to belong to her great-grandmother? (4)

9. Your father is describing your house to a delivery man over the telephone. He says:

   La casa es muy moderna. Tiene un piso y es de ladrillos. El techo es gris y tiene un garaje para dos autos.

   Which house is being described? (2)

10. Alfredo's mother wants to know why he is in her room. He explains:

    No tengo espejo en mi dormitorio y papá se ducha ahora en el baño. Cuando me visto para una fiesta prefiero mirarme en el espejo antes de salir con mis amigos. El espejo del tocador en tu dormitorio es muy grande.

    What is Alfredo doing in his mother's bedroom? (2)

Listening Comprehension Answers:
For all chapters, the answers are indicated in parentheses following each question. (See
questions 1-10 on the previous pages.)

Reading Comprehension answers:

3a. (8%)	11. __1__	12. __4__	13. __3__	14. __2__
3b (12%)	15. __3__	16. __1__	17. __3__	18. __2__

HOUSE AND HOME 2

Nombre ___________________________ Fecha _______________

EXAMINATION

Part 1 SPEAKING (30%)
Part 2 LISTENING (30%)

Part 2a Directions: For each question, you will hear some background information in English. Then you will hear a passage in Spanish twice, followed by a question in English. Listen carefully. After you have heard the question, read the question and the four suggested answers. Choose the best answer and write its number in the appropriate space on your answer sheet (9%).

1. Where does Teresa choose to sleep?
   1. in the kitchen
   2. on the top floor
   3. in the basement
   4. at her cousin´s house

2. What do you expect Maria and her husband to eventually do?
   1. look for an apartment with more bedrooms
   2. buy a new queen-size bed
   3. invite the grandmother to move in
   4. hire a full-time nanny

3. In order to get his game, what will Pedro do next?
   1. pick up the phone
   2. look under his bed
   3. go outside
   4. go upstairs

Part 2b Directions: For each question, you will hear some background information in English. Then you will hear a passage in Spanish twice, followed by a question in Spanish. Listen carefully. After you have heard the question, read the question and the four suggested answers. Choose the best answer and write its number in the appropriate space on your answer sheet (9 %).

4. ¿Qué hace la abuela los domingos?
   1. Ella toca el piano.
   2. Ella cocina.
   3. Ella nada en la piscina
   4. Ella canta.

5. ¿Quién está enfermo?
   1. el doctor
   2. tu madre
   3. tu hermano menor.
   4. tu amigo.

6. ¿Cuál es su habitación favorita?
   1. la sala
   2. el comedor
   3. la cocina
   4. el baño

HOUSE AND HOME 2

Part 2c Directions: For each question, you will hear some background information in English. Then you will hear a passage in Spanish twice, followed by a question in English. Listen carefully. After you have heard the question, read the question and look at the 4 pictures on your test. Choose the picture that best answers the question and write its number in the appropriate space on your answer sheet. (12%)

7. Where is your aunt speaking to you on her cell phone?

8. Which item is most likely from Paco's room?

9. Which house is being described?

10. What is Alfredo doing in his mother's bedroom?

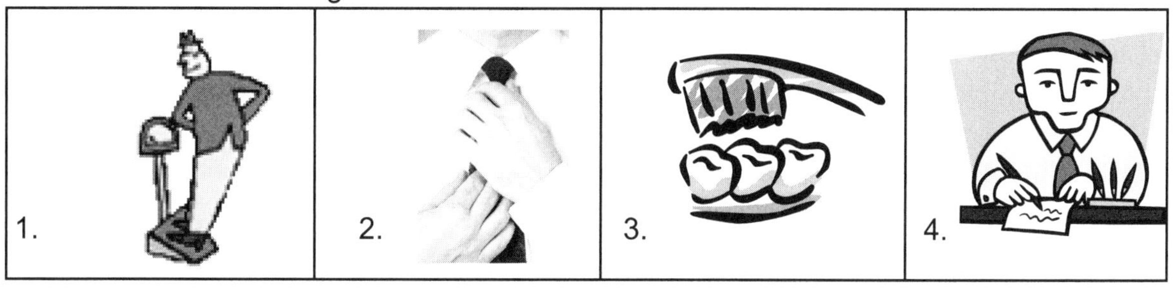

Part 3 READING (20%)

Part 3a Directions: Answer the questions in English based on the reading selections in Spanish. Choose the best answer to each question. Base your choice on the content of the reading selection. Write the number of your answer in the appropriate space on your answer sheet (8%).

CLASIFICADOS

A. TORREMOLINOS
¡Véalo!
Aquilo apartamento con 1 dormitorio, amueblado, cocina, sala, baño. Primer piso, tranquilo y bien decorado. A 150 metros de la playa. Julio y agosto.
Tel. 555-768-456

B. MARBELLA
¡Estupendo!
Alquilo apartamento con 2 dormitorios, cocina y baño, terraza magnífica. Parking incluído, muy bonito. 2º piso Enero y febrero.
Tel. 555-398-996

C. SEVILLA
¡Preciosa! Vendo casa 3 pisos, 4 dormitorios, 2 baños, cocina completa, sala, garaje para 2 coches, jardín grande. Da al Río Guadalquivir.
Tel. 555-770-107

D. MALAGA
¡ Perfecto !
Vendo casa, 3 dormitorios, cocina, sala, baño, garaje y piscina. Aire acondicionado central.
Tel. 555-101-884

11. In which city can one rent an apartment in the summer?
 1. Torremolinos 3. Marbella
 2. Sevilla 4. Málaga

12. Which listing advertises a swimming pool?
 1. A 2. B 3. C 4. D

ANUNCIO

¿Eres un buen estudiante? ¿Estás confortable cuando estudias? Nosotros tenemos muebles para tí. Tenemos escritorios, sillas confortables, lámparas de pie y lámparas de mesa. Tenemos mesas de computadoras y estantes para libros.

Visítanos a HERMANOS LOPEZ
Calle Goya, 33 Barcelona
abierto: lunes - martes 9.00 - 11.00 / 14.00 - 18.00
jueves - viernes 9.00 - 12.00 / 14.00 - 19.00
sábado 8.30 / 13.00

13. Who would be interested in this advertisement?
    1. a janitor
    2. an artist
    3. a university student
    4. a chef

14. On what days is this store closed?
    1. Monday and Tuesday
    2. Sunday and Wednesday
    3. Thursday and Friday
    4. Tuesday and Saturday

Part 3b Directions: Answer the question in Spanish based on the reading selection in Spanish. Choose the best answer to each question. Base your choice on the content of the reading selection. Write the number of your answer in the appropriate space on your answer sheet (12%).

> Querida Consuelo Consejera,
>
> ¡Ayudéme! Mi hijo Carlos no es ordenado. Su dormitorio pequeño está siempre en desorden. No hace la cama. No limpia los muebles. No pone la ropa en el armario. Deja la ropa en la alfombra. Sus libros de colegio están por todos lados.
>
> Una Mamá Infeliz

15. ¿ Quién es la persona que escribe a Consuelo Consejera?

1. un hijo
3. una hija
3. una madre
4. un padre

16. ¿ Cómo es el dormitorio de Carlos?

1. Está siempre en desorden
3. Es muy elegante
2. Es muy limpio
4. No está amueblado

<u>LEYENDA</u>
A. el dormitorio de los padres
B. el comedor
C. la cocina
D. el dormitorio de la abuela
E. mi dormitorio
F. el cuarto de baño
G. la cocina

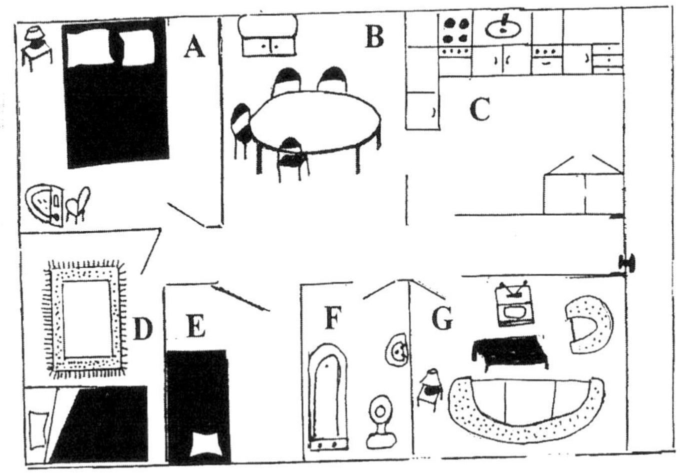

17. ¿ Cuántas sillas hay en comedor ?
    1. uno
    2. tres
    3. cuatro
    4. seis

18. ¿ Dónde está la alfombra ?
    1. en la sala
    2. en la cocina
    3. en el dormitorio de la abuela
    4. en el dormitorio de los padres

HOUSE AND HOME 2

Part 4 Writing (20%)

Part 4 Directions: Choose two of the three writing tasks provided below. Your answer to each of the two questions should be written entirely in Spanish and should contain a minimum of **30 words**.

Place names and brand names written in Spanish count as one word. Contractions are counted as one word. Salutations, closings and commonly used abbreviations are included in the word count. Numbers, unless written as words, and names of people do not count as words.

Be sure that you have satisfied the purpose of the task. The sentence structure and /or expressions used should be connected logically and demonstrate a wide range of vocabulary with minimal repetition.

4a. You have moved to a new home. Write a letter to your pen pal in the target language and describe your new home. You may wish to include:

- Where you new home is located
- The size of your house or apartment
- The number and names of the rooms
- Which room is your favorite and why

4b. You are living with a family in a country where Spanish is spoken. Write a letter describing one room in that house. You may wish to include:

- The color of the room
- The size of the room
- What activity one does in that room
- A description of the furniture found there

4c. Your local newspaper is having a contest entitled "My Dream House". Write a composition on what you consider to be an ideal house. You may wish to include:

- The number of floors, windows and exterior doors
- The number of rooms
- What the house is made of. (i.e. brick, wood)
- Whether it should have a garage, and if so where
- Whether the house should have a backyard or garden

ANSWER SHEET

Nombre y Apellido ______________________________ Fecha ______________

Part I **Speaking** __________ (30%)
Part 2 **Listening (30%)**

PART 3: READING (20%)

2a.	2b.	2c.	3a.(8%)	3b.(12%)
1._____	4._____	7._____	11._____	15._____
2._____	5._____	8._____	12._____	16._____
3._____	6._____	9._____	13._____	17._____
		10._____	14._____	18._____

Part 4 **Writing (20%)** **20 words** **Write 2 paragraphs** **4a , 4b or 4c**

1____

2____

HOUSE AND HOME 2

EDUCATION

EDUCATION 2

EDUCATION 2

TEACHER'S SCRIPT FOR THE EXAM, PART II (Listening, 30%)

Part 2a Directions: For each question, you will hear some background information in English. Then you will hear a passage in Spanish twice, followed by a question in English. Listen carefully. After you have heard the question, read the question and the four suggested answers. Choose the best answer and write its number in the appropriate space on your answer sheet (9%).

1. Luisa is speaking to you on the telephone. She says:

   No me gusta mi horario porque no veo a mis amigos. Tengo el almuerzo en el período 4. Pero todos mis amigos comen el almuerzo en el período 5. Veo a mis amigos sólo antes o después de las clases.

   What is Luisa complaining about? (3)

2. María meets her cousin Consuelo from Puerto Rico at a family gathering. They talk about the schools that they attend. María makes the first comment.

   María: En mi escuela hay quinientos alumnos. ¿Cuántos alumnos hay en tu escuela?
   Consuelo: Hay trescientos ochenta estudiantes y veintinueve profesores.
   María: ¡Ay! Es una escuela pequeña.

   What are the two cousins comparing? (2)

3. You telephone your best friend about a sports game that is about to start on television. Your friend says:

   No es posible. No puedo mirar el partido. Mi familia tiene sólo un televisor en casa. Mi hermana está mirando un documentario en la televisión para su clase de historia.

   Why can't your friend watch television? (4)

Part 2b Directions: For each question, you will hear some background information in English. Then you will hear a passage in Spanish twice, followed by a question in Spanish. Listen carefully. After you have heard the question, read the question and the four suggested answers. Choose the best answer and write its number in the appropriate space on your answer sheet. (9%)

4. Felipe is walking into his next class with you. He says to you:

   Me gusta mucho esta clase. Me gusta cantar y un día quiero ser cantante como Plácido Domingo. Es mi clase favorita.

   ¿Cuál es la clase favorita de Felipe? (3)

5. Beatriz is showing you her report card. She says:

   Me gusta dibujar y pintar. Por eso, saco buenas notas en la clase de la Señora López. Ella dice que soy muy artística. Me gusta trabajar con colores.

   ¿Qué aprende Beatriz en la clase de la Señora López? (3)

6. Gregorio is getting acquainted with a new student in his school. He says to her:

   Me gusta correr y esquiar. Soy capitán del equipo de básquetbol y soy miembro también del equipo de fútbol. Me gustan todos los deportes.

   ¿Cómo es Gregorio? (1)

Part 2c Directions: For each question, you will hear some background information in English. Then you will hear a passage in Spanish twice, followed by a question in English. Listen carefully. After you have heard the question, read the question and look at the 4 pictures on your test. Choose the picture that best answers the question and write its number in the appropriate space on your answer sheet. (12%)

7. A student from the previous class has come back looking for an item he left inside the desk where you are now seated. He asks:

   ¿Ves un papel blanco en el pupitre? Es un examen. Mi profesor de matemáticas quiere ver el nombre de mi padre en el examen.

   What did this student forget? (2)

8. Your aunt, who is a teacher in Puerto Rico, is showing you some photos that she had taken at work. She says:

   Enseño en una escuela pública. Tengo 20 alumnos en mi clase. Los niños tienen 6 años. En mi clase, ellos aprenden a escribir y a leer. Aprenden también a dibujar con colores.

   Which of these photos is from her album? (1)

9. You are having difficulty with an assignment from your textbook. At lunch time you ask Maria, one of your classmates, if she can help you. She replies:

   El inglés es fácil para mí. Mis padres son de los Estados Unidos y lo hablamos siempre en casa.

   Which textbook do you show her? (3)

10. You are helping your geography teacher put things away in his classroom. You notice something and question him. You say:

    ¿De quién es la foto? ¿La foto sobre su escritorio?
    ¿Es su esposa? Es una mujer muy bonita

    What item on your teacher's desk are you referring to? (1)

Listening Comprehension Answers:
For all chapters, the answers are indicated in parentheses following each question. (See question 1-10 on the previous pages.)

Reading Comprehension answers:

3a (8%) 11. __4__ 12. __1__ 13. __4__ 14. __3__

3b (12%) 15. __1__ 16. __4__ 17. __2__ 18. __2__

EDUCATION 2

Nombre ____________________________ Fecha ________________

EXAMINATION

Part 1 SPEAKING (30%)
Part 2 LISTENING (30%)

Part 2a Directions: For each question, you will hear some background information in English. Then you will hear a passage in Spanish twice, followed by a question in English. Listen carefully. After you have heard the question, read the question and the four suggested answers. Choose the best answer and write its number in the appropriate space on your answer sheet (9%).

1. What is Luisa complaining about?
    1. that the food in the cafeteria is not to her liking
    2. that her homework assignments are too hard
    3. that she doesn't see her friends at lunch time
    4. that she has a very difficult test tomorrow

2. What are the two cousins comparing?
    1. the subjects offered
    2. the school size
    3. the number of clubs available
    4. the ages of their teachers

3. Why can't your friend watch television?
    1. He is being punished.
    2. The television is broken
    3. He has to study for a test
    4. His sister is watching a program for school

Part 2b Directions: For each question, you will hear some background information in English. Then you will hear a passage in Spanish twice, followed by a question in Spanish. Listen carefully. After you have heard the question, read the question and the four suggested answers. Choose the best answer and write its number in the appropriate space on your
answer sheet. (9%)

4. ¿Cuál es la clase favorita de Felipe?
    1. la clase de español
    2. la clase de historia
    3. la clase de música
    4. la clase de ciencias

5. ¿Qué aprende Beatriz en la clase de la Señora López?
    1. geografía
    2. matemáticas
    3. arte
    4. educación física

6. ¿Cómo es Gregorio?
    1. Es muy atlético.
    2. Es muy débil.
    3. Es muy perezoso.
    4. Es muy inteligente.

EDUCATION 2

Part 2c Directions: For each question, you will hear some background information in English. Then you will hear a passage in Spanish twice, followed by a question in English. Listen carefully. After you have heard the question, read the question and look at the 4 pictures on your test. Choose the picture that best answers the question and write its number in the appropriate space on your answer sheet. (12%)

7. What did this student forget?

8. Which of these photos is from her album?

9. Which textbook do you show her?

7. What item on the teacher's desk are you referring to?

EDUCATION 2

Part 3 READING (20%)

Part 3a Directions: Answer the question in English based on the reading selection in Spanish. Choose the best answer to each question. Base your choice on the content of the reading selection. Write the number of your answer in the appropriate space on your answer sheet (8%).

En mi escuela hay cuatrocientos muchachos y trescientas muchachas. Hay también ochenta profesores. Por la mañana hay clases desde las nueve hasta mediodía. El almuerzo dura noventa minutos. La comida es desde el mediodía hasta la una y media. Por la tarde hay clases desde la una y media hasta las cinco. Hay una hora de recreo excepto los viernes.

En el sótano están la cafetería, la cocina y una aula grande de música. En la planta baja hay la oficina del director, el gimnasio, la clínica médica y la biblioteca. En el primer piso hay muchas aulas para las ciencias y las artes manuales. Hay también laboratorios. En el segundo piso hay clases de lenguas, de estudios sociales y otras aulas.

11. How long is lunch time at this school?
    1. thirty minutes
    2. forty-five minutes
    3. sixty minutes
    4. ninety minutes

12. Where is the music class?
    1. in the basement
    2. on the second floor
    3. on the ground floor
    4. on the third floor

De: Silvia < silviah7@dahoo.com>
A: Pedro < pjl1986@aol.com>
Enviado: martes, 29 de enero de 2002 18:33
Objeto: la clase favorita

¡Hola Pedro!

Tú quieres noticias de mi clase favorita. Es la clase de ciencias. Mi clase de ciencias es muy interesante. Cada mes hacemos actividades diferentes. En septiembre visitamos un jardín botánico. En octubre visitamos el acuario. En noviembre visitamos el jardín zoológico. En diciembre visitamos un museo de historia natural. Antes de los viajes, la clase ve una película. Mañana mi clase va a visitar un planetario. ¿Ves tú películas o videos en tu clase de ciencias?

Silvia

13. What was most likely the topic in this class in September?
    1. algebraic equations
    2. fossils
    3. stars and planets
    4. flowers and plants

14. What does this class do prior to each field trip?
    1. visit the library
    2. listen to a guest speaker
    3. see a film
    4. take a test

Part 3b Directions: Answer the question in Spanish based on the reading selection in Spanish. Choose the best answer to each question. Base your choice on the content of the reading selection. Write the number of your answer in the appropriate space on your answer sheet (12%).

Colegio Simon Bolivar
Horario escolar

ESTUDIANTE: **José Luis García López**

Hora	Asignatura	Sala	Profesor
9:00	Historial 8	205	Sr. Bernal
9:45	Matemáticas 8	311	Srta Lara
10:30	Español	106	Sr. Rivera
11:15	Inglés	48	Sra. Londres
12:00	Aula de estudio	33	Srta. Santana
12:45	Almuerzo	cafetería	--------------
1:30	Educación física	gimnasio	Sr. Maradona
2:15	Música	18	Sra Segovia

Firma del director: *María-Carmen Fuentes de Montoya*

15. ¿A qué hora es la primera clase?
    1. a las nueve
    2. a la una y media
    3. a las diez menos cuarto
    4. a las tres

16. ¿Dónde enseña el Sr. Rivera?
    1. en un laboratorio de ciencia
    2. en el gimnasio
    3. en la cafetería
    4. en la sala número 106

ESCUELA FRANCISCO PIZARRO

77 Calle F. Pizarro Luanco tel. 56 - 01 - 99
DIRECTOR Alfredo Oñate

Boletín de Evaluación Progresiva

para

Gómez Hurtado Bernardo
primer apellido segundo apellido nombre

dirección: *41/ Avenida Narvaéz*
telef. 56 - 78 - 33 .

MATERIAS	Nota	Profesor
Español	*Excelente*	*A. Ortega*
Matemáticas	*Muy deficiente*	*E. López*
Historia	*Muy bien*	*B. Quiñones*
Arte	*Bien*	*B. Fuentes*
Educación física	*Bien*	*B. Muñez*
Biología	*Insuficiente*	*R. Ruíz*
Francés	*Bien*	*P. Castillo*

Bernardo tiene que estudiar más en las asignaturas de biología y matemáticas. Él tiene que mejorar su conducta en las mismas clases.

17. ¿Cómo se llama el alumno?
    1. Francisco Pizarro
    2. Bernardo Gómez
    3. Alfredo Oñate
    4. Avenida Narváez

18. ¿ En qué asignatura es muy fuerte el alumno?
    1. matemáticas
    2. español
    3. biología
    4. francés

Part 4 WRITING (20%)

Part 4 Directions: Choose two of the three writing tasks provided below. Your answer to each one of the two questions should be written entirely in Spanish and should contain a minimum of **30 words**.

Place names and brand names written in Spanish count as one word. Contractions are counted as one word. Salutations, closings and commonly used abbreviations are included in the word count. Numbers, unless written as words, and names of people do not count as words.

Be sure that you have satisfied the purpose of the task. The sentence structure and /or expressions used should be connected logically and demonstrate a wide range of vocabulary with minimal repetition.

4a. A group of Mexican visitors is coming to your school. Your Spanish teacher has asked you to write an introductory article about your school. In your article you may wish to include:

- The size of your school: big, small
- How many students there are in your school
- How many teachers there are
- Which subjects are taught in the school
- Whether there are lab rooms, a library or a gymnasium
- Why you think your school is special

4b. Your pen pal in Spain would like to know something about your class schedule. In your reply, you may wish to include

- How many periods or classes you have each day
- How long each period is
- At what time each period begins and ends
- At what time you have lunch
- Whether you like you class schedule and why

4c. You participate in an after school activity. Your pen pal would like to know about your extra curriculum activity. Write a letter to your friend. In your letter you may wish to include:

- The name of the clubs or sports in which you participate
- On which day and at what time this extracurricular activity meets
- The number of members / participants
- The name of the moderator / coach
- Specify what you do in this club / activity
- Say if you like or dislike this club

ANSWER SHEET

Nombre y Apellido ______________________________ Fecha ______________

Part I **Speaking** __________ (30%)
Part 2 **Listening (30%)**

2a.	2b.	2c.
1._____	4._____	7._____
2._____	5._____	8._____
3._____	6._____	9._____
		10._____

PART 3: READING (20%)

3a.(8%)	3b.(12%)
11._____	15._____
12._____	16._____
13._____	17._____
14._____	18._____

Part 4 **Writing (20%) 20 words** **Write 2 paragraphs** **4a , 4b or 4c**

1____

2____

Community and Neighborhood

COMMUNITY/ NEIGHBORHOOD 2

TEACHER'S SCRIPT FOR THE EXAM, PART II (Listening, 30%)

Part 2a Directions: For each question, you will hear some background information in English. Then you will hear a passage in Spanish twice, followed by a question in English. Listen carefully. After you have heard the question, read the question and the four suggested answers. Choose the best answer and write its number in the appropriate space on your answer sheet. (9%)

1. An elderly woman stops to ask you for directions to the local hospital. You reply:

   ¡ Oh no ! Ud. no puede caminar al hospital. Está muy lejos de aquí.
   En la esquina de mi calle hay una parada de autobús. Tome el autobús.
   Cuando Ud. baja del autobús, el hospital estará enfrente de Ud.

   What is your suggestion? (2)

2. David is asking Dorothy out for a date. He asks her:

   ¿Te gusta la comida española? Hay un restaurante excelente en
   mi pueblo donde se come bien. Ellos hacen una paella muy deliciosa.
   ¿Quieres ir conmigo?

   What is David suggesting? (4)

3. You are traveling in Mexico. You have stopped in the Tourist Office for directions to the Hotel Cortés. The tourist office clerk explains:

   Camine seis cuadras y doble a la izquierda. Ahora Ud. está en la Calle Jorge Wáshington. Ud. va a ver una iglesia blanca. Enfrente de la iglesia está el Hotel Cortés.

   Where will you find the Hotel Cortés? (3)

Part 2b Directions: For each question, you will hear some background information in English. Then you will hear a passage in Spanish twice, followed by a question in Spanish. Listen carefully. After you have heard the question, read the question and the four suggested answers. Choose the best answer and write its number in the appropriate space on your answer sheet. (9%)

4. Your friend tells you that he had seen your brother earlier that day. He asks you for an explanation

   Mi hermano, Arturo se levanta a las seis de la mañana cada día. A él le gusta dar un paseo por una hora. El dice que no hay mucho tráfico en las calles por la mañana. Cuando mi hermano regresa a la casa se ducha y después, sale a las ocho.

   ¿A qué hora se levanta Arturo por la mañana?

5. Juanita is an new exchange student from Peru. She is telling you about her grandmother. She says:

   Mi abuela tiene noventa y dos años pero es una mujer activa. Ella vive con su hermana Adelina en una casa en Puerto Rico. En julio, mi abuela visita a su hijo mayor en California. En octubre ella visita a mi familia en el Perú. Mi abuela viaja siempre en avión y ella viaja siempre con su hermana Adelina. Ellas son inseparables.

   ¿Con quién viaja la abuela de Juanita? (3)

6. Your older brother is late. You call him on his cell phone. He replies.

   Lo siento. Estoy en mi coche en la Avenida de la Reforma. Hubo un accidente entre una motocicleta y un autobús. Yo no puedo doblar a la derecha y no puedo doblar a la izquierda. Hay mucho tráfico alrededor de mí y yo no puedo continuar.

   ¿Dónde está su hermano? (2)

Part 2c Directions: For each question, you will hear some background information in English. Then you will hear a passage in Spanish twice, followed by a question in English. Listen carefully. After you have heard the question, read the question and look at the four pictures on your test. Choose the picture that best answers the question and write its number in the appropriate space on your answer sheet. (12%)

7. Your teacher mentions that on her way to school this morning she had seen your father in a local coffee shop. She asks where he works. You say:

   Mi padre trabaja con mi tío. A los dos hombres les gustan los carros. Mi tío tiene una gasolinera cerca de aquí. A la derecha de la gasolinera hay un garaje donde trabaja mi padre. Si Ud. tiene un problema con su auto, hable con mi padre. Es un mecánico excelente.

   What does your father do for a living? (1)

8. It is Saturday and you meet a classmate at the bus stop. She says:

   En la escuela estudio francés. El profesor dice que es muy importante escuchar la lengua hablada. Yo voy al centro hoy para ver una película francesa en el cine.

   Where is this person going on Saturday? (4)

9. Carlos and his brother Diego are discussing what kind of gift they should buy their father for Father´s Day. Carlos says:

   A papá le gusta escuchar la música latinoamericana. El tiene más de doscientos discos y casetes. Vamos a comprar un regalo diferente. A papá le gusta leer también. Vamos a la librería y vamos a comprar un libro sobre la música de Argentina

   What will Carlos and Diego buy for their father? (2)

10. Your uncle works overseas in Panama. He likes to have an uncluttered desk at work and tells you about the very few items he keeps on it. He says:

    Yo trabajo en un banco en Panamá. En mi escritorio tenía cuatro cosas: un papel secante, una pluma, un teléfono, y la bandera panameña. Ahora tengo también una bandera norteamericana en mi escritorio. Fue un regalo recente de un cliente de Nueva York.

    What is the most recent item your uncle added to his desk at work? (2)

Listening Comprehension Answers:
For all chapters, the answers are indicated in parentheses following each question. (See questions 1-10 on the previous pages.)

Reading Comprehension answers:

3a (8%) 11. __3__ 12. __4__ 13. __1__ 14. __3__

3b (12%) 15. __2__ 16. __4__ 17. __3__ 18. __1__

Nombre ____________________________ Fecha ________________________

EXAMINATION

Part I SPEAKING (30%)
Part 2 LISTENING (30%)

Part 2a Directions: For each question, you will hear some background information in English. Then you will hear a passage in Spanish twice, followed by a question in English. Listen carefully. After you have heard the question, read the question and the four suggested answers. Choose the best answer and write its number in the appropriate space on your answer sheet. (9%)

1. What is your suggestion?
   1. that she walk
   2. that she take a bus
   3. that she call for an ambulance
   4. that she hail a taxicab

2. What is David suggesting?
   1. that they go see a movie
   2. that they go to the beach
   3. that they go to an amusement park
   4. that they have lunch together

3. Where will you find the Hotel Cortés?
   1. to the left of a supermarket.
   2. behind a red building.
   3. across the street from a church
   4 next to the American Embassy

Part 2b Directions: For each question, you will hear some background information in English. Then you will hear a passage in Spanish twice, followed by a question in Spanish. Listen carefully. After you have heard the question, read the question and the four suggested answers. Choose the best answer and write its number in the appropriate space on your answer sheet (9%).

4. ¿A qué hora se levanta Arturo por la mañana?
   1. a las ocho
   2. a la una
   3. a las diez
   4. a las seis

5. ¿Con quién viaja la abuela de Juanita?
   1. con su padre
   2. con su tío
   3. con su hermana Adelina
   4. con su sobrina

6. ¿Dónde está su hermano?
   1. en un autobús
   2. en un auto
   3. en un hospital
   4. en una tienda de bicicletas

Part 2c Directions: For each question, you will hear some background information in English. Then you will hear a passage in Spanish twice, followed by a question in English. Listen carefully. After you have heard the question, read the question and look at the 4 pictures on your test. Choose the picture that best answers the question and write its number in the appropriate space on your answer sheet. (8%)

7. What does your father do for a living?

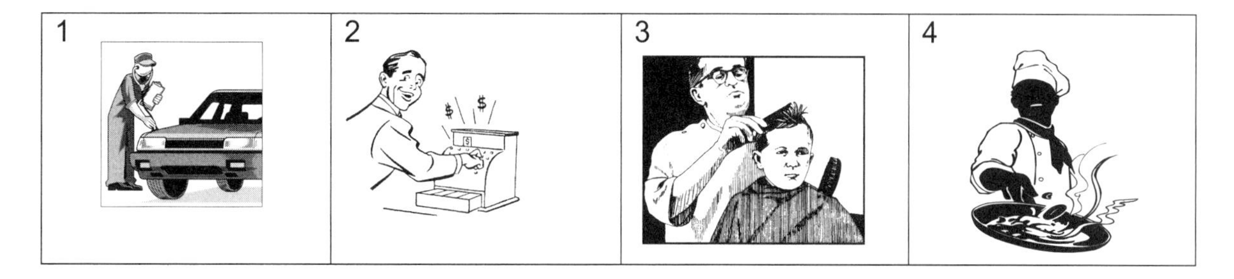

8. Where is this person going on Saturday?

9. What will Carlos and Diego buy for their father?

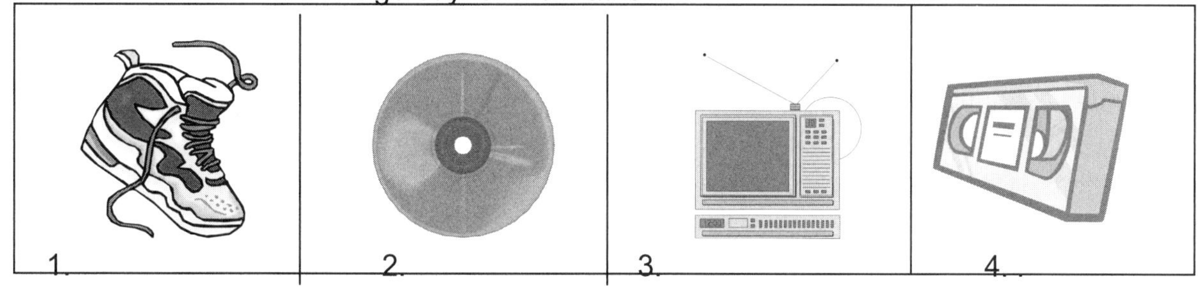

10. What is the most recent item that your uncle added to his desk at work?

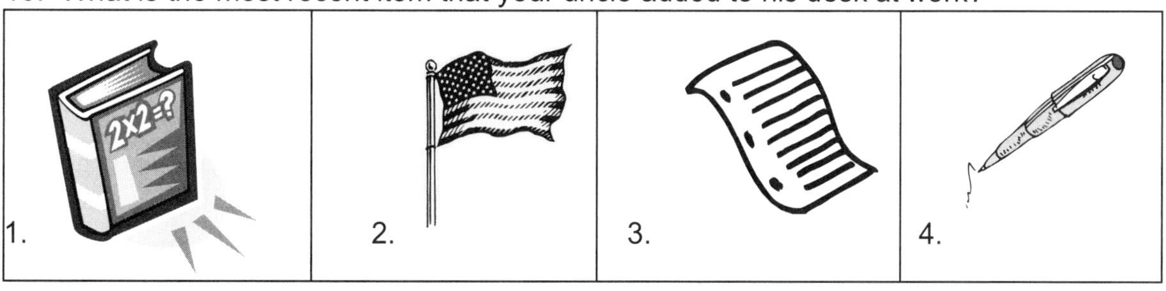

Part 3a Directions: Answer the question in English based on the reading selection in Spanish. Choose the best answer to each question. Base your choice on the content of the reading selection. Write the number of your answer in the appropriate space on your answer sheet.

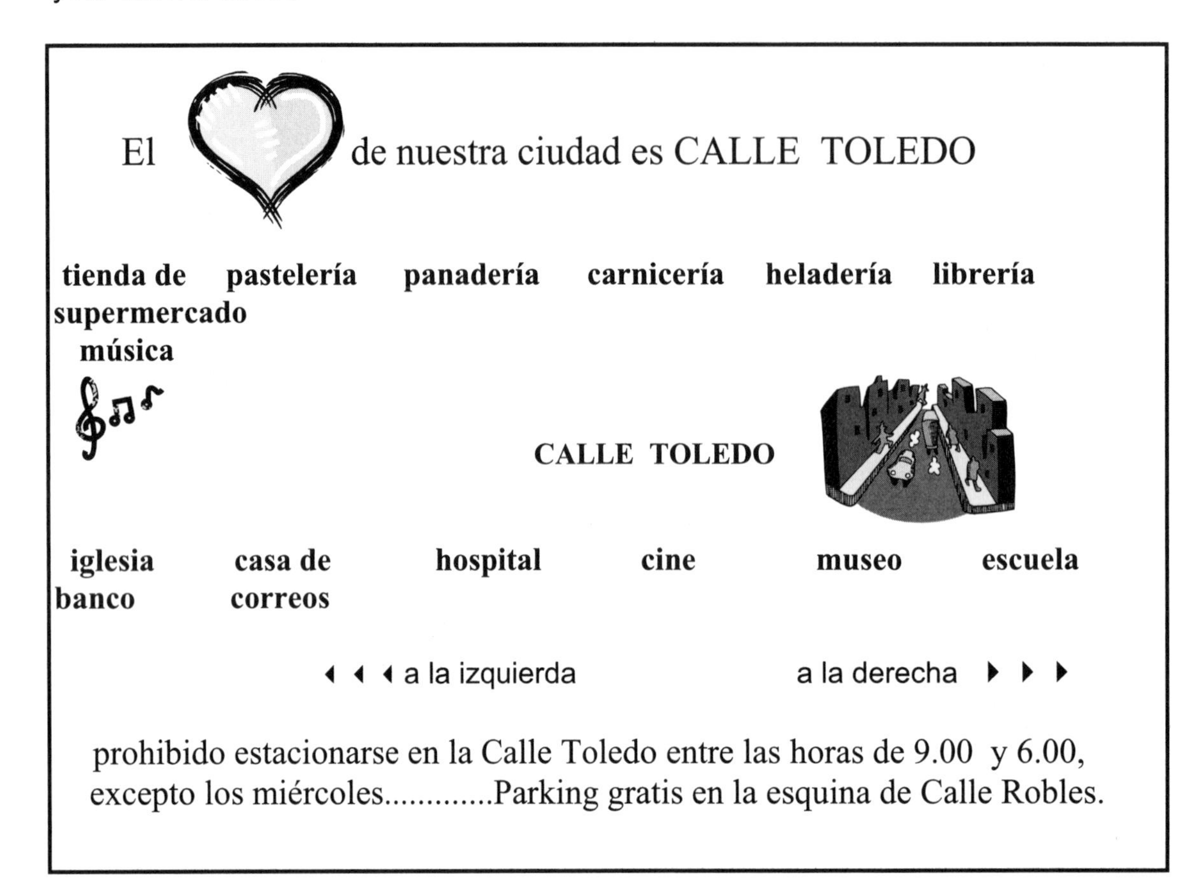

11. What is the price for parking on Robles Street?

    1. $9   2. $6   3. Free   4. $10

12. One can park a car on this street at anytime on ....

    1. Sunday   3. Monday
    2. Tuesday   4. Wednesday

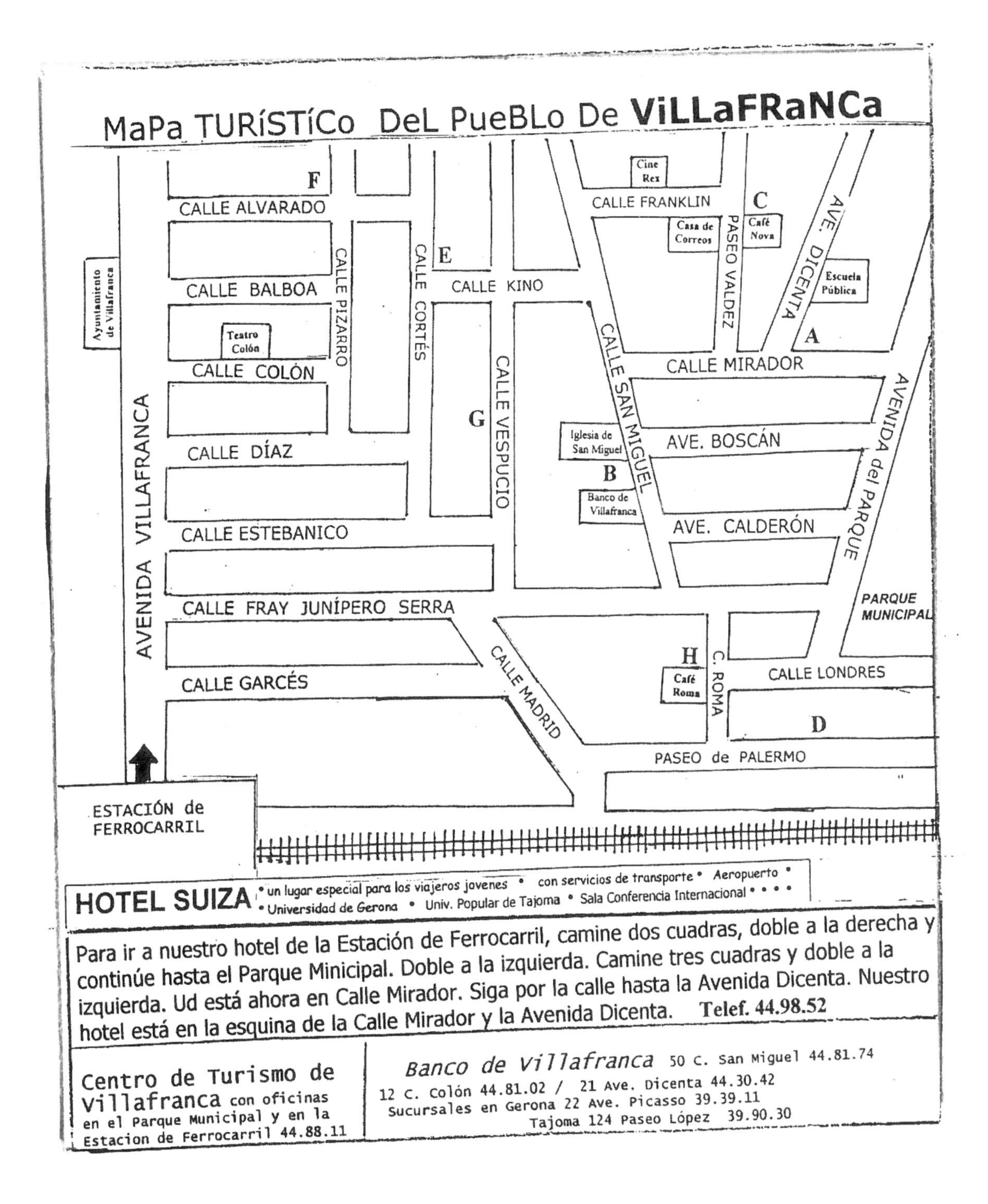

13. According to the directions given on the above map, what letter marks the location of the Hotel Suiza?

1. A 2. B 3. D 4. G

14. What is the name of this town?

1. Gerona 2. San Miguel 3. Villafranca 4. Tajoma

Part 3b Directions: Answer the question in Spanish based on the reading selection in Spanish. Choose the best answer to each question. Base your choice on the content of the reading selection. Write the number of your answer in the appropriate space on your answer sheet. (8%)

EL PARQUE DE SANTO DOMINGO

ES EL PARQUE DE TODOS LOS DIAS

¡ Hay 7 razones buenas para visitar este parque excitante !

1. El **Museo de Arte** con una gran colección de arte pre-colombiana.
2. El **Teatro Colón** con las obras de Lope de Vega y Alarcón.
3. El **Zoológico** con animales domésticos y exóticos de antilopes a los zorrillos.
4. El **Estadio Municipal** con partidos de béisbol, de hockey, fútbol, volibol, tenís.
5. El **Centro Acuático** con cuatro piscinas interiores.
6. El **Jardín Botánico** con las fragrancias de quinientas flores.
7. El **Café del Parque** con comidas internacionales muy sabrosas.

15. ¿Qué puede hacer una familia en el Centro Acuático ?
    1. Jugar al fútbol
    2. Nadar
    3. Ver una comedia musical
    4. Comer nachos y burritos

16. ¿Adónde va una familia para ver los elefantes, los leones y los gorilas?
    1. al centro acuático
    2. al jardín botánico
    3. al museo de arte
    4. al parque zoológico

Querido David,

Salamanca es una ciudad importante en España. Hay muchos estudiantes.

La Universidad de Salamanca es muy histórica y famosa. Fue fundada en 1218. Hay muchas diversiones: cines, teatros, discotecas, parques, estadios y cafés. Para el estudiante serio hay bibliotecas y librerías. Para una estudiante como yo hay muchas tiendas en el centro. Pero, no voy de compras. Soy una estudiante responsable, y tengo que trabajar para ganar dinero. Yo trabajo en una tienda de muebles los viernes, los sábados y los domingos. Camino todos los días desde mi casa hasta la universidad donde estudio ciencias. Por eso, soy muy delgada. Después de las clases yo voy a la biblioteca central. Salamanca es una ciudad hermosa y estoy muy contenta de vivir aquí.

Tu amiga,

Silvia

17. ¿Cómo es Silvia?
    1. perezosa y antipática
    2. tonta e indiferente
    3. estudiosa y responsable
    4. gorda y rubia

18. ¿Cómo va Silvia a la universidad cada día?
    1. va a pie
    2. en taxí
    3. en moto
    4. en coche

Part 4 Writing (20%)

Part 4 Directions: Choose two of the three writing tasks provided below. Your answer to each of the two questions should be written entirely in Spanish and should contain a minimum of **20 words**.

Place names and brand names written in Spanish count as one word. Contractions are counted as one word. Salutations, closings and commonly used abbreviations are included in the word count. Numbers, unless written as words, and names of people do not count as words.

Be sure that you have satisfied the purpose of the task. The sentence structure and /or expressions used should be connected logically and demonstrate a wide range of vocabulary with minimal repetition.

4a. You are spending your summer vacation at a resort town in a country where the language you are studying is spoken. Write a letter to your friend asking him/her questions about the town. You may wish to include questions concerning:

- Where the town is located
- What the town is like
- How many people live there
- What kind of buildings there are
- What activities one can do in the summertime here

4b. Your pen pal from Spain has asked you to describe an important building in your town. You may wish to include the following ideas:

- The name and description of this place
- Why you go to this place
- With whom you go there
- Who works there
- When you go there

4c. You will be hosting a student from a Spanish-speaking country for a few months. He/she has asked you to describe the shopping area in your town. Write a letter. You may wish to include:

- What stores are located in your neighborhood
- What can be bought in these stores
- When these stores are open
- Where these stores are located in relationship to each other

ANSWER SHEET

Nombre y Apellido ______________________________ Fecha ______________

Part I **Speaking** __________ (30%)
Part 2 **Listening (30%)**

PART 3: READING (20%)

2a.	2b.	2c.	3a.(8%)	3b.(12%)
1._____	4._____	7._____	11._____	15._____
2._____	5._____	8._____	12._____	16._____
3._____	6._____	9._____	13._____	17._____
		10._____	14._____	18._____

Part 4 **Writing (20%) 20 words** **Write 2 paragraphs** **4a , 4b or 4c**

1____

____

____

____

____

____

____

____

____

2____

____

____

____

____

____

____

____

____

____

____

____

COMMUNITY/ NEIGHBORHOOD 2

Food and Meal Taking

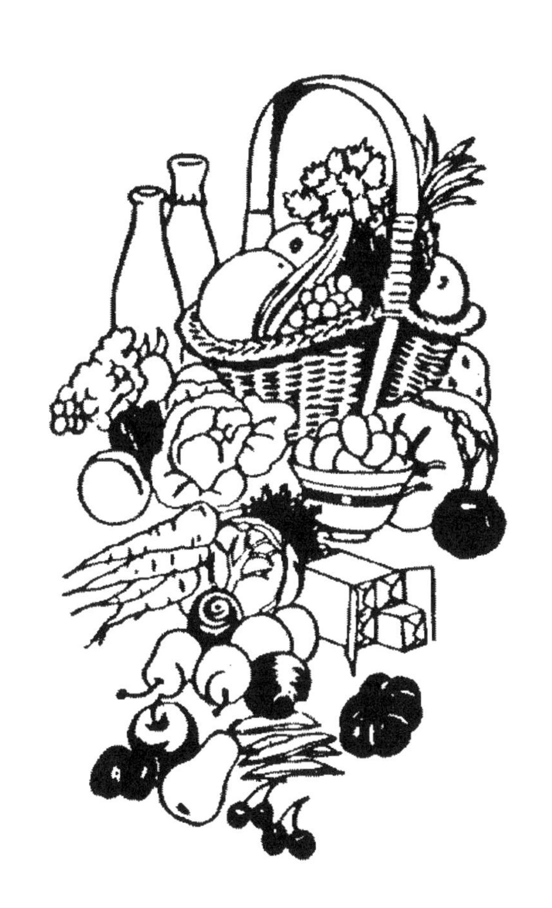

MEAL TAKING/ FOOD/ DRINK 2

MEAL TAKING/ FOOD/ DRINK 2

TEACHER'S SCRIPT FOR THE EXAM, PART II (Listening, 30%)

Part 2a Directions: For each question, you will hear some background information in English. Then you will hear a passage in Spanish twice, followed by a question in English. Listen carefully. After you have heard the question, read the question and the four suggested answers. Choose the best answer and write its number in the appropriate space on your answer sheet. (9%)

1. You are ordering lunch in a restaurant in Colombia with your parents. Your mother orders first. She says:

   Yo quisiera sopa de legumbres, luego pollo con papas fritas y zanahorias. Para beber, una taza de café con leche. Me gusta mucho el café colombiano.

   What did your mother order to drink? (2)

2. You are having a luncheon in your school for some visitors from Ecuador. Your teacher is looking over the menu list that you have prepared. She says:

   La carne es pavo...bravo. La bebida es leche...bueno.. Pero las legumbres son espinacas, guisantes y bróculi. Las legumbres son todas verdes y esto no me gusta. Cuando yo miro un plato, quiero ver colores diferentes. Prefiero las papas, las zanahorias y los guisantes. Ahora hay muchos colores.

   Why did the teacher criticize your choice of vegetables? (4)

3. You and your friend are watching a Spanish TV movie. In one scene you hear the actress say to the actor:

   Ponga el tenedor a la izquierda del plato. El cuchillo va a la derecha. Al lado del cuchillo están la cuchara y la cucharita. Ponga la servilleta encima del plato. Va a estar cerca de la taza.

   What is happening in this scene? (1)

Part 2b Directions: For each question, you will hear some background information in English. Then you will hear a passage in Spanish twice, followed by a question in Spanish. Listen carefully. After you have heard the question, read the question and the four suggested answers. Choose the best answer and write its number in the appropriate space on your answer sheet. (9%)

4. Marisol and Luisa are at the beach. Marisol asks Luisa how she stays thin. Luisa replies:

   Yo soy delgada porque no como mucho. No como ni pan, ni arroz y ni papas. Para el postre no como ni tortas ni dulces. Prefiero comer una manzana o una pera. Pero, hoy yo tengo una naranja para postre. Es muy sabrosa.

   ¿Qué come Luisa para postre? (3)

5. At an international picnic your classmate David is telling one of the Spanish-speaking guests what he does on certain days. He says:

   Los lunes y los jueves tomo un huevo, pan tostado y jugo de tomate por la mañana. Los martes y los viernes tomo cereal con leche. Los miércoles y los sábados me gustan panqueques con jugo de uva. Los domingos mi familia come en un restaurante a las nueve antes de ir a la iglesia. En el restaurante me gusta pedir el especial del día: huevos revueltos con tocino y café.

   ¿De qué comida habla David? (1)

6. You telephone your classmate Rosalia to ask her about a Spanish assignment. She apologizes that she cannot speak to you at that moment. She explains:

   Son las cuatro y voy al apartamento de mi abuela ahora. Mi abuela tiene ochenta y dos años. Ella es inglesa. Todos los días a las cuatro de la tarde mi abuela toma una taza de té y unas galletas. Yo tomo la merienda con ella. Es una tradición inglesa.

   ¿A qué hora toma merienda Rosalia? (3)

Part 2c Directions: For each question, you will hear some background information in English. Then you will hear a passage in Spanish twice, followed by a question in English. Listen carefully. After you have heard the question, read the question and look at the 4 pictures on your test. Choose the picture that best answers the question and write its number in the appropriate space on your answer sheet. (12%)

7. You are food shopping with your parents. Your father is about to go into the supermarket, when your mother stops him. She says:

   Prefiero ir a la carnicería en la esquina de la calle. La carne está siempre fresca. Voy a comprar chuletas de cerdo para la cena de esta noche.

   What does your mother want to buy? (3)

8. You are listening to a TV cook show. The television chef says:

   Para hacer una ensalada Ud. necesita lechuga, cebolla y tomate. Yo prefiero poner jugo de limón y un poco de sal.

   What is this chef preparing? (2)

9. It is lunch time and you and your friend Pedro stop in a cafe. Your friend says:

No tengo hambre. Pero tengo sed. Sólo me gustaría un vaso de jugo de naranja. La naranja es mi fruta favorita.

What is Pedro going to order? (3)

10. You are in a store with your grandmother in Madrid. She is speaking to the man behind the counter. He says.

    Las galletas de chocolate cuestan tres euros por kilo. Todos los pasteles cuestan nueve euros, excepto el pastel de cereza. La torta de fresas es muy deliciosa. La torta de fresas y el pastel de cerezas cuestan diez euros.

    Where are you and your grandmother? (2)

Listening Comprehension answer:
For all chapters, the answers are indicated in parentheses following each question. (See questions 1-10 on the previous pages.)

Reading Comprehension answers:

3a (8%) 11. __1__ 12. __4__ 13. __4__ 14. __1__

3b (12%) 15. __2__ 16. __1__ 17. __4__ 18. __3__

MEAL TAKING/ FOOD/ DRINK 2

Nombre ______________________________ Fecha ______________________

EXAMINATION

Part 1 SPEAKING (30%)
Part 2 LISTENING (30%)

Part 2a Directions: For each question, you will hear some background information in English. Then you will hear a passage in Spanish twice, followed by a question in English. Listen carefully. After you have heard the question, read the question and the four suggested answers. Choose the best answer and write its number in the appropriate space on your answer sheet. (9%)

1. What did your mother order to drink?
   1. carrot juice
   2. coffee
   3. mineral water
   4. lemonade

2. Why did the teacher criticize your choice of vegetables?
   1. They were not nutritious.
   2. You did not include peas.
   3. She wanted you to pick only 1 vegetable, not 3.
   4. She'd prefer to see a variety of colors on the plate.

3. What is happening in this scene?
   1. The actor is setting the table
   2. The actor is driving a car
   3. The actress is buying jewelry
   4. The actress is cooking a meal.

Part 2b Directions: For each question, you will hear some background information in English. Then you will hear a passage in Spanish twice, followed by a question in Spanish. Listen carefully. After you have heard the question, read the question and the four suggested answers. Choose the best answer and write its number in the appropriate space on your answer sheet.

4. ¿Qué toma Luisa para postre?
   1. queso
   2. pan dulce
   3. fruta
   4. helado

5. ¿De qué comida habla David?
   1. el desayuno
   2. el almuerzo
   3. la cena
   4. la merienda

6. ¿A qué hora toma merienda Rosalia?
   1. a las nueve de la mañana.
   2. a las dos de la tarde
   3. a las cuatro de la tarde
   4. a las siete de la noche

Part 2c Directions: For each question, you will hear some background information in English. Then you will hear a passage in Spanish twice, followed by a question in English. Listen carefully. After you have heard the question, read the question and look at the 4 pictures on your test. Choose the picture that best answers the question and write its number in the appropriate space on your answer sheet. (12%)

7. What does your mother want to buy?

8. What is the chef preparing?

9. What is Pedro going to order?

10. Where are you and your grandmother going?

Part 3a Directions: Answer the question in English based on the reading selection in Spanish. Choose the best answer to each question. Base your choice on the content of the reading selection. Write the number of your answer in the appropriate space on your answer sheet (8%)

REFRESCO TROPICAL

Para 6 personas

Ingredientes

1 litro de agua	1 taza de jugo de piña
3 limones	1 toronja
1 naranja	1/2 taza de azúcar

Preparación

Esta bebida es muy fácil de preparar. Ponga el jugo de piña y el agua en un jarro grande. Añada azúcar. Exprima los jugos de los limones, la toronja y la naranja en el jarro y mezcle todos los ingredientes. Ponga el jarro en la nevera. Sirva la bebida con cubitos de hielo.

11. What would this recipe be used for making?
    1. a beverage
    2. an omelet
    3. ice cream
    4. a soup

12. Which of the following is **NOT** an added ingredient of this recipe?
    1. water
    2. fruit juice
    3. sugar
    4. egg

MEAL TAKING/ FOOD/ DRINK 2

cocina mexicana BUSCAR

Los Sitios Web

1. **La Cocina Yanqui** - un restaurante en el centro de Veracruz con comida auténtica de los Estados Unidos: perros calientes, hamburguesa con papas fritas, macarrones y queso, pastel de manzana, los frijoles de Boston, pollo frito a la Kentucky.
www.cocinayanqui.com

2. **Paradero Casal** - una tienda con muebles para toda la casa: lavaplatos y neveras para la **cocina**, bañeras e inodoros para el baño, camas y cómodas para el dormitorio, sofás y sillones para la sala, mesas y sillas para el comedor.
www.paradero.com

3. Instituto de Protocolo - una escuela donde Ud. aprende a ser camarero para eventos diplomáticos. Trabaje en una **cocina** y un comedor. Aprenda como poner una mesa, servir la comida a los presidentes, a los reyes, a los diplomáticos.
www.instidiplomat.com

4. Nuestra **Cocina** - un sitio dedicado a los platos típicos de nuestro país. Maíz, chiles, chocolate y cactus son exclusivos de nuestra **cocina**. Aprenda como nuestros bisabuelos cocinaron enchiladas, tacos, tamales, tortillas, pollo de limón.
www.historiamexico.com

5. La Clase de **Cocina** - sitio oficial de " la Película mexicana del año ". Con el gran talento del actor cómico Juan Báez. Le gustarán a Ud. las acciones tontas de un mecánico que se enamora de una profesora de **cocina**.
www.peliculamexico.org

13. Which website would you click if you were doing a report on the origins of Mexican food?

1. La Cocina Yanqui
2. La Clase de Cocina
3. Paradero Casal
4. Nuestra Cocina

14. Who would be interested in reading the website of the Instituto de Protocolo?

1. someone wishing to be a waiter
2. someone wishing to be a teacher
3. someone wishing to be a butcher
4. someone wishing to be an interpreter

Part 3b Directions: Answer the question in Spanish based on the reading selection in Spanish. Choose the best answer to each question. Base your choice on the content of the reading selection. Write the number of your answer in the appropriate space on your answer sheet.

LA SOPERA

116/ Avenida Rey Carlos de Borbón

Estamos enfrente de la estación de ferrocarril a la derecha del cine

Gazpacho andaluz ......3,00 euros
Sopa de legumbres......2,75 euros
Sopa de pescado....... .5,00 euros
Sopa de pollo.............4,00 euros

Ensalada de espinacas..............4 euros
Ensalada mixta ....3 euros
Ensalada de frijoles................. 4 euros
Ensalada griega........................7 euros

Nosotros servimos sólamente quesos españoles: mahón - manchego - majorero - cabrales - zamorano

Cada plato de queso 5 euros

Abierto todos los días excepto los jueves
lunes - miércoles 10.00 - 4.00
viernes - domingo 9.30 - 3.30

15. ¿En qué día está cerrada este restaurante?
   1. lunes
   2. jueves
   3. miércoles
   4. domingo

16. ¿Cuánto cuesta un plato del queso manchego?
   1. cinco euros
   2. tres euros
   3. cuatro euros
   4. siete euros

Acto II, Escena 3

(A la derecha hay una mesa con mantel rojo y dos sillas.
Un hombre y una mujer joven caminan hasta la mesa y se sientan.
Un camarero camina hasta ellos desde la izquierda.)

CAMARERO: ¿En qué puedo servirle ?
HOMBRE: ¿Cuál es el especial del día?.
CAMARERO: Salmón frito con arroz y judias verdes.
HOMBRE: Muy bien. Me gusta mucho el pescado. Tráigame el salmón, por favor.
CAMARERO: ¿Y para Usted, señora?
MUJER: ¿Hay pavo?
CAMARERO: Lo siento. Hoy, no. Le recomiendo el pollo a la parilla con papas fritas y frijoles. Es muy sabroso.
MUJER: Muy bien...El pollo, por favor.

(El camarero se va y regresa en dos minutos.)

CAMARERO: Aquí están los platos. Buen provecho.
HOMBRE: ¡Qué rápido!
CAMARERO: Con el microondas de hoy la cocina es muy rápida.

(El telón se cierra)

17. ¿Qué pide el señor?
    1. carne 2. pavo 3. pollo 4. pescado

18. Las personas están ......
    1. en la panadería
    2. en una iglesia
    3. en un restaurante
    4. en un dormitorio

MEAL TAKING/ FOOD/ DRINK 2

Part 4 WRITING (20%)

Part 4 Directions: Choose two of the three writing tasks provided below. Your answer to each of the two questions should be written entirely in Spanish and should contain a minimum of 30 words.

Place names and brand names written in Spanish count as one word. Contractions are counted as one word. Salutations, closings and commonly used abbreviations are included in the word count. Numbers, unless written as words, and names of people do not count as words.

Be sure that you have satisfied the purpose of the task. The sentence structure and /or expressions used should be connected logically and demonstrate a wide range of vocabulary with minimal repetition.

4a. You are staying with a family in a Spanish speaking country in an exchange student program. Write a letter to your Spanish class in your home school telling them about one of the meals served by your host family. You may wish to include:

- The meal you are writing about
- The time this meal is usually eaten
- Who prepares this meal
- What is served at this meal including vegetables, desserts and beverages
- Whether you like or dislike this meal and why

4b. You are staying in a country where the language you are studying is spoken. You will be meeting a pen pal from that country. Invite him/her to a restaurant for lunch. You may include:

- The name and location of this restaurant
- The type of restaurant that it is
- What kind of food is served in this restaurant
- What is the specialty of this restaurant

4c. Your pen pal has asked you to describe your favorite snack foods. Write him a letter about them. You may wish to include:

- How many snack foods you like
- The names of the snacks
- The type of foods they are
- Where you buy them
- How much they cost
- Why you like them

MEAL TAKING/ FOOD/ DRINK 2

ANSWER SHEET

Nombre y Apellido ______________________________ Fecha _____________

Part I **Speaking** __________ (30%)
Part 2 **Listening (30%)** **PART 3: READING** (20%)

2a.	2b.	2c.	3a.(8%)	3b.(12%)
1._____	4._____	7._____	11._____	15._____
2._____	5._____	8._____	12._____	16._____
3._____	6._____	9._____	13._____	17._____
		10._____	14._____	18._____

Part 4 **Writing (20%) 20 words** **Write 2 paragraphs** **4a , 4b or 4c**

1____

2____

MEAL TAKING/ FOOD/ DRINK 2

Shopping

SHOPPING 2

SHOPPING 2

TEACHER'S SCRIPT FOR THE EXAM, PART II (Listening, 30%)

Part 2a Directions: For each question, you will hear some background information in English. Then you will hear a passage in Spanish twice, followed by a question in English. Listen carefully. After you have heard the question, read the question and the four suggested answers. Choose the best answer and write its number in the appropriate space on your answer sheet. (9%)

1. You are shopping for a gift to give your host mother. The salesman says to you:

   Aquí tengo anillos y aretes. La pulsera de oro cuesta cincuenta dólares. Tengo joyas caras y joyas baratas. ¿Cuánto dinero quiere Ud. gastar?

   What is this salesman selling? (2)

2. Your friend David is looking for a job at the restaurant El Sombrero Pardo. He says:

   Los precios de la comida son muy altos en el restaurante El Sombrero Pardo. Una taza de café cuesta cinco dólares y un vaso de vino cuesta treinta dólares. Los clientes son personas muy ricas y ellos son muy generosos. Mi primo trabaja aquí como camarero. El me dice que recibe cuatrocientos dólares en propinas en una noche.

   Why does David want a job at this restaurant? (1)

3. Carmen and Luisa are in a department store. Carmen says to Luisa:

   Mira, Luisa. Las blusas y las faldas son una ganga. La blusa amarilla es muy bonita. Me gustan mucho los vestidos verdes. ¿Qué talla usas tú?

   In what department of the store are these girls? (3)

Part 2b Directions: For each question, you will hear some background information in English. Then you will hear a passage in Spanish twice, followed by a question in Spanish. Listen carefully. After you have heard the question, read the question and the four suggested answers. Choose the best answer and write its number in the appropriate space on your answer sheet. (9%)

4. You are visiting your uncle at his place of business. He is speaking to a customer. He says:

   El pollo cuesta tres pesos por kilo. Y el biftec es cuatro pesos por kilo. Hoy la especialidad es el jamón.

   ¿Qué vende tu tío? (2)

5. You are about to board a plane. You hear a man speaking to his wife. He says:

   Tengo el dinero y las tarjetas de crédito en mi cartera. Los pasaportes están aquí en mi chaqueta. ¡Ay! Los cheques de viajero. ¿Dónde están los cheques de viajero? ¡Ay! ahora recuerdo. Los cheques de viajero están en la maleta negra y la maleta negra está ahora en el avión.

   ¿Qué busca el señor? (4)

6. You and your friend María are passing a store inside a shopping mall. María says:

   Esta tienda vende ropa excelente y los precios son bajos. Pero yo no voy de compras más allí. No me gustan las personas que trabajan en esta tienda. Los empleados no son amables. Ellos son terribles y perezosos. ¿Y la cajera? Ella es siempre antipática.

   ¿Por que María no va de compras en esta tienda? (3)

Part 2c Directions: For each question, you will hear some background information in English. Then you will hear a passage in Spanish twice, followed by a question in English. Listen carefully. After you have heard the question, read the question and look at the 4 pictures on your test. Choose the picture that best answers the question and write its number in the appropriate space on your answer sheet. (12%)

7. You are living with a family in Ecuador. Your host mother says to you:

   Mi esposo no va a trabajar hoy. Está enfermo y está en la cama ahora. Voy a la farmacia para comprarle medicina.

   Where is your host father? (2)

8. Teresa is getting ready to go out with friends. She says to her mother:

   Mamá, ¿dónde está mi traje de baño nuevo? Es rosado. Mis amigas y yo vamos a la playa por la tarde. Vamos a nadar.

   What is Teresa looking for? (1)

9. Pedro is at home. His mother says to him:

   Ve a mirarte en el espejo en mi dormitorio. La corbata azul va muy bien con la camisa blanca y el traje. Tú vas a ser el muchacho más guapo a la quinceañera de María Teresa.

   What does he do next? (2)

10. Pilar is shopping for clothes with her mother. She says to her mother:

    En mi escuela necesito llevar zapatos negros y calcetines azules. Pero hay un baile este sábado y necesito unas medias y un par de tacones altos.

    Where are these items worn? (1)

Listening Comprehension Answers:
For all chapters, the answers are indicated in parentheses following each question. (See questions 1-10 on the previous pages.)

Reading Comprehension answers:

3a. (8%) 11. __2__ 12. __1__ 13. __1__ 14. __4__

3b (12%) 15. __1__ 16. __3__ 17. __4__ 18. __3__

SHOPPING 2

Nombre ______________________________ Fecha ______________________

EXAMINATION

Part I SPEAKING (30%)
Part II LISTENING (30%)

Part 2a Directions: For each question, you will hear some background information in English. Then you will hear a passage in Spanish twice, followed by a question in English. Listen carefully. After you have heard the question, read the question and the four suggested answers. Choose the best answer and write its number in the appropriate space on your answer sheet (9%)

1. What is this salesman selling?
   1. perfume
   2. jewelry
   3. gloves
   4. scarves

2. Why does David want a job at this restaurant?
   1. He would make a lot of money in tips
   2. He would get a free meal.
   3. It is in walking distance of his house
   4. He gets to wear a mariachi costume

3. In what department of the store are these girls?
   1. the shoes department
   2. the jewelry department
   3. the women´s clothing department
   4. the housewares department

Part 2b Directions: For each question, you will hear some background information in English. Then you will hear a passage in Spanish twice, followed by a question in Spanish. Listen carefully. After you have heard the question, read the question and the four suggested answers. Choose the best answer and write its number in the appropriate space on your answer sheet. (9%)

4. ¿Que vende tu tío?
   1. pan
   2. carne
   3. dulces
   4. legumbres

5. ¿Qué busca el señor?
   1. la cartera
   2. la maleta azul
   3. la chaqueta
   4. los cheques de viajero

6. ¿Por que María no va de compras en esta tienda?
   1. Los precios son muy altos.
   2. La ropa no es buena.
   3. Los empleados no son simpáticos
   4. La tienda está en un barrio malo.

SHOPPING 2

Part 2c Directions: For each question, you will hear some background information in English. Then you will hear a passage in Spanish twice, followed by a question in English. Listen carefully. After you have heard the question, read the question and look at the 4 pictures on your test. Choose the picture that best answers the question and write its number in the appropriate space on your answer sheet. (12%)

7. Where is your host father?

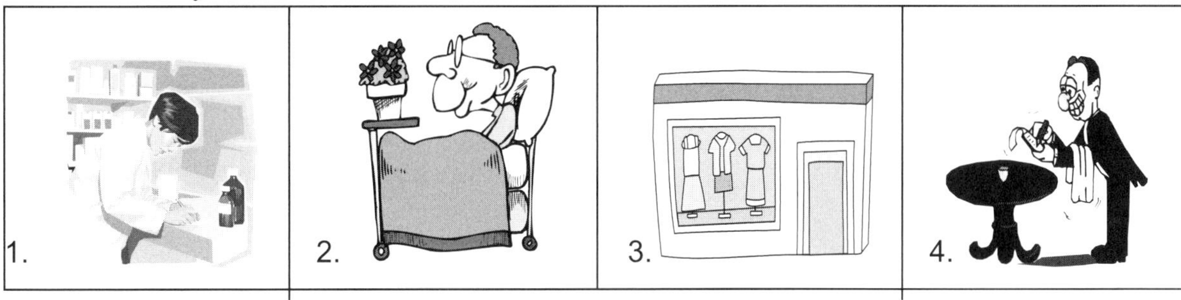

8. What is Teresa looking for?

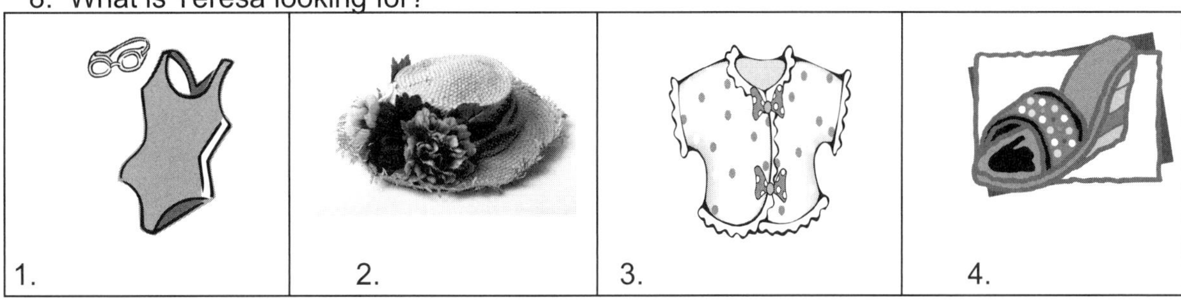

8. What does he do next?

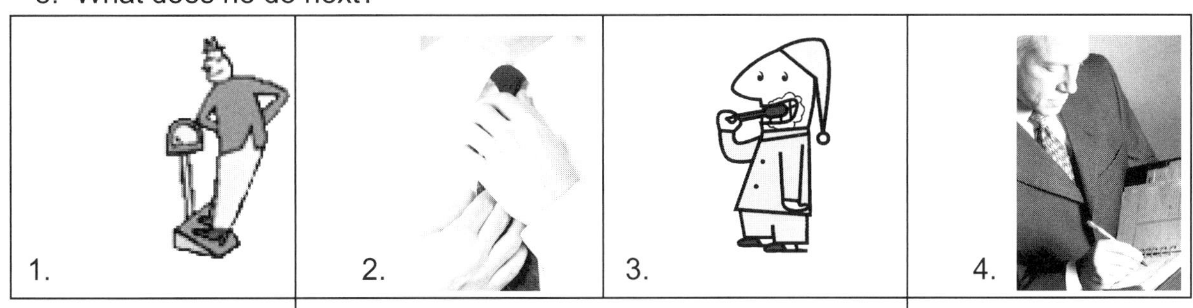

9. Where are these items worn?

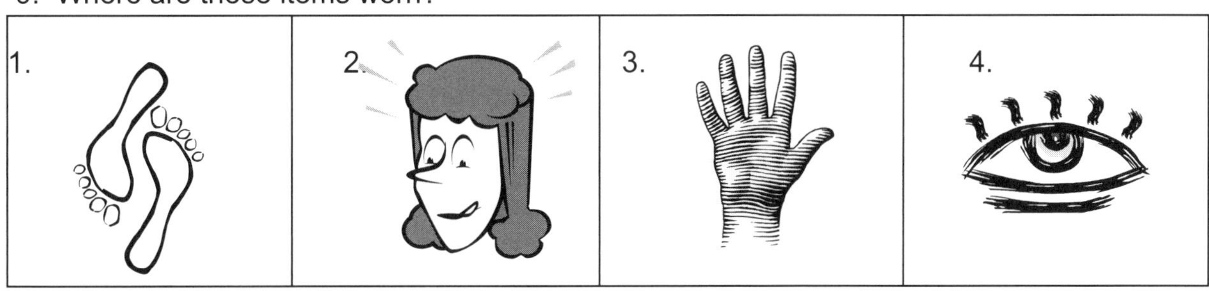

SHOPPING 2

Part 3a Directions: Answer the question in English based on the reading selection in Spanish. Choose the best answer to each question. Base your choice on the content of the reading selection. Write the number of your answer in the appropriate space on your answer sheet (8%).

DEPARTAMENTO	PLANTA	DEPARTAMENTO	PLANTA
Cristalería	2	Perfumería	1
Electrodómesticos	2	Rejolería	1
Joyería	1	Restaurante	4
Juguetería	5	Ropa para hombres	3
Librería	5	Ropa para niños	5
Material para deportes	3	Ropa para señoras	4
Muebles	2	Zapatería	5

11. On what floor does one buy furniture?
    1. First floor
    2. Second floor
    3. Third floor
    4. Fourth floor

12. What can one buy on the fifth floor?
    1. books, toys and children´s clothing
    2. tennis racket, baseball caps and neckties
    3. women's clothing
    4. men's cologne, clocks, bracelets

SHOPPING 2

A

3 cuadernos
papel de impresora láser
lápices
calculadora
bolígrafos

B

una docena de huevos
mantequilla
sal
pimienta
queso

C

una bufanda
botas de cuero 11 1/2
guantes
un suéter ex-grande

D

pantalones cortos (azul)
camiseta (amarilla)
zapatos de deportes
medias de algodón (amarillas)

E

gafas de sol
sombrero de paja
sandalias
toalla de playa
traje de baño

13. Which shopping list belongs to a student getting ready for school?
    1. A   3. B
    2. D   4. E

14. The person with shopping list C.....
    1. is going on a boat cruise to a tropical island
    2. is going to make a cheese omelets
    3. has joined a soccer team
    4. lives in a region where it snows a lot

SHOPPING 2

Part 3b Directions: Answer the question in Spanish based on the reading selection in Spanish. Choose the best answer to each question. Base your choice on the content of the reading selection. Write the number of your answer in the appropriate space on your answer sheet.

Cartoon

scene 1

Pepe: Lulu, ¿qué haces para ser tan flaca?
Lulu: Yo corro. Yo corro todos los días ¿por qué no corres tú?

scene 2

Pepe: Es una buena idea. Yo voy a correr cada día .

scene 3

Pepe: ¡Ah! una heladería. Voy a comprar un helado de pistacho. Es mi sabor favorito.

scene 4

Pepe: ¡Ah! una pastelería. Esta pastelería es famosa para sus galletas de chocolate. Tengo que comprarlas.

scene 5

Pepe: ¡Ah! un quiosco de limonada. Tengo sed ahora. Compro el tamaño mediana.

scene 6

Pepe: Hamburguesas y tacos. Sabrosos.

scene 7

Pepe: Tú sabes, Lulu que me gusta correr, pero soy todavía gordo.

15. ¿Cómo es Lulu?
    1. delgada y atlética
    2. rubia e indiferente
    3. gorda y perezosa
    4. indisciplinada y antipática

16. ¿Dónde compra Pepe una bebida?
    1. en la pastelería
    2. en la heladería
    3. en el quiosco de limonada
    4. en el quiosco de tacos

A
Pijamas para hombres
50% algodón/ 50% rayón
Tamaños P/ M/ G / XG
azul claro / azul marino /
verde / marrón
. ...14 Euros

B
Abrigo para señoras
Pura lana 100%
Tallas 44 - 54
18-555 rojo
18-556 negro
18-678 azul oscuro
...................255 Euros

C
Vestidos de noche
Pura seda 100%
Tallas 40 - 48
30-354 blanco
30-500 rosado
30-355 negro
...................85 Euros

D
Impermeable para niños
en Vinyl
Tamaños P/ M/ G
amarillo
anaranjado
azul
....................30 Euros

17. ¿Cuál es la cosa más cara?
    1. C
    3. A
    3. D
    4. B

18. ¿Qué clase de ropa se pone para acostarse en la cama?
    1. C
    3. A
    3. D
    4. B

Part 4 WRITING (20%)

Part 4 Directions: Choose two of the three writing tasks provided below. Your answer to each of the two questions should be written entirely in Spanish and should contain a minimum of **30 words**.

Place names and brand names written in Spanish count as one word. Contractions are counted as one word. Salutations, closing, and commonly used abbreviations are included in the word count. Numbers, unless written as words, and names of people do not count as words.

Be sure that you have satisfied the purpose of the task. The sentence structure and-or expressions used should be connected logically and demonstrate a wide range of vocabulary with minimal repetition.

4a. You are going to spend your vacation with a pen pal who has never met you. Your pen pal is going to meet you at a very busy airport. In order for your pen pal to recognize you easily, you send out an e-mail message prior to departure. In your message you may wish to include:

- A physical description of yourself
- A description of what you will be wearing, including the colors, size and fabric of your clothes
- The kind of luggage you will be carrying, including the color, size and number of pieces

4b. You ordered an item from a mail order company. Unfortunately, the company sent you the wrong item. Write a letter of complaint explaining the problem. In your letter you may wish to include:

- The item you ordered, including its size, color, fabric, price as applicable
- A description of the item the mail order company sent you
- An explanation of what the company must do to correct the problem

4c. Your local Merchants' Association is holding a written contest on the best store in your community. Write a letter on your favorite store. In your letter you may wish to include:

- The name of the store
- A reason why you shop there
- What items are sold in this store
- A description of the quality of goods sold there
- A description of the kind of service given

ANSWER SHEET

Nombre y Apellido ______________________________ Fecha ______________

Part I **Speaking** __________ (30%)
Part 2 **Listening (30%)**

2a.	2b.	2c.
1._____	4._____	7._____
2._____	5._____	8._____
3._____	6._____	9._____
		10._____

PART 3: READING (20%)

3a.(8%)	3b.(12%)
11._____	15._____
12._____	16._____
13._____	17._____
14._____	18._____

Part 4 **Writing (20%) 20 words** **Write 2 paragraphs** **4a , 4b or 4c**

1____

____

____

____

____

____

____

____

____

2____

____

____

____

____

____

____

____

____

____

____

____

Health and Welfare

HEALTH AND WELFARE 2

TEACHER'S SCRIPT FOR THE EXAM, Part 2 (LISTENING 30%)

Part 2a Directions: For each question, you will hear some background information in English. Then you will hear a passage in Spanish twice, followed by a question in English. Listen carefully. After you have heard the question, read the question and the four suggested answers. Choose the best answer and write its number in the appropriate space on your answer sheet. (9%)

1. Carlos is at his doctor´s office. The doctor says to him:

   Tú no puedes jugar al básquetbol. Tú tienes el dedo indice roto en la mano izquierda. Es una buena cosa que tú escribes con la mano derecha.

   What did Carlos break? (3)

2. A policeman is speaking to Señorita Robles. He is filling an accident report. He wants to know the exact time of the accident. Señorita Robles answers:

   Eran las siete y nueve. Tomo siempre el tren a las siete y diez. Yo estaba corriendo hacía el tren cuando me caí. Ahora me duele la rodilla.

   What was Señorita Robles doing prior to her accident? (4)

3. Your family doctor has left a message for your parents on the answering machine in your home. He wants to emphasize a point. He says:

   Su hijo tiene la varicela. No le recomiendo aspirinas. Repito. Su hijo no puede tomar aspirinas porque él tiene menos de doce años.

   What advice did the doctor wish to emphasize? (1)

Part 2b Directions: For each question, you will hear some background information in English. Then you will hear a passage in Spanish twice, followed by a question in Spanish. Listen carefully. After you have heard the question, read the question and the four suggested answers. Choose the best answer and write its number in the appropriate space on your answer sheet. (9%)

4. You are listening to the radio and hear this announcement. The announcer says:

   ¿Está Ud. siempre enojado? ¿Está siempre triste? ¿ Si Ud. está nervioso o preocupado...si Ud. tiene un problema mental, Ud. tiene que hablar con el doctor Catapano, psicólogo reconocido del Hospital Cubano de la Salud Mental.

   ¿Por qué va una persona al doctor Catapano? (3)

5. David is talking to a salesman. He says:

   ¿Puede Ud. ayudarme? El número de mis viejas botas es once. Ahora necesito zapatos de deportes y medias blancas.

   ¿Dónde está David? (1)

6. You are in the doctor´s examination room. He says to you:

   ¿No puedes leer la línea número 6? Tú ves bien las cosas cerca de ti, pero cuando miras las cosas de lejos, tú no ves bien. Pienso que tú necesitas anteojos.

   ¿Por qué vas a este doctor? (4)

Part 2c Directions: For each question, you will hear some background information in English. Then you will hear a passage in Spanish twice, followed by a question in English. Listen carefully. After you have heard the question, read the question and look at the four pictures on your test. Choose the picture that best answers the question and write its number in the appropriate space on your answer sheet. (12%)

7. Your uncle is telling you about his job. He says:

   Yo trabajo en un hospital. Pero no soy médico y no soy enfermero. Yo trabajo en la cocina donde yo preparo comida para los pacientes. Para mejorarse, necesita comer bien.

   What is your uncle's profession? (2)

8. Your health class teacher is speaking to the class. She says:

   Es muy importante beber leche cada día para tener dientes fuertes. La leche contiene la vitamina D y muchos minerales como el calcio.

   What does she recommend that one drinks? (1)

9. Your mother is speaking to you. She says:

   Tú tienes dolor de cabeza y dolor de oído porque no llevas una gorra.
   What does your mother want you to protect? (2)

10. You are staying with a family in Uruguay. Your host mother says to you:

Yo voy a la farmacia. Tengo que comprar aspirinas para mi hijo.
El tiene un resfriado.

To what store is your host mother going? (1)

Listening Comprehension answers:
For all chapters, the answers are indicated in parentheses following each question. (See
questions 1-10 on the previous pages.)

Reading Comprehension answers:

3a (8%)	11. __1__	12. __2__	13. __3__	14. __4__
3b (12%)	15. __1__	16.__3__	17. __4__	18. __4__

HEALTH AND WELFARE 2

Nombre ______________________________ Fecha ______________________________

EXAMINATION

Part 1 SPEAKING (30%)
Part 2 LISTENING (30%)

Part 2a Directions: For each question, you will hear some background information in English. Then you will hear a passage in Spanish twice, followed by a question in English. Listen carefully. After you have heard the question, read the question and the four suggested answers. Choose the best answer and write its number in the appropriate space on your answer sheet. (9%)

1. What did Carlos break?
   1. his right leg
   2. his nose
   3. his index finger
   4. a tooth

2. What was Señorita Robles doing prior to her accident?
   1. ice-skating
   2. driving
   3. skiing
   4. running

3. What advice did the doctor wish to emphasize?
   1. He is not to be given aspirin as a medication
   2. He is to stay in bed all the time.
   3. He should use calamine lotion on his skin
   4. He must avoid contact with others his age.

Part 2b Directions: For each question, you will hear some background information in English. Then you will hear a passage in Spanish twice, followed by a question in Spanish. Listen carefully. After you have heard the question, read the question and the four suggested answers. Choose the best answer and write its number in the appropriate space on your answer sheet. (9%)

4. ¿Por qué va una persona al doctor Catapano?
   1. El tiene un brazo roto.
   2. El quiere vender vitaminas.
   3. El tiene un problema mental
   4. El tiene dolor de muelas.

5. ¿Dónde está David?
   1. en la zapatería
   2. en la carnicería
   3. en una tienda de sombreros
   4. en una iglesia

6. ¿Por qué vas a este doctor?
   1. Tengo una pierna rota
   2. Tengo indigestión
   3. Tengo la rubeola.
   4. Tengo un problema con los ojos

Part 2c Directions: For each question, you will hear some background information in English. Then you will hear a passage in Spanish twice, followed by a question in English. Listen carefully. After you have heard the question, read the question and look at the 4 pictures on your test. Choose the picture that best answers the question and write its number in the appropriate space on your answer sheet. (12%)

What is your uncle's profession?

8. What does she recommend that one drinks?

9. What does your mother want you to protect?

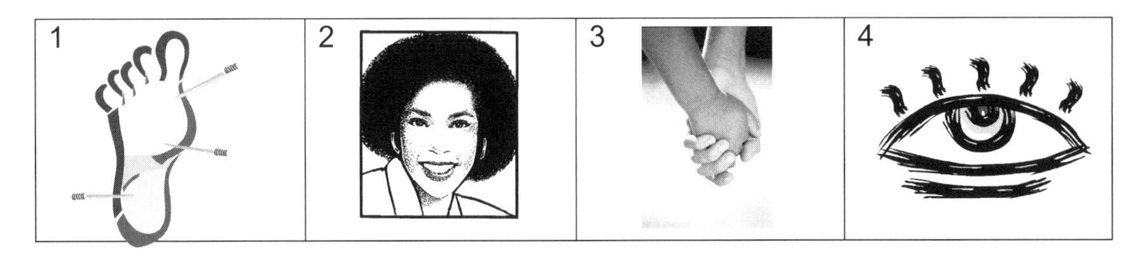

10. Where is your host mother going?

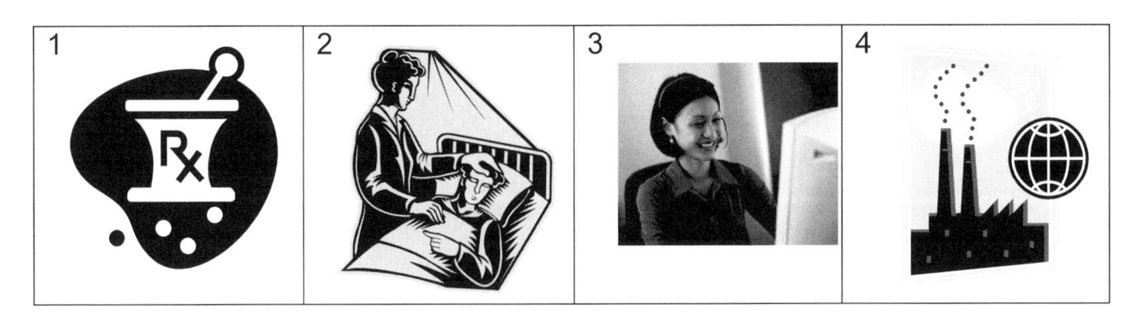

Part 3a Directions: Answer the question in English based on the reading selection in Spanish. Choose the best answer to each question. Base your choice on the content of the reading selection. Write the number of your answer in the appropriate space on your answer sheet. (8%)

REMEDIOS PARA MI GATO

Yo tengo un gato delgado
Que tiene un mal resfriado.
Le doy un pescado asado
Y un jarro de vino rosado.

Cuando tiene dolor de cabeza
Le doy un barril de cerveza
Y si él camina con torpeza
Le doy coñac de cereza.

11. According to the poem, when is the cat given a baked fish?
    1. when it has a bad cold.
    2. when it is hungry.
    3. when it is dizzy.
    4. when it is thirsty.

12. What other illnesses does the cat have?
    1. sore throat
    2. headache
    3. ear ache
    4. fever

BLANDEX

Para la higiene oral
Cepíllese los dientes
con esta pasta dental
tres veces al día y Ud.
tiendrá dientes blancos

FINALEX

Este repelente de
insectos es el más
eficaz del mundo.
Una aplicación de
este producto sobre
la piel dura 30 horas

LIMONEX

Este jarabe a base de
limón y de cereza silvestre
le ayudará a Ud. si tiene
fiebre, dolor de garganta,
dolor en el pecho o espalda,
y mucosidad.

ZANOREX

Crema dermatólogica
a base de zanahoria
para el cuidado y la
protección de la cara
contra los rayos peligrosos
del sol.

13. Which product would you take for a chest or back pain?

    1. Blandex 2. Finalex 3. Limonex 4. Zanorex

14. Which product uses carrots in its ingredients?

    1. Blandex 2. Finalex 3. Limonex 4. Zanorex

Part 3b Directions: Answer the question in Spanish based on the reading selection in Spanish. Choose the best answer to each question. Base your choice on the content of the reading selection. Write the number of your answer in the appropriate space on your answer sheet (12%)

Para escribir una buena composición Ud. tiene que usar los cinco sentidos: la vista, el oído, el tacto, el olfacto y el gusto. Lea este ejemplo:

Estoy escuchando la música de guitarra. El camarero me toca el hombro. El me da un vaso frío. Yo puedo oler el aroma de los limones y la naranja. La bebida, roja como la sangre, es muy dulce y sabrosa. Me siento bien y contenta.

15. ¿Qué oye esta persona?
    1. música
    2. el aroma de frutas
    3. el color del refresco
    4. el sabor dulce de una bebida

16. El camarero toca ....
    1. la pierna de la cliente.
    2. la sangre de la cliente.
    3. el hombro de la cliente
    4. el cuello de la cliente.

Francisco Xavier Balmis era un médico español. El nació en la ciudad de Alicante en el año 1753. En 1803 Balmis leyó un libro francés por el doctor Jacques-Louis Moreau. El leyó en el libro que un médico inglés había descubierto la vacuna contra la viruela en el año 1796. Este médico inglés se llamaba Eduardo Jenner. Balmis tradujo el libro de francés al español.

En el año 1804 el doctor Balmis llegó a México con la vacuna. El habló del descubrimiento del doctor Jenner con los médicos mexicanos. El doctor Balmis era instrumental en la erradicación de la viruela en México y en América Latina. Antes de la introducción de la vacuna, la viruela era la causa principal de la mortalidad entre los niños mexicanos. Hoy la viruela es inexistente.

17. ¿Cuál es la nacionalidad de Eduardo Jenner?
    1. francés
    2. español
    3. mexicano
    4. inglés

18. ¿Cuándo llegó a México el doctor Balmis con la vacuna contra la viruela?
    1. en 1753
    2. en 1803
    3. en 1796
    4. en 1804

Part 4 WRITING (20%)

Part 4 Directions: Choose two of the three writing tasks provided below. Your answer to each of the two questions should be written entirely in Spanish and should contain a minimum of 30 words.

Place names and brand names written in Spanish count as one word. Contractions are counted as one word. Salutations, closings and commonly used abbreviations are included in the word count. Numbers, unless written as words, and names of people do not count as words.

Be sure that you have satisfied the purpose of the task. The sentence structure and /or expressions used should be connected logically and demonstrate a wide range of vocabulary with minimal repetition.

4a. You have seen a robbery. The police have asked you to write down a description of the person you saw. In your written report you may wish to include:

- The sex, height and built of the person you saw
- The color of his/her hair and eyes
- Facial characteristics such as whether the person had a big/ small nose, large ears etc.
- What the person was wearing
- Whether the person was young or old

4b. You like to draw cartoons of unusual creatures. You have won a prize for your picture. Your pen pal in Spain has asked you to send him a written description to see if he or she can duplicate it. In your description you may wish to include:

- How big your "creature" is
- How many arms, legs, eyes, ears etc. it has
- Whether the arms, legs are long
- Whether the eyes, ears, mouth are big
- What color it is

4c. You are on vacation with your family in a Spanish-speaking country. You were due to meet your pen pal and his family in their hometown the next day, but an illness has befallen your group. Your hotel has allowed you to e-mail your pen pal on their computer. Write a message canceling your meeting. You may wish to include:

- A statement canceling your meeting
- The member of your family who became ill
- The illness that this person has
- Whether this person had to go to a doctor/dentist/or hospital
- What kind of medication this person is taking
- A possible future date for a meeting

ANSWER SHEET

Nombre y Apellido ________________________________ Fecha ______________

Part I **Speaking** __________ (30%)
Part 2 **Listening (30%)** **PART 3: READING** (20%)

2a.	2b.	2c.	3a.(8%)	3b.(12%)
1._____	4._____	7._____	11._____	15._____
2._____	5._____	8._____	12._____	16._____
3._____	6._____	9._____	13._____	17._____
		10._____	14._____	18._____

Part 4 **Writing (20%) 20 words** **Write 2 paragraphs** **4a , 4b or 4c**

1____

2____

HEALTH AND WELFARE 2

PHYSICAL ENVIRONMENT

PHYSICAL ENVIRONMENT 2

TEACHER´S SCRIPT FOR THE EXAM, PART II (Listening, 30%)

Part 2a Directions: For each question, you will hear some background information in English. Then you will hear a passage in Spanish twice, followed by a question in English. Listen carefully. After you have heard the question, read the question and the four suggested answers. Choose the best answer and write its number in the appropriate space on your answer sheet. (9%)

1. You are interviewing Carlos, a teenager from Peru, for a summer job. He says:

   Me gusta mucho la naturaleza: los árboles, los animales, las montañas. Me gusta acampar en el aire fresco, pescar en los lagos y escalar las montañas.

   Where might a person do these activities? (2)

2. You are an exchange student in Venezuela. Your host mother is speaking to her husband. She explains:

   Sí, la tienda está cerca de aquí pero no camino. Voy en carro.
   Mira. Hace viento ahora y está lloviendo. Necesito el paraguas y el impermeable.

   Why isn't she walking to the store? (3)

3. Juanita is speaking to her cousin on the phone. She says:

   Yo vivo en el piso ochenta de un rascacielos. Mi escuela está en la próxima calle. Pero, necesito quince minutos para ir de mi apartamento a mi escuela porque en mi vecindario hay mucho tráfico y gente en las calles. Me gustaría vivir en el campo! Es tan tranquilo allí.

   What is Juanita's complaint? (4)

Part 2b Directions: For each question, you will hear some background information in English. Then you will hear a passage in Spanish twice, followed by a question in Spanish. Listen carefully. After you have heard the question, read the question and the four suggested answers. Choose the best answer and write its number in the appropriate space on your answer sheet.

4. Marisol tells you want she does on winter vacation. She says:

   En el mes de febrero estoy de vacaciones por una semana. Yo viajo por avión a una isla en el Caribe. Me gustan las playas allí porque son muy limpias. Yo nado y yo tomo sol todos los días.

   ¿Adónde va Marisol en el invierno? (4)

5. You are watching TV in Puerto Rico. The weather reporter says:

    Hoy es el diez de junio. Hace sol. La temperatura es 24 ° centigrados.
    Es un día perfecto para caminar en el parque.

    ¿Qué tiempo hace hoy? (3)

6. You meet your Spanish teacher at the florist´s. He says:

    Mañana es el catorce de febrero. Es el Día de San Valentín.
    Voy a comprar flores y chocolates para mi esposa. Por la noche
    vamos a un restaurante. Hace frío este mes y este restaurante
    tiene una chimenea. ¡Qué romántico!

    ¿En qué estación estamos? (4)

Part 2c Directions: For each question, you will hear some background information in English. Then you will hear a passage in Spanish twice, followed by a question in English. Listen carefully. After you have heard the question, read the question and look at the four pictures on your test. Choose the picture that best answers the question and write its number in the appropriate space on your answer sheet.

7. Diego is explaining something to his younger brother. He says:

    El proceso es muy fácil. Tú haces dos bolas de nieve enormes y las pones una sobre la otra. Luego, tú utilizas una zanahoria para la nariz, dos manzanas para los ojos y dos ramas de árbol para los brazos. Después, tú vistes al hombre de nieve con un sombrero viejo y una bufanda.

    What is Diego's brother going to do? (1)

8. You are traveling by car in northern Mexico. You come to a fork in the road and you ask a native where the road to the right leads. He tells you:

    A la derecha hay un desierto. Pero, tenga cuidado. Es peligroso viajar sin bastante agua y sin teléfono celular. Hace mucho calor y no hay tiendas o gasolineras por noventa kilómetros. El desierto es bonito y le gustaría tomar fotos de las plantas, especialmente el cacto.

    What will you see from your car? (2)

9. Your cousin from Uruguay is going to visit the museums and churches in your local city with your sister. She says to your sister:

    En agosto hace mucho calor. Y hoy hay sol. Mi piel es muy delicada. ¿Tienes algo que puedo ponerme sobre la cabeza?

    What would your cousin like to borrow? (2)

10. You turn on the car radio and hear this message. The speaker says:

    La nieve va a continuar hasta las once de la noche.Tenga cuidado en las calles. El hielo está peligroso y hace mucho frío. Es el día perfecto de estar dentro de la casa y beber un chocolate caliente.

    Who is speaking? (3)

Listening Comprehension Answers:
For all chapters, the answers are indicated in parentheses following each question. (See
questions 1-10 on the previous pages.)

Reading Comprehension answers:

3a. (8%) 11. __3__ 12. __4__ 13. __3__ 14. __4__

3b (12%) 15. __2__ 16. __2__ 17. __3__ 18. __4__

Nombre ______________________________ Fecha ______________________

EXAMINATION

Part 1 SPEAKING (30%)
Part 2 LISTENING (30%)

Part 2a Directions: For each question, you will hear some background information in
English. Then you will hear a passage in Spanish twice, followed by a question in English. Listen carefully. After you have heard the question, read the question and the four suggested answers. Choose the best answer and write its number in the appropriate space on your answer sheet. (9%)

1. Where might a person do these activities?
   1. on an ocean liner
   2. in the mountains
   3. in the desert
   4. in a large city

2. Why isn't she walking to the store?
   1. She is tired.
   2. She has a lot of groceries to buy.
   3. It is raining.
   4. She is going far.

3. What is Juanita's complaint?
   1. She gets too much homework at school.
   2. The library is closed on the weekends.
   3. The school bus is always late.
   4. There is too much traffic where she lives.

Part 2b Directions: For each question, you will hear some background information in English. Then you will hear a passage in Spanish twice, followed by a question in Spanish. Listen carefully. After you have heard the question, read the question and the four suggested answers. Choose the best answer and write its number in the appropriate space on your answer sheet. (9%)

4. ¿Adónde va Marisol en el invierno?
   1. a las montañas
   2. a una granja
   3. al campo
   4. al mar

5. ¿Que tiempo hace hoy?
   1. Hace mal tiempo.
   2. Hace buen tiempo.
   3. Hace viento.
   4. Está nevando.

6. ¿En qué estación estamos?
   1. la primavera
   2. el otoño
   3. el verano
   4. el invierno

Part 2c Directions: For each question, you will hear some background information in English. Then you will hear a passage in Spanish twice, followed by a question in English. Listen carefully. After you have heard the question, read the question and look at the four pictures on your test. Choose the picture that best answers the question and write its number in the appropriate space on your answer sheet. (12%)

7. What is Diego's brother going to do?

8. What will you see from your car?

9. What would your cousin like to borrow?

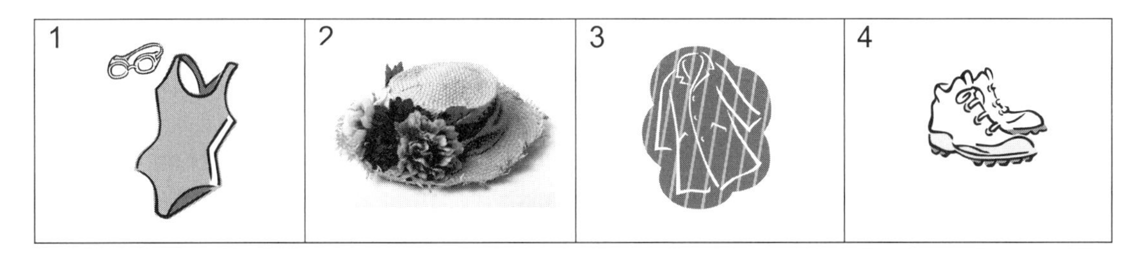

10. Who is speaking?

Part 3a Directions: Answer the question in English based on the reading selection in Spanish. Choose the best answer to each question. Base your choice on the content of the reading selection. Write the number of your answer in the appropriate space on your answer sheet. (8%)

BernH2O: ¡Hola! Juan
Juanbug: ¡Hola! Bernardo. ¿Qué hay de nuevo?
BernH2O: Mi padre está en Argentina.
Juanbug: ¿En Argentina? ¿Por qué?
BernH2O: Él trabaja para una agencia internacional de ecología. Está estudiando el problema de la contaminación en el Río de la Plata.
Juanbug: ¿El Río de la Plata? ¿Qué es?
BernH2O: Es el segundo río en importancia en la América Latina.
Juanbug: Tu padre tiene un trabajo muy interesante.
BernH2O: Yo sé.

11. What kind of pollution problem is being studied in Argentina?
   1. air pollution
   3. noise pollution
   3. water pollution
   4. land pollution

Casa de Tranquilidad

Nuestra casa está encima de una montaña baja en un florido jardín tropical. Es el lugar ideal para las personas que busquen descanso. Es un lugar tranquilo para aquellos que aman paseos en el mundo de la naturaleza. Huelan las flores y los árboles frutales. Oigan el mar que está cerca de nuestra casa. Y por la noche miren las estrellas en un cielo todo azul.

12. Who would **NOT** want to vacation at this place?
   1. Someone who just wants to relax
   2. Someone who enjoys walking along the beach
   3. Someone who is interested in tropical plants
   4. Someone who likes to go roller-blading

Martes, 5 de julio

Querido Profesor Alarcón,

Estoy aquí en Chile donde estoy trabajando en una granja de animales. Aquí hay alpacas, guanacos, vicuñas y llamas. La llama es mi animal favorito. Estoy aprendiendo mucho sobre estos animales y un día espero trabajar en un parque zoológico como veterinaria.

Mañana mi grupo va a los Andes para esquiar y patinar sobre hielo. Pero yo tengo que ir de compras a Santiago, la capital. Necesito guantes y calcetines de lana. Hace mucho frío aquí porque ahora es invierno.

Su estudiante favorita,

Luisa Lasala

13. Where is Luisa according to her letter?
    1. at a summer resort
    2. at a department store
    3. on a farm
    4. at the ice skating rink

14. What is Luisa going to do on July 6th?
    1. take a trip to the mountains.
    2. visit a zoo.
    3. go row boating.
    4. go shopping.

Part 3b Directions: Answer the question in Spanish based on the reading selection in Spanish. Choose the best answer to each question. Base your choice on the content of the reading selection. Write the number of your answer in the appropriate space on your answer sheet. (12%)

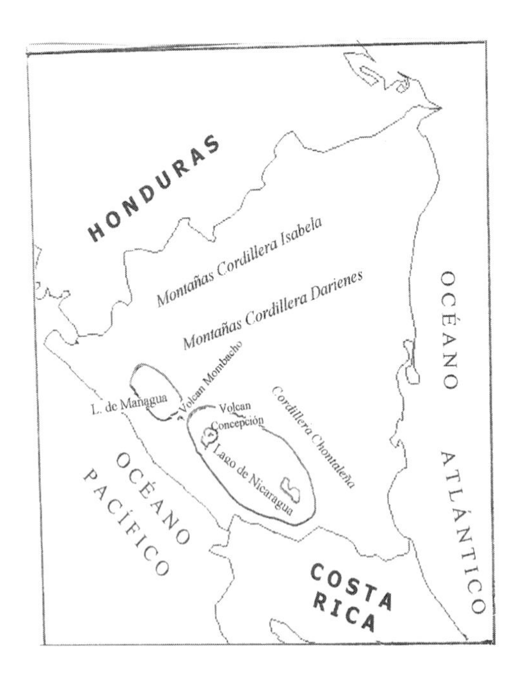

Nicaragua está casi en el centro del hemisferio occidental. Al norte hay el país de Honduras, y al sur el país de Costa Rica. Nicaragua está entre dos océanos, con el Pacífico al oeste y el Atlántico al este.

A lo largo de la costa Pacífico el clima es seco y tropical. En la región montañosa hace fresco. En la zona del Mar Caribe la humedad es alta. La temperatura normal es 27 º centigrados.

En Nicaragua hay sólo dos estaciones. De mayo a noviembre se observa la estación lluviosa. Y de diciembre a abril es el período de clima seco.

La posición de este país lo hace famoso por sus bellezas variadas. En este país centroamericano hay inmensos lagos, volcanes activos, lagunas bonitas en antiguos crateres, islas ricas en vegetación verde, playas hermosas, montañas altas y selvas tropicales.

15. ¿Qué hay directamente al norte de Nicaragua?
    1. el océano Pacífico
    2. Honduras
    3. el mar Caribe
    4. Costa Rica

16. ¿Cuántas estaciones se observan en Nicaragua?
    1. una
    2. dos
    3. tres
    4. cuatro

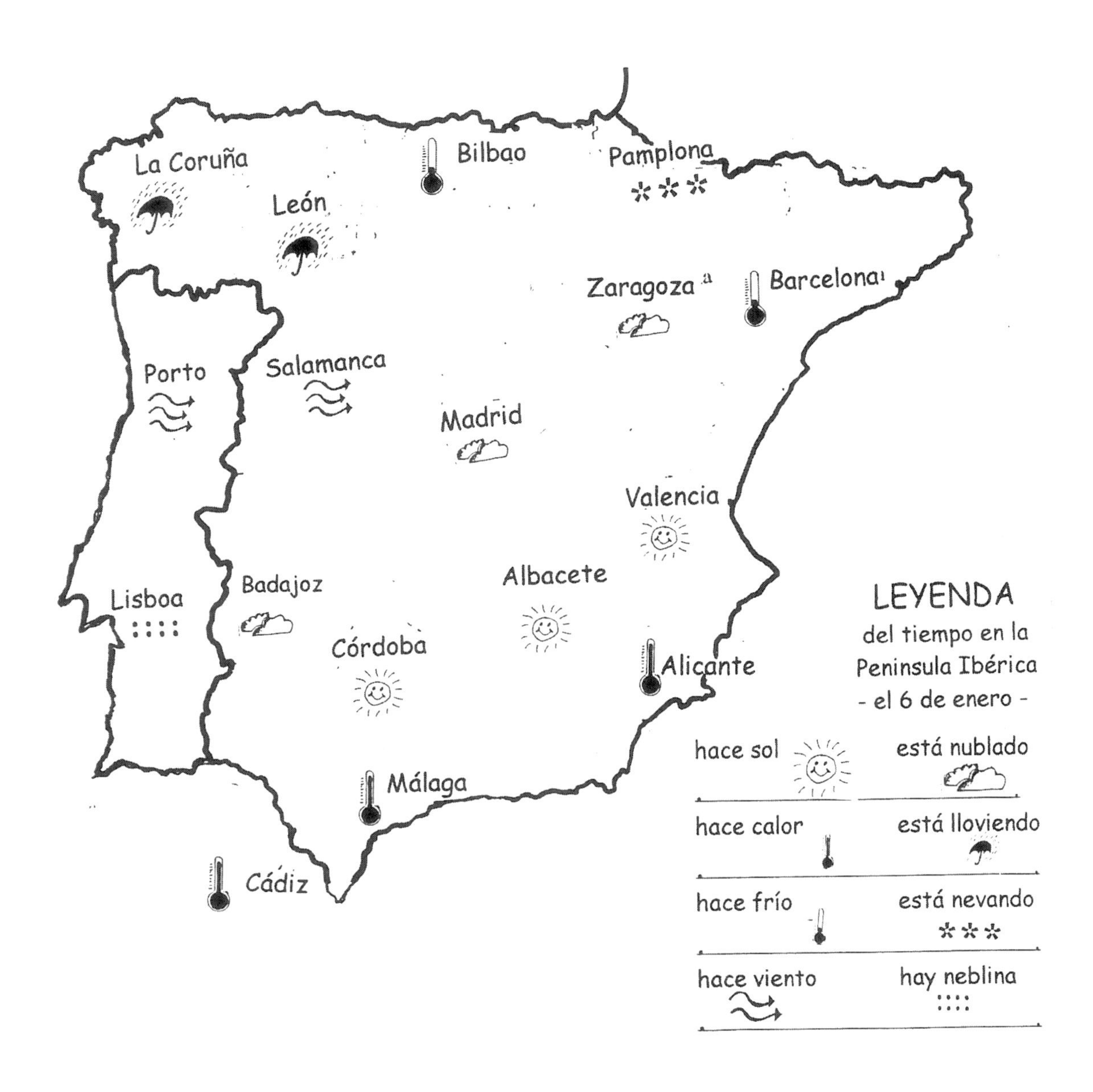

17. ¿ Dónde está nevando?
   1. Lisboa
   2. Bilbao
   3. Pamplona
   4. Badajoz

18. ¿Qué tiempo hace en Córdoba?
   1. Hace mal tiempo
   2. Está lloviendo
   3. Está nevando
   4. Hace buen tiempo

Part 4 WRITING (20%)

Part 4 Directions: Choose two of the three writing tasks provided below. Your answer to each of the two questions should be written entirely in Spanish and should contain a minimum of **30 words**.

Place names and brand names written in Spanish count as one word. Contractions are counted as one word. Salutations, closings and commonly used abbreviations are included in the word count. Numbers, unless written as words, and names of people do not count as words.

Be sure that you have satisfied the purpose of the task. The sentence structure and /or expressions used should be connected logically and demonstrate a wide range of vocabulary with minimal repetition.

4a. Write a letter to your Spanish-speaking pen pal telling him/her about the area in which you live. You may wish to include:

- The name of the town or region where you live
- What the physical features of the area look like
- What activities you can do because of the topography e.g. swimming in a lake/ river; skiing in the mountains etc.
- Why you like or dislike living in that area

4b. You are on a summer vacation. Write a letter in the target language to your friend telling him or her about your experience. You may wish to include the following items:

- Where you went on vacation
- Why you chose that area for vacation
- What means of transportation you took to arrive there
- What you saw there
- What the weather is like

4c. Your class had gone on a field trip recently where you were able to observe animals. Write a letter to a pen pal describing one of these animals. In your letter you may wish to include:

- The place where you had seen this animal: zoo, farm, aquarium, museum of natural history, a pet store, a veterinary clinic etc.
- What animal you saw
- A physical description of the animal
- The animal's usual habitat
- Whether you liked or disliked the animal and why

ANSWER SHEET

Nombre y Apellido ______________________________ Fecha ______________

Part I **Speaking** __________ (30%)
Part 2 **Listening (30%)**

2a.	2b.	2c.
1._____	4._____	7._____
2._____	5._____	8._____
3._____	6._____	9._____
		10._____

PART 3: READING (20%)

3a.(8%)	3b.(12%)
11._____	15._____
12._____	16._____
13._____	17._____
14._____	18._____

Part 4 **Writing (20%) 20 words** **Write 2 paragraphs** **4a , 4b or 4c**

1____

2____

PHYSICAL ENVIRONMENT 2

EARNING A LIVING

EARNING A LIVING 2

TEACHER'S SCRIPT FOR THE EXAM, Part 2 (LISTENING 30%)

Part 2a Directions: For each question, you will hear some background information in English. Then you will hear a passage in Spanish twice, followed by a question in English. Listen carefully. After you have heard the question, read the question and the four suggested answers. Choose the best answer and write its number in the appropriate space on your answer sheet. (9%)

1. Elena is telling her friend about her grandfather. She says:

   Mi abuelo trabaja en Hollywood. Conoce a muchos actores y actrices; pero, no es actor. Es peluquero y ha cortado el pelo de muchos actores famosos.

   What does Elena's grandfather do for a living? (1)

2. Roberto is reading a want ad in a Spanish-language newspaper. He reads:

   Esta compañía busca a una persona responsable y cooperativa. La persona tiene que hablar alemán, francés e italiano. La entrevista será el sábado desde las nueve hasta la una.

   What is the main requirement for this position? (2)

3. Pablo is talking to his guidance counselor about his future career goal. He says:

   Yo quiero ser contador porque me gusta mucho trabajar con los números. Mi asignatura favorita es las matemáticas.

   What would Pablo like to be? (1)

Part 2b Directions: For each question, you will hear some background information in English. Then you will hear a passage in Spanish twice, followed by a question in Spanish. Listen carefully. After you have heard the question, read the question and the four suggested answers. Choose the best answer and write its number in the appropriate space on your answer sheet. (9%)

4. Teresa is telling her classmate Juanita what kind of part-time work she is looking for. She says:

   Me gustaría trabajar en una oficina de un veterinario. Como yo tengo un perro y dos gatos en casa, yo puedo dar un baño a los animales y puedo darles de comer también.

   ¿Dónde quiere trabajar Teresa? (1)

5. You are walking to school. You hear someone speak. He says:

   ¡Alto! No cruces ahora. Hay mucho tráfico en la calle. La luz del semáforo es roja. Espera la luz verde.

   ¿Quién está hablando? (1)

6. María is talking to her cousin about her future. She says:

   Mi madre quiere que yo sea secretaria y mi padre quiere que yo estudie la medicina. Pero, yo quiero ser cantante. Yo toco el piano y yo canto muy bien. Me gusta mucho la música.

   ¿Qué quiere ser María? (4)

Part 2c Directions: For each question, you will hear some background information in English. Then you will hear a passage in Spanish twice, followed by a question in English. Listen carefully. After you have heard the question, read the question and look at the four pictures on your test. Choose the picture that best answers the question and write its number in the appropriate space on your answer sheet. (12%)

7. You are at Antonio's house. He is telling you about his uncle. He says:

   Mi tío trabaja para una compañía de ropa. El es diseñador de trajes y camisas para hombres. El ecribió un libro sobre la ropa de moda. Aquí tiene su libro. Esta es la versión inglesa.

   Which book did Antonio´s uncle write? (4)

8. Raúl is speaking to his guidance counselor. He says:

   Yo no quiero ser bombero. Es muy peligroso. Yo no quiero ser mecánico. No es un trabajo limpio. Quisiera ser cocinero y trabajar en un restaurante elegante. Hay una escuela famosa de cocina en Madrid donde me gustaría estudiar.

   What career is Raul interested in? (2)

9. You are interviewing a teacher for the school newspaper. He tells you:

   Hace cuatro años que cambié mi carrera. Fue dentista por treinta años. Ahora soy profesor de biología y química en esta escuela secundaria. Los estudiantes aquí son muy simpáticos y yo soy muy feliz.

   Which class does this man teach? (3)

10. Students are giving an oral report on their parents' occupations. Your classmate Alicia says:

    Mi madre es enfermera. Ella ayuda a los médicos durante las operaciones. Ella da las píldoras a los pacientes enfermos. A ella le gusta ayudar a la gente.

    Where does Alicia's mother work? (4)

Listening Comprehension Answers:
For all chapters, the answers are indicated in parentheses following each question. (See
question 1-10 on the previous pages.)

Reading Comprehension answers:

3a (8%) 11. __1__ 12. __2_ 13. __3__ 14. __1__

3b (12%) 15. __4__ 16. __3__ 17. __1_ 18. __3__

EARNING A LIVING 2

Nombre ____________________________ Fecha ___________________________

EXAMINATION

Part 1 SPEAKING (30%)
Part 2 LISTENING (30%)

Part 2a Directions: For each question, you will hear some background information in English. Then you will hear a passage in Spanish twice, followed by a question in English. Listen carefully. After you have heard the question, read the question and the four suggested answers. Choose the best answer and write its number in the appropriate space on your answer sheet. (9%)

1. What does Elena's grandfather do for a living?
   1. He cuts hair.
   2. He takes pictures.
   3. He's an usher in a movie theater.
   4. He drives a limousine.

2. What is the main requirement for this position?
   1. that the applicant own a car
   2. that the applicant be fluent in certain languages
   3. that the applicant be computer-literate.
   4. that the applicant have a university degree.

3. What would Pablo like to be?
   1. an accountant
   2. a waiter
   3. a history teacher
   4. a detective

Part 2b Directions: For each question, you will hear some background information in English. Then you will hear a passage in Spanish twice, followed by a question in Spanish. Listen carefully. After you have heard the question, read the question and the four suggested answers. Choose the best answer and write its number in the appropriate space on your answer sheet. (9%)

4. ¿Dónde quiere trabajar Teresa?
   1. Ella prefiere trabajar en una clínica para animales.
   2. Ella prefiere trabajar a la piscina
   3. Ella prefiere trabajar en una casa de correos
   4. Ella prefiere trabajar en una tienda

5. ¿Quién está hablando?
   1. Un policía
   2. Un arquitecto
   3. Un enfermero
   4. Un criado

6. ¿Qué quiere ser María?
   1. dentista
   2. abogada
   3. programadora
   4. cantante

EARNING A LIVING 2

Part 2c Directions: For each question, you will hear some background information in English. Then you will hear a passage in Spanish twice, followed by a question in English. Listen carefully. After you have heard the question, read the question and look at the four pictures on your test. Choose the picture that best answers the question and write its number in the appropriate space on your answer sheet. (12%)

7. Which book did Antonio's uncle write?

8. What career is Raul interested in?

9. Which class does this man teach?

10. Where does Alicia's mother work?

Part 3a Directions: Answer the question in English based on the reading selection in Spanish. Choose the best answer to each question. Base your choice on the content of the reading selection. Write the number of your answer in the appropriate space on your answer sheet. (8%)

Cada primavera las escuelas de mi districto tienen una *Semana de la Prensa en la Escuela*. Hay muchas actividades durante esta semana. Los reporteros de los periódicos locales visitan las escuelas y explican la importancia de la comunicación.... escrita y hablada.

Durante la semana los estudiantes visitan los estudios de TV. Ellos visitan también las fábricas de prensa. Ellos organizan debates y conferencias. Hay también una exhibición de los periódicos escolares. La Semana de la Prensa ayuda a los estudiantes a comprender el mundo del periodista. Al fin de la semana se da un premio al mejor periódico escolar.

11. In what season is "Press Week" celebrated in this school district?
   1. in the spring
   2. in the fall
   3. in the summer
   4. in the winter

12. At the end of "Press Week", a prize is given ....
   1. to a local radio station
   2. to the best school newspaper
   3. to a guest speaker
   4. to a foreign reporter

EARNING A LIVING 2

A: Hilda Hurtado <hildahurt@oogle.com.ar>
De: Betsy Waite <betsyw8@zeronet.com
Objeto: Take Our Daughters to Work Day
Fecha: 24 de abril de 2002

Querida Hilda,

En el pasado, las mujeres eran amas de casa. Algunas eran secretarias, maestras y enfermeras. Eran los hombres que tenían la mayoría de los trabajos importantes. Hoy es diferente. Mi madre, por ejemplo, es arquitecta. Trabaja para una compañía que construye edificios. Mi tía Adela es ingeniera para la misma compañía.

Mi hermana mayor es basurera. Ella es fuerte y recoge la basura. Mi prima Olivia es abogada. Sus clientes son médicos, enfermeros, cirujanos y otros que trabajan en un hospital. Ella es muy inteligente y trabaja en una corte.

Pero, es mi vecina Señora Codella que tiene un trabajo muy diferente. Un día hubo un fuego en mi escuela. Y ¿quién era la persona que lo apagó? ¡Señora Codella! Sí, ella es bombera.

En cuánto a mí, yo quiero ser maestra. Sí, es un trabajo tradicional, pero me gustan a los niños y yo sé que seré una maestra excepcional.

Betsy

13. What does Betsy's mother do for a living?
    1. She's a secretary
    2. She's a teacher
    3. She's an architect
    4. She's a plumber

14. When did Betsy find out about Mrs. Codella's occupation?

1. when the woman came to her school.
2. when she read about it in the newspaper.
3. when she met her at a party.
4. when Mrs. Codella was arrested.

. **La Prensa de Asunción** el 22 de diciembre de 2000 pag. 45

OBITUARIO

Juan A. Larrauri, compositor español, murió el 21 de diciembre en Bilbao a la edad de 68 años. Maestro Larrauri nació el 30 de abril de 1932 en una familia con tradición musical. El dedicó su vida a este arte. Sus composiciones para orquesta le ganaron el reconomiento de la comunidad musical del mundo. Larrauri deja mujer y cuatro hijos.

15. Este obituario da información de
    1. un policía
    2. un artista
    3. un profesor de español
    4. un músico

16. ¿En qué año murió Juan Larrauri?
    1. en 1932
    2. en 1968
    3. en 2000
    4. en 1945

TABLÓN WEB DE ANUNCIOS PARA EMPLEO

Soy María. Tengo 18 años y me gustaría trabajar en algún hotel este verano en el sur de España.
e-mail: marirome88@hotmail.com

Hola. Mi nombre es Cecilia y estoy buscando trabajo de camarera para fines de semana en algún restaurante de Barcelona. Hablo inglés.
Tengo experiencia como camarera.
e-mail: cecimore99@hotmail.com

Me llamo Heinrich. Busco trabajo como profesor de alemán, matemáticas o biología en un instituto privado en Madrid. Hablo un español perfectamente.
e-mail: heinzald77@dahoo.com

Se necesitan enfermeros con experiencia en emergencias y transporte sanitario aereo para Islas Canarias. Interesados por favor escriban
e-mail: aeromed66@boogle.com

17. ¿Qué clase de empleo quiere *heinzald77@dahoo.com*?
    1. Quiere trabajar en una escuela.
    2. Quiere trabajar en un hotel.
    3. Quiere trabajar en un restaurante.
    4. Quiere trabajar en un hospital.

18. ¿ A quién le interesa contestar el anuncio de *aeromed66@boogle.com*?
    1. un camarero
    2. una criada
    3. un enfermero
    4. un contador

EARNING A LIVING 2

Part 4 WRITING (20%)

Part 4 Directions: Choose two of the three writing tasks provided below. Your answer to each of the two questions should be written entirely in Spanish and should contain a minimum of 30 words.

Place names and brand names written in Spanish count as one word. Contractions are counted as one word. Salutations, closings and commonly used abbreviations are included in the word count. Numbers, unless written as words, and names of people do not count as words.

Be sure that you have satisfied the purpose of the task. The sentence structure and /or expressions used should be connected logically and demonstrate a wide range of vocabulary with minimal repetition.

4a. You had the opportunity recently to accompany a member of your family to his/her workplace. Write a letter to your pen pal about this experience. You may wish to include:

- The name and relationship of the person you accompanied
- Where this person works
- How you traveled to this workplace
- When you went with this person
- What this person does there
- Whether you enjoyed this experience

4b. Your school newspaper has asked students to write about which school subject they consider important to study for a future career. Respond in writing with your opinion. You may wish to include:

- The school subject you consider important
- What skills you learn in that particular subject
- The name of one or more careers in which one would use those skills
- How that career would implement those skills

4c. Your local newspaper has a job advice column to which one can write. You want a job and are interested in suggestions. Write a letter to the columnist. You may wish to include:

- The fact that you are looking for employment
- What your interests or preferences are: e.g. sports, writing, computers, cars
- What kind of environment you like: e.g. working outdoors, working with animals, working with children, working in a store
- A description of your work habits: e.g. responsible, cooperative, active

ANSWER SHEET

Nombre y Apellido ______________________________ Fecha ______________

Part I **Speaking** __________ (30%)
Part 2 **Listening (30%)**

2a.	2b.	2c.
1._____	4._____	7._____
2._____	5._____	8._____
3._____	6._____	9._____
		10._____

PART 3: READING (20%)

3a.(8%)	3b.(12%)
11._____	15._____
12._____	16._____
13._____	17._____
14._____	18._____

Part 4 **Writing (20%) 20 words** **Write 2 paragraphs** **4a , 4b or 4c**

1____

2____

LEISURE

LEISURE 2

LEISURE 2

TEACHER´S SCRIPT FOR THE EXAM, PART II (Listening, 30%)

Part 2a Directions: For each question, you will hear some background information in English. Then you will hear a passage in Spanish twice, followed by a question in English. Listen carefully. After you have heard the question, read the question and the four suggested answers. Choose the best answer and write its number in the appropriate space on your answer sheet. (9%)

1 It's Saturday and you are speaking to your friend by phone. You say:

¿Vamos al parque hoy? Hace buen tiempo y yo quiero practicar al tenis. Yo reservé una corte para las dos. ¿Quieres jugar conmigo?

What should you bring with you? (3)

2. When you get home from school, you call up your friend, Carolina. She says:

Yo no puedo hablar contigo ahora. Estoy mirando mi programa favorita en la televisión. Tú sabes que me gusta mucho mirar las telenovelas.

What was Carolina doing? (3)

3. Your friend Pedro is telling you about his family's vacation home. He says:

Mi familia tiene una casa pequeña en las montañas. Cada fin de semana en enero y en febrero mi familia va allí. Nos gusta esquiar y patinar sobre hielo. A veces, damos un paseo en trineo en la nieve.

What is Pedro's favorite season? (4)

Part 2b Directions: For each question, you will hear some background information in English. Then you will hear a passage in Spanish twice, followed by a question in Spanish. Listen carefully. After you have heard the question, read the question and the four suggested answers. Choose the best answer and write its number in the appropriate space on your answer sheet. (9%)

4. You and your cousin Marta are deciding on a weekend activity. She says:

Yo soy una persona muy activa. No me gusta sentarme todos los tiempos. No me gusta ir al cine ni mirar la televisión. Prefiero bailar, correr o jugar a los deportes o hacer alguna cosa activa.

¿Cuál actividad le gustaría mucho hacer a Marta? (4)

5. Your father is dropping you off at the movies. You tell him when to pick you up. You say:

   La película empieza a las tres y dura dos horas. La película termina a las cinco. Ven a las cinco y diez. Yo voy a esperarte delante del cine.

. ¿Cuánto tiempo dura la película? (2)

6. You are watching the news on TV. The announcer says:

   Mañana se presenta en todos los cines la nueva película cómica, *Drácula Celebra el Día de los Muertos* con el gran talento del actor español Roberto González. El señor González no hace el papel del vampiro. En vez, él hace el papel de un científico tonto.

   ¿De qué habla el anunciador? (1)

Part 2c Directions: For each question, you will hear some background information in English. Then you will hear a passage in Spanish twice, followed by a question in English. Listen carefully. After you have heard the question, read the question and look at the 4 pictures on your test. Choose the picture that best answers the question and write its number in the appropriate space on your answer sheet. (12%)

7. Marisol is at the doctor's. He says to her:

   Ud. tiene dolor de pie porque patina sobre hielo mucho. Necesita usar dos pares de calcetines de lana, en vez de un par. Le recomiendo que no patines por algunos días.

   What did the doctor examine? (3)

8. Pablo is telling you about his favorite sport. He says:

   Yo necesito sólo mi traje de baño y una toalla. Pero, mi hermana tiene que traer sombrero, anteojos de sol, crema anti-solar y un buen libro a leer.

   What is Pablo's favorite sport? (2)

9. Serafina and Luisa are at the Olympics. They are deciding which event to attend that afternoon. Serafina says:

   Para mí, el boxeo es un deporte más violento y la gimnasia es muy aburrida. Vamos a ver un partido de básquetbol. Prefiero ver un deporte de equipo. Me gusta mucho la acción de este deporte.

   What event does Serafina want to see? (3)

10. Marta is talking about her father. She says:

    Mi padre es policía para la ciudad de Caracas. Cada día él ve bastante violencia. El no va a menudo al cine, pero cuando él va, él prefiere ver una película romántica. Siempre hay un fin alegre.

    What kind of movie does Marta's father enjoy seeing? (4)

Listening Comprehension Answers:
For all chapters, the answers are indicated in parentheses following each question. (See questions 1-10 on the previous pages.)

Reading Comprehension answers:

3a. (8%) 11. __2__ 12. __4__ 13. __1__ 14. __4__

3b (12%) 15. __3__ 16. __4__ 17. __2__ 18. __3__

LEISURE 2

Nombre ______________________________ Fecha ____________________

EXAMINATION

Part 1 SPEAKING (30%)
Part 2 LISTENING (30%)

Part 2a Directions: For each question, you will hear some background information in English. Then you will hear a passage in Spanish twice, followed by a question in English. Listen carefully. After you have heard the question, read the question and the four suggested answers. Choose the best answer and write its number in the appropriate space on your answer sheet. (9%)

1. What should you bring with you?
   1. a folding chair
   2. an umbrella
   3. a racket
   4. skates

2. What was Carolina doing?
   1. practicing the piano
   2. putting on her skates
   3. watching TV
   4. reading the newspaper

3. What is Pedro´s favorite season?
   1. spring
   2. summer
   3. autumn
   4. winter

Part 2b Directions: For each question, you will hear some background information in English. Then you will hear a passage in Spanish twice, followed by a question in Spanish. Listen carefully. After you have heard the question, read the question and the four suggested answers. Choose the best answer and write its number in the appropriate space on your answer sheet. (9%)

4. ¿Cuál actividad le gustaría mucho hacer a Marta?
   1. jugar al ajedrez
   2. ver una película
   3. mirar una telenovela
   4. nadar

5. ¿Cuánto tiempo dura la película?
   1. una hora
   2. dos horas
   3. tres horas
   4. cinco horas

6. ¿De qué habla el anunciador?
   1. una nueva película cómica
   2. el tiempo
   3. la muerta de una actriz famosa
   4. un documentario sobre la historia del cine

Part 2c Directions: For each question, you will hear some background information in English. Then you will hear a passage in Spanish twice, followed by a question in English. Listen carefully. After you have heard the question, read the question and look at the four pictures on your test. Choose the picture that best answers the question and write its number in the appropriate space on your answer sheet.

7. What did the doctor examine?

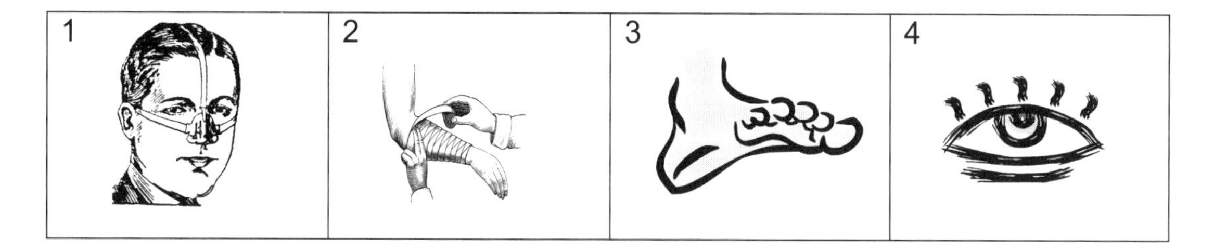

8. What is Pablo's favorite sport?

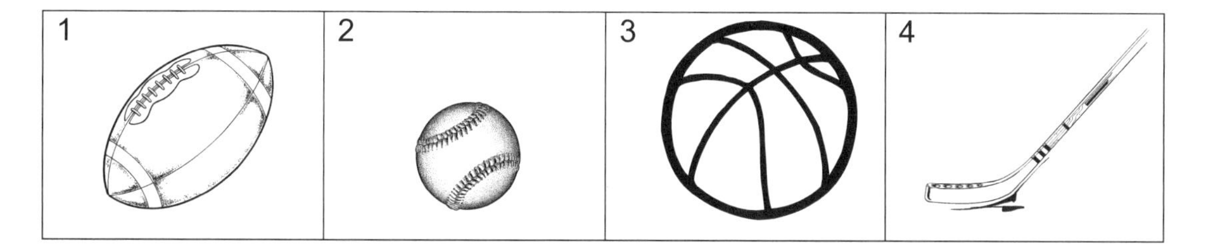

9. What event does Serafina want to see?

10. What kind of movie does Marta's father prefer to see?

Part 3a Directions: Answer the question in English based on the reading selection in Spanish. Choose the best answer to each question. Base your choice on the content of the reading selection. Write the number of your answer in the appropriate space on your answer sheet. (8%)

Acto 2, Escena 1

En un cuarto de un hotel. Una mujer está en el sofá mirando la televisión. Un hombre está mirando por la ventana. El se vuelve y habla a la mujer.

Benson: ¿Qué estás mirando, Gloria?
Gloria: Estoy mirando las noticias, Benson.
Benson: Este es nuestro primer día de vacaciones en México, y tú estás mirando la televisión. Hay muchas cosas que hacer en México.
Gloria: ¿Dígame, que vamos a hacer por la noche, por ejemplo?
Benson: Podemos ir de compras en el mercado al aire fresco. Podemos tomar un refresco en la plaza y escuchar la música de los mariachis.
Gloria: Nuestra decisión no será fácil. ¿Y por la tarde?
Benson: Podemos visitar las pirámides. o podemos asistir a una corrida de toros.
Gloria: ¡Caramba! Nuestra decisión no será fácil. ¿Y por la mañana?
Benson: Podemos ir en bicicleta, o podemos jugar al golf, o podemos jugar al tenis.
Gloria: Hay muchas cosas que hacer en México. Nuestra decisión no será fácil. Me gustaría ir a la playa
Benson: Nosotros podemos nadar en la piscina del hotel. Mira por la ventana, Gloria. La piscina del hotel es muy bonita.

Gloria mira por la ventana.

Gloria: ¡Oh! ¡Oh! Está nublado.
Benson: [*mirando la televisión*] Oh, escucha, Gloria. El anunciador va a hablar del tiempo de hoy.

El Anunciador: Malas noticias para los turistas en México. Va a llover todo el día hoy, y toda la semana.

Se oye el ruido de la lluvia.

Gloria: Oh, Benson, está lloviendo. ¿Qué vamos a hacer?
Benson: Oh, Gloria, nuestra decisión será fácil ahora. Vamos a mirar la televisión por toda la semana.

11. Where are Gloria and Benson?
    1. at a movie theater
    2. on vacation
    3. at a travel agency
    4. at a bull fight

12. What is the bad news that the TV announcer gives?
    1. the buses are on strike
    2. the bull fight has been cancelled.
    3. there is an electrical power outage.
    4. the weather will be nasty all week.

Programas del TV - Jueves

4.00 Los Días Mágicos (telenovela argentina)
4.30 Babar y sus amigos (programa para los niños)
5.00 Las Llamas de Chile (documentario)
6.00 Las Noticias a las Seis
6.30 Meteo-boletin - El tiempo de mañana
6.35 La Rueda de la Fortuna (programa de juego)
6.45 Los Tres Tenores en Madrid (concierto especial)
7.30 Tele-película "Invasión del Extraterrestre de Júpiter"

13. What would you watch at 4:30?
    1. a children's show
    2. a sports event
    3. a game show
    4. a soap opera

14. At what time is a science-fiction movie?
    1. at 4 o´clock
    2. at 5 o´clock
    3. at 6:30
    4. at 7:30

Part 3b Directions: Answer the question in Spanish based on the reading selection in Spanish. Choose the best answer to each question. Base your choice on the content of the reading selection. Write the number of your answer in the appropriate space on your answer sheet. (12%)

HORARIO DE EVENTOS:

TORNEO INTERNACIONAL
de AJEDREZ
PARA AFICIONADOS

GRAN HOTEL INCA
Salón Bolivar: Registro de inscripciones 8 am - 9:30 am
11 de Septiembre
500$ US en premios

BAILE
con la orquesta de
Ferdinando Rivera
cada viernes a las 9 PM

Terraza del Lago
el 18 de octubre con
el tenor, José Belso

Rick Robles amansador
de leones y tigres feroces
CIRCO
de los Hermanos
ZANZINI

DOMINGO
4 AGOSTO
PATINAJE ARTISTICO SOBRE HIELO
6 PM
Campeonato de Chile
ESTADIO O'HIGGINS

Koko el Payaso
jueves, 25 de julio
PARQUE MEMORIAL

15. ¿Qué día de la semana hay siempre un baile ?
    1. domingo
    2. jueves
    3. viernes
    4. sábado

16. ¿Dónde se puede ver un partido de deporte?
    1. en la Terraza del Lago
    2. en el Parque Memorial
    3. en el Gran Hotel Inca
    4. en el Estadio O´Higgins

LA PRENSA SECCIONES

17. ¿ En cuál sección del periódico ve Ud. para saber el horario de una película?
    1. en la Sección A
    2. en la Sección B
    3. En la Sección C
    4. en la Sección E

18. ¿ Dónde puede leer un artículo sobre su jugador de béisbol favorito?
    1. en la sección B
    2. en la sección D
    3. en la sección C
    4. en la sección E

Part 4 WRITING (20%)

Part 4 Directions: Choose two of the three writing tasks provided below. Your answer to each of the two questions should be written entirely in Spanish and should contain a minimum of **30 words.**

Place names and brand names written in Spanish count as one word. Contractions are counted as one word. Salutations, closings and commonly used abbreviations are included in the word count. Numbers, unless written as words, and names of people do not count as words.

Be sure that you have satisfied the purpose of the task. The sentence structure and /or expressions used should be connected logically and demonstrate a wide range of vocabulary with minimal repetition.

4a. In a note in the target language to your pen pal, write him or her about a movie you have seen recently. You may wish to include:

- The name of the movie
- When and where you saw it
- What kind of movie it was
- Who were the principal actors
- Your feelings about the movie

4b. You have recently read the biography of your favorite sports figure. Write a letter to your pen pal. In your letter you may wish to include:

- The name of this sports figure
- The sport this person is engaged in
- Biographical information about this person: date and place of birth
- Where this person played
- What this person's accomplishments were

4c. In a note in Spanish, write about a leisure activity in which you are a participant (and not a spectator). You may wish to include:

- The type of activity
- When and where you engage in this activity
- What equipment is needed, if any
- Who is with you
- Your feelings about this activity

ANSWER SHEET

Nombre y Apellido ______________________________ Fecha ______________

Part I **Speaking** __________ (30%)
Part 2 **Listening (30%)**

2a.	2b.	2c.
1._____	4._____	7._____
2._____	5._____	8._____
3._____	6._____	9._____
		10._____

PART 3: READING (20%)

3a.(8%)	3b.(12%)
11._____	15._____
12._____	16._____
13._____	17._____
14._____	18._____

Part 4 **Writing (20%) 20 words** **Write 2 paragraphs** **4a , 4b or 4c**

1 ____

2 ____

Public and Private Services

TEACHER'S SCRIPT FOR THE EXAM, PART II (Listening, 30%)

Part 2a Directions: For each question, you will hear some background information in English. Then you will hear a passage in Spanish twice, followed by a question in English. Listen carefully. After you have heard the question, read the question and the four suggested answers. Choose the best answer and write its number in the appropriate space on your answer sheet (9%).

1. It is lunchtime and you take your out-of-town cousin to a particular restaurant in your neighborhood. You explain:

   Este restaurante es el más extraordinario de la ciudad. Sobre cada mesa hay una computadora. Mientras que comemos, yo puedo enviar un correo electrónico a mis amigos.

   Why did you take your cousin to this restaurant? (3)

2. At a hotel in Buenos Aires, a tourist stops to ask the doorman for information. The doorman says:

   Sí, señora, hay un buzón dentro del hotel al lado del ascensor. Hay otro buzón allí en la esquina de la calle.

   What is this tourist looking for ? (1)

3. Your mother is talking to the new mailman. You hear your mother say to him:

   No se preocupe. Estos perros me conocen bien. Yo voy a caminar con Ud. toda esta semana hasta que los perros lo conozcan a Ud. también. Después, Ud. no tendrá ningún problema.

   What problem is this mailman encountering on this delivery route? (3)

Part 2b Directions: For each question, you will hear some background information in English. Then you will hear a passage in Spanish twice, followed by a question in Spanish. Listen carefully. After you have heard the question, read the question and the four suggested answers. Choose the best answer and write its number in the appropriate space on your answer sheet (9%).

4. You are on a double date. Your friend, Maria Luisa, answers her cell phone. You hear her say:

   Mamí, ¿por qué me llamas tantas veces? Esta es la séptima llamada que haces. Yo no soy una bebé. Yo tengo dieciséis años y yo estoy bien. ¡No te preocupes! Yo regresaré antes de las diez.

   ¿Cuántos años tiene María Luisa? (4)

5. Your grandfather and you are doing research online on your home computer. Suddenly an instant message appears on the screen. You explain to your grandfather.

   Es un mensaje instanténeo de mi amigo Pablo. El me está escribiendo de Puerto Rico. El fue a Puerto Rico para la boda de su prima puertorriqueña.

   ¿Por qué está Pablo en Puerto Rico? (1)

6. Your sister Marisol is about to leave the house. Your father says to her:

   Comprendo que tú vas a regresar de la fiesta después de medianoche. Es muy tarde, y yo estaré preocupado. Toma mi teléfono celular. Si tienes un problema tú puedes llamarme. No importa a que hora.

   ¿Qué le da el padre a Marisol? (4)

Part 2c Directions: For each question, you will hear some background information in English. Then you will hear a passage in Spanish twice, followed by a question in English. Listen carefully. After you have heard the question, read the question and look at the 4 pictures on your test. Choose the picture that best answers the question and write its number in the appropriate space on your answer sheet. (12%)

7. You are with your mother. She says to the person on the other side of the counter:

   Necesito veinte sellos de treinta y siete centavos para enviar estas tarjetas de Navidad. Y dígame ¿cuánto cuesta enviar una tarjeta por correo aéreo a Venezuela?

   What is this woman buying? (1)

8. You are at the post office with your friend. The postal clerk behind the counter says:

   Primero, su paquete es muy grande. Pués, pesa setenta y cinco libras. El peso máximo que el Servicio Postal puede aceptar es treinta y cinco libras. Lo siento pero Ud. tiene que llevar su paquete a un servicio privado de envío.

   Which of the following items was in your friend's package? (4)

9. Your grandfather is telling you about a job he had as a young man. He says:

   Cuando era un joven de quince años, yo trabajaba para una compañía telegráfica. Yo entregaba los telegramas a todas las casas en mi bicicleta.

   What vehicle did your grandfather use? (3)

10. Carmen is showing you her stamp album. She says:

    El sello con la imagen del elefante completa ahora la serie comemorativa que tengo sobre los animales exóticos. Mi sello favorito es el sello con la imagen del tigre..

    What series of commemorative stamps was Carmen collecting? (2)

Listening Comprehension Answers:
For all chapters, the answers are indicated in parentheses following each question. (See question 1-10 on the previous pages.)

Reading Comprehension answers:

3a (8%) 11. __1__ 12. __3__ 13. __4__ 14. __3__

3b (12%) 15. __1__ 16. __4__ 17. __2__ 18. __1__

PUBLIC AND PRIVATE SERVICES 2

Nombre ______________________________ Fecha __________________________

EXAMINATION

Part 1 SPEAKING (30%)
Part 2 LISTENING (30%)

Part 2a Directions: For each question, you will hear some background information in English. Then you will hear a passage in Spanish twice, followed by a question in English. Listen carefully. After you have heard the question, read the question and the four suggested answers. Choose the best answer and write its number in the appropriate space on your answer sheet (9%).

1. Why did you take your cousin to this restaurant?

1. They serve very unusual food
2. Your best friend works there.
3. The patrons can use its computers.
4. Every table is given a free newspaper.

2. What is this tourist looking for?
   1. a mailbox
   2. a souvenir shop
   3. a bank
   4. a phone booth

3. What problem is this mailman encountering on this delivery route?
   1. There are no numbers on the houses.
   2. There are many cracks in the sidewalk.
   3. The neighborhood dogs are nervous about strangers.
   4. Some of the houses don't have mailboxes.

Part 2b Directions: For each question, you will hear some background information in English. Then you will hear a passage in Spanish twice, followed by a question in Spanish. Listen carefully. After you have heard the question, read the question and the four suggested answers. Choose the best answer and write its number in the appropriate space on your answer sheet (9%).

4. ¿Cuántos años tiene María Luisa?
   1. veinte y siete años
   2. trece años
   3. diez años
   4. deiciséis años

5. ¿Por qué está Pablo en Puerto Rico?
   1. El está asistiendo al matrimonio de una pariente.
   2. El está asistiendo a una universidad.
   3. El trabaja en un hotel en la ciudad de Ponce.
   4. El está viajando con su clase de español.

6. ¿Qué le da el padre a Marisol?
   1. una tarjeta de crédito
   2. llaves
   3. dinero
   4. un teléfono celular

Part 2c Directions: For each question, you will hear some background information in English. Then you will hear a passage in Spanish twice, followed by a question in English. Listen carefully. After you have heard the question, read the question and look at the 4 pictures on your test. Choose the picture that best answers the question and write its number in the appropriate space on your answer sheet. (12%)

9. What is this woman buying?

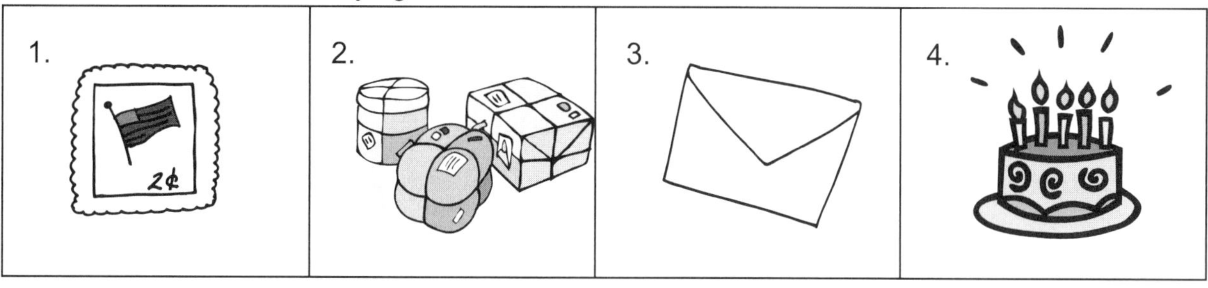

7. Which of the following items was in your friend's package?

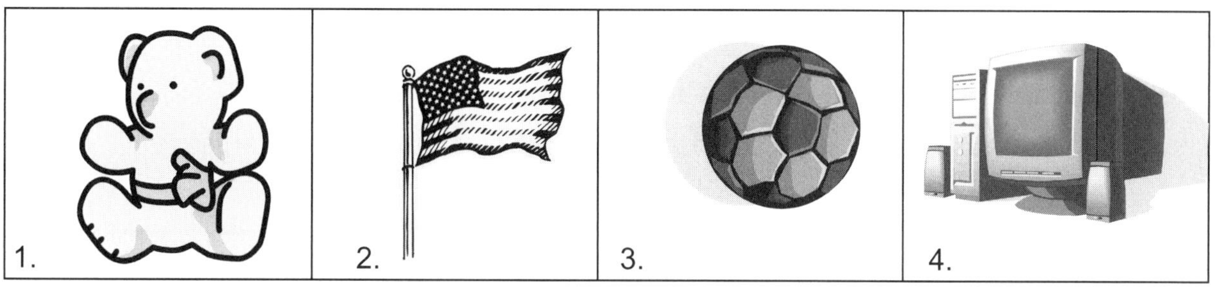

8. What vehicle did your grandfather use?

9. What series of commemorative stamps is Carmen collecting?

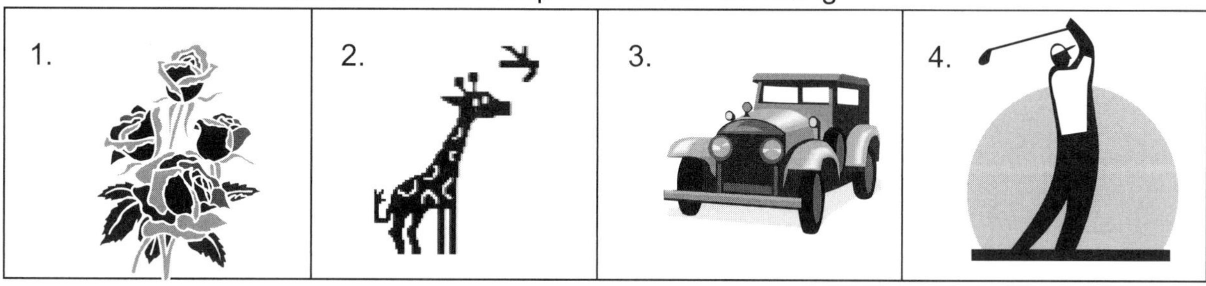

Part 3 READING (20%)

Part 3a Directions: Answer the question in English based on the reading selection in Spanish. Choose the best answer to each question. Base your choice on the content of the reading selection. Write the number of your answer in the appropriate space on your answer sheet (8%).

Números de Teléfono:

A. Llamadas Locales: el número de teléfono tiene siete dígitos para marcar.

B. Llamadas de larga distancia: este número tiene once dígitos.
Marcar "1" + (el código del área) + (los siete dígitos del número de teléfono).

C. Llamadas sin cargo: Marcar "1" + "800" + los siete dígitos del número de teléfono.

D. Llamadas Internacionales directas: Marcar "011" + (el código del país) + (el código de la ciudad) + (los siete dígitos del número de teléfono).

E. Llamadas Internacionales con la asistencia de un telefonista: Marcar el "01" + (el código del país) + (el código de la ciudad) + (los siete dígitos del número de teléfono

11. Which is considered a local number?
    1. 555-3490
    2. 01-52-66-555-3490
    3. 011-52-66-555-3490
    4. 1-787-555-3490

Directorio de Sitios Web

Arte y cultura Poesía, Pinturas, Literatura...	Familia y sociedad Comida, Salud, Casa...
Diversiones Juegos, Teatro, Deportes ...	Internet y tecnología Correo, Chat, Antivirus ...
Economía y negocios Empleo, Tiendas, Finanzas...	Noticias Periódicos, Revistas, Radio, TV...
Educación y formación Escuelas, Ciencias, Idiomas...	Política y gobierno Países, Historia, Mapas...

12. Which web site would you access for information on the geography and history of Paraguay?

1. Familia y sociedad
2. Arte y cultura
3. Política y gobierno
4. Economía y negocios

A

¡Nuestra compañía tiene el regalo ideal! Tenemos una gran selección d tarjetas de teléfono pre-pagadas con tarifas muy bajas. Tarjetas de treinta minutos cuestan cinco dólares. Y tarjetas de cien minutos cuestan diez dólares.

B

No importa si su cliente está a la vuelta de la esquina o al otro lado del globo, nuestra compañía puede enviar su documento via fax en pocos minutos. Nuestra compañía le ofrece tarifas competivas de transmisíon local, regional e internacional.

C

Nuestra compañía tiene una línea completa de materiales de empaque. Tenemos cajas de envío, sobres para fotos, tubos de envío, y sobres de todos tamaños y todos colores.

D

Nuestra compañía le ofrece servicio de empaque profesional. Los expertos de nuestra compañía empacarán el paquete para Ud. y lo enviarán también a todas partes del mundo. Desde cosas más delicatas y frágiles hasta artículos grandes, trataremos su artículo con mucha atención.

13. If you needed to have a very delicate crystal vase shipped to South America, to which ad would you respond?

1. A 2. B 3. C 4. D

14. Which company sells oversized envelopes in an assortment of colors?

1. A 2. B 3. C 4. D

125 Calle Simon Bolivar
Bahía Blanca, Bs. As.
Jueves, el 3 de mayo

Escuela E. Policastro
Bahía Blanca, Bs. As.

Querida Sra. DeBartolo,

Por favor, disculpe Ud. a mi hijo Arturo por su ausencia el martes y el miércoles. Tuvo un resfriado y dolor de estómago.

Sinceramente,

Sr. Carlos Zarra

P.D. Arturo completará todas las tareas..

****

15. ¿Dónde está la fecha de esta carta?
    1. A 2. B 3. C. 4. D

16. ¿Cuál es la razón para esta carta?
    1. El padre quiere una conferencia con la maestra.
    2. Arturo perdió su libro.
    3. Arturo no se portó bien en clase.
    4. Arturo estuvo enfermo.

Guía telefónico

Números de Emergencia

BOMBEROS
POLICIA
AMBULANCIA

Otros números útiles

Servicio de recolección de basura	597 - 7301
Centro ecológico de reciclaje	597 - 7322
Hospital General de San José	594 - 5321
Centro de control de envenenamiento	877 - 3207
Compañía de teléfono	597 - 2100
Farmacia de noche	594 - 5300
Centro contra la violencia doméstica	877 - 4707
Departamento de la Salud Pública	594 - 2718

17. ¿ A quién llama Ud. si marca " cinco - nueve - cuatro - cinco - tres - dos - uno ? "

1. el departamento de la Salud Pública
2. un hospital
3. farmacia de noche
4. el servicio de recolección de basura

18. Si es medinoche y Ud. necesita medicina , ¿cuál número va a marcar?

1. 594-5300   3. 9-1-1
2. 597-7322 | 4. 597-2100

Part 4 WRITING (20%)

Part 4 Directions: Choose two of the three writing tasks provided below. Your answer to each of the two questions should be written entirely in Spanish and should contain a minimum of **30 words**.

Place names and brand names written in Spanish count as one word. Contractions are counted as one word. Salutations, closing, and commonly used abbreviations are included in the word count. Numbers, unless written as words, and names of people do not count as words.

Be sure that you have satisfied the purpose of the task. The sentence structure and-or expressions used should be connected logically and demonstrate a wide range of vocabulary with minimal repetition.

4a. Your Spanish class exchanges e-mails with a school in a Spanish speaking country. That school has sent your class some items [maps, brochures, flags, dolls, recipes etc.] which are representative of its country. Your teacher has asked you to write a thank you letter. In that letter you may wish to include:

- A list of the various items that were sent
- Your class's opinions of the items sent
- What your class plans to do with those items
- What your class is sending their school

4b. A Spanish-speaking country has recently issued a commemorative stamp on a subject of which you have a strong viewpoint. In your letter you may wish to include:

- A description of the subject on the stamp
- The value of the stamp
- Whether you like or dislike the stamp
- The reason for your feelings

4c. You recently ordered a telephone through a mail-order catalogue. The telephone arrived and you are not satisfied. Write a letter to the mail order catalogue company with your complaint. In the letter you may wish to include:

- Your name and address
- A description of the phone that was sent
- An explanation of why you are not satisfied
- What you expect this company to do to rectify the situation

ANSWER SHEET

Nombre y Apellido ______________________________ Fecha ______________

Part I **Speaking** __________ (30%)
Part 2 **Listening (30%)** **PART 3: READING** (20%)

2a.	2b.	2c.	3a.(8%)	3b.(12%)
1._____	4._____	7._____	11._____	15._____
2._____	5._____	8._____	12._____	16._____
3._____	6._____	9._____	13._____	17._____
		10._____	14._____	18._____

Part 4 **Writing (20%) 20 words** **Write 2 paragraphs** **4a , 4b or 4c**

1____

____

____

____

____

____

____

____

____

2____

____

____

____

____

____

____

____

____

____

____

____

TRAVEL

TRAVEL 2

TEACHER'S SCRIPT FOR THE EXAM, PART II (Listening, 30%)

Part 2a Directions: For each question, you will hear some background information in English. Then you will hear a passage in Spanish twice, followed by a question in English. Listen carefully. After you have heard the question, read the question and the four suggested answers. Choose the best answer and write its number in the appropriate space on your answer sheet (9%).

1. You work in the Peruvian tourist office. A woman calls you and says:

   Vamos a pasar quince días en agosto en Perú. ¿Me puede decir que excursiones hay? Quiero ver las ciudades más importantes.

   This caller wants to know ....(3)

2. You have arrived at the airport when you discover that the non-stop flight to Madrid has been cancelled. The airline ticket agent says:

   Lo siento. Se canceló el viaje porque el avión tuvo un problema mecánico. Pero Ud. puede tomar un vuelo a Barcelona y cambiar allí para otro a Madrid.

   What does the ticket agent suggest? (4)

3. You are speaking to a woman at the airport. You say to her:

   No, no tengo nada que declarar. En mi maleta tengo mi ropa y mi cámara. Y en mi bolso tengo regalos para mis amigos.

   To whom are you speaking? (2)

Part 2b Directions: For each question, you will hear some background information in English. Then you will hear a passage in Spanish twice, followed by a question in Spanish. Listen carefully. After you have heard the question, read the question and the four suggested answers. Choose the best answer and write its number in the appropriate space on your answer sheet (9%).

4. You work at the Hotel Intercontinental in Santo Domingo. The telephone rings and a voice at the other end says:

   Estoy llamando de Nueva York. Voy a su hotel la semana que viene. Me puede decir si hay autobuses que pasen cerca de su hotel?

   ¿Qué información quiere esta persona? (1)

5. You are going to visit your grandparents in Chicago. The passenger next to you says:

   Este vuelo es directo y rápido pero hoy va a ser un día largo para mí. Tengo que ir a Chicago para una conferencia esta mañana. Más tarde, tengo que regresar en el vuelo de las cinco y diez. Mi esposa va a recogerme al aeropuerto y vamos a cenar con amigos en un restaurante mexicano.

   ¿Dónde estás tú? (1)

6. Your friend Pedro tells you how he stays fit and healthy. He says:

   Después de las clases trabajo en un restaurante italiano. Yo entrego pizzas con mi bicicleta. Gano dinero y hago ejercicios al mismo tiempo.

   ¿Qué tipo de ejercicios hace Pedro? (2)

Part 2c Directions: For each question, you will hear some background information in English. Then you will hear a passage in Spanish twice, followed by a question in English. Listen carefully. After you heard the question, read the question and look at the 4 pictures on your test. Choose the picture that best answers the question and write its number in the appropriate space on your answer sheet. (12%)

7. You and your friend are in Mexico City for the day. You are debating as to which means of transportation you should take. Your friend says:

   Es verdad que vamos a ver más con un taxi que en metro. Pero, el taxi es más caro y el metro es sucio. Prefiero tomar un autobus turístico. Es más cómodo y hay siempre un guía que nos puede explicar todo.

   What means of transportation does your friend prefer? (4)

8. You are in your friend´s house. His uncle has just come in. Your friend´s father says:

   Tengo el camión de mi hermano. Quiero llevar estos muebles a la casa de mi hijo casado. El sofá es muy largo y el piano es pesado.

   What did the uncle bring to your friend´s house? (4)

9. You and your friend Veronica are talking about different vacation spots. Veronica says to you:

   A mi familia le gustan mucho los deportes acuáticos. Cuando vamos de vacaciones, vamos siempre al mar o al lago. Jugamos al polo acuático. Hacemos el esquí acuático. Y naturalmente, nadamos.

.

   Where does Veronica's family like to vacation? (4)

10. You are on vacation in South America. You stop at a souvenir shop with your parents. Your mother says:

    Yo quiero comprar un recuerdo típico de este país. Me gusta mucho esta blusa hecha a mano. El diseño es bonito y yo puedo llevarla con mi falda azul.

    What will your mother buy as a souvenir? (2)

Listening Comprehension Answers:
For all chapters, the answers are indicated in parenthesis following each question. (See questions 1-10 on the previous pages.)

Reading Comprehension answers:
3a. (8%) 11. __1__ 12. __3__ 13. __3__ 14. __2__
3b (12%) 15. __3__ 16. __ 1__ 17. __ 2__ 18. __4__

TRAVEL 2

Nombre ____________________________ Fecha ________________

EXAMINATION

Part 1 SPEAKING (30%)
Part 2 LISTENING (30%)

Part 2a Directions: For each question, you will hear some background information in English. Then you will hear a passage in Spanish twice, followed by a question in English. Listen carefully. After you have heard the question, read the question and the four suggested answers. Choose the best answer and write its number in the appropriate space on your answer sheet (9%).

1. This caller wants to know ....
   1. what is the money exchange
   2. the name of a good hotel
   3. what kind of tours are available
   4. what the weather is like

2. What does the ticket agent suggest?
   1. that you take the train
   2. that you take a bus
   3. that you come back tomorrow
   4. that you take another flight

3. To whom are you speaking?
   1. the pilot
   2. the customs agent
   3. the stewardess
   4. the shop keeper

Part 2b Directions: For each question, you will hear some background information in English. Then you will hear a passage in Spanish twice, followed by a question in Spanish. Listen carefully. After you have heard the question, read the question and the four suggested answers. Choose the best answer and write its number in the appropriate space on your answer sheet (9%).

4. ¿Qué información quiere esta persona?
   1. quiere saber como llegar al hotel.
   2. si se admiten animales en el hotel
   3. el horario del almuerzo
   4. si el hotel tiene una piscina interior

5. ¿Dónde estás tú?
   1. en un avión
   2. en un restaurante
   3. en un tren
   4. en un barco

6. ¿Qué tipo de ejercicios hace Pedro?
   1. El juega al básquetbol.
   2. El anda en bicicleta
   3. El corre.
   4. El no hace nada.

Part 2c Directions: For each question, you will hear some background information in English. Then you will hear a passage in Spanish twice, followed by a question in English. Listen carefully. After you heard the question, read the question and look at the 4 pictures on your test. Choose the picture that best answers the question and write its number in the appropriate space on your answer sheet. (12%)

7. What means of transportation does your friend prefer?

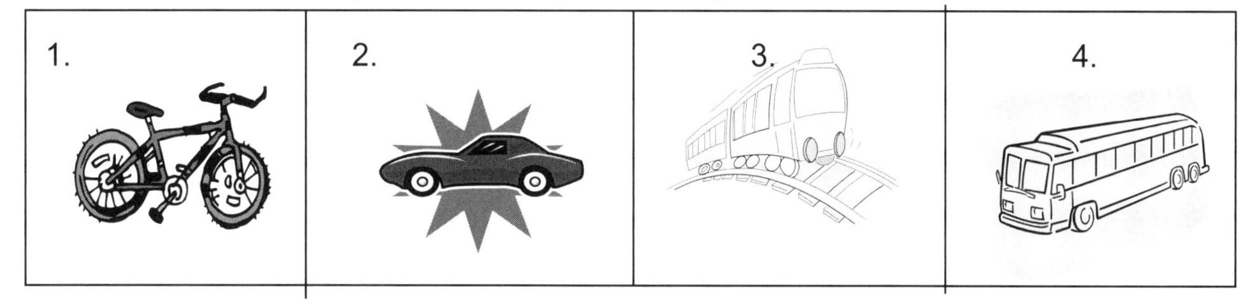

8. What did the uncle bring to your friend's house?

9. Where does Veronica's family like to vacation?

10. What will your mother buy as a souvenir?

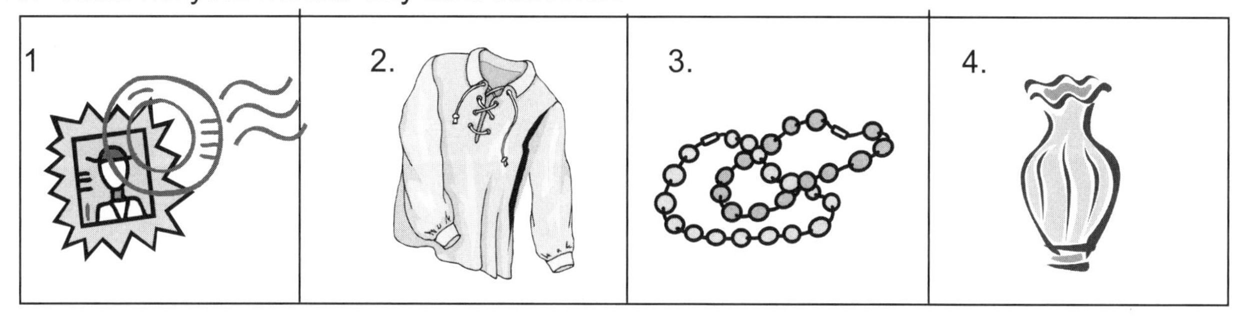

Part 3 READING (20%)
Part 3a Directions: Answer the questions in English based on the reading selections in Spanish. Choose the best answer to each question. Base your choice on the content of the reading selection. Write the number of your answer in the appropriate space on your answer sheet (8%).

Aprenda el español en las Islas Galápagos, un lugar de belleza exótica. Con profesores muy calificados, nuestro programa incluye muchas actividades y excursiones. Aprenda un idioma mientras que Ud descubra una isla.

El precio del programa incluye instrucción, comida, habitación, todas excursiones, y el viaje por barco desde el continente.

11. What means of transportation is included in the program cost?
    1. boat trip from the mainland
    2. plane flight from your home city
    3. railway
    4. car rental

12. Who would be interested in this program?
    1. someone wishing to learn how to sail a boat
    2. someone wishing to lose weight
    3. someone interested in learning a language
    4. someone who is looking for solitary relaxation

SU PEQUEÑO VIAJERO ES NUESTRA CARGA PRECIOSA

Marta Sánchez, agente de viajes

Para viajar solo en un vuelo internacional, su hijo debe tener 6 años de edad o más..

Rodolfo Castro, aduanero

Su hijo debe portar documentos necesarios: pasaporte, registro civil, y autorización de los padres para salir del país.

Miguel Brunetti, aeromozo

Su hijo tiene que llegar al aeropuerto dos horas antes de la salida del vuelo

Ana Ruíz, guardia de seguridad

No deje al niño en el aeropuerto sin antes confirmar la hora de salida del vuelo.

Velma Borgos, azafata

Los niños que viajan solos son cuidados por azafatas responsables y autorizadas. Ellas deben saber la identidad de las personas que van a recoger a los niños.

Daniel Orozco, piloto

Siga estas reglas y todos tendrán un buen viaje.

13. The above poster discusses
    1. opinions on how to improve airport security
    2. the various careers in the airline industry
    3. the procedure to follow if a child travels alone
    4. facilities at the air terminal.

14. Velma Borgos most likely...
    1. sells airline tickets
    2. serves refreshments
    3. stamps passports
    4. searches luggage

Part 3b Directions: Answer the question in Spanish based on the reading selection in Spanish. Choose the best answer to each question. Base your choice on the content of the reading selection. Write the number of your answer in the appropriate space on your answer sheet. (12%)

ESTACION DE FERROCARRIL

LLEGADAS

hora	vía	
11:30	7	BARCELONA
11:45	8	LEON
11:55	10	CORDOBA
12:05	6	VALENCIA
2:40	4	MALAGA
3:15	6	LISBOA

SALIDAS

hora	vía	
11:40	6	GRANADA
12:00	7	PARIS
13:00	6	SALAMANCA
13:30	5	MURCIA
14:39	9	TOLEDO
14:05	6	AMSTERDAM

15. ¿A qué hora llega el tren de Málaga?
    1. a la una y media de la tarde
    2. a las dos y cuarto
    3. a la una menos veinte
    4. a las doce y treinta

16. ¿Adónde va el tren en vía número 6 a las dos y cinco?
    1. Amsterdam
    2. Salamanca
    3. Valencia
    4. Lisboa

Asunción el 10 de ago.

Queridos Miguel y Luisa,

Paso una semana aquí en Paraguay con mis primos. Mi tío Carlos es chofer de taxi y hacemos excursiones en su vehículo. Estoy viendo muchos puntos de interés. Ayer fuimos a Itauguá, un pueblo conocido por el ñandutí. Mañana, vamos de camping en las montañas.

Abrazos,
Irene

Sr. y Sra. M. Reyes
Calle Roma, 551
Santo Domingo, R.D.

PHOTO NOVEX
Ñanduti: Tejido de encaje hecho por las mujeres de Itaugua
Ñanduti lace woven by the women of Itaugua, Paraguay
Dentelles ñanduti fabriquées par les femmes d'Itaugua

17. ¿De quién es la tarjeta postal?

1. Miguel
2. Irene
3. Carlos
4. Itaugua

De: smcateer317@oogle.com
A: hotellatina@bahoo.com
Enviado: 10 de octubre de 2002 09:53 a m
Objeto: hacer una reservación

Quisiera reservar una habitación con cama matrimonial, con baño y con vista al mar. Tengo intención de estar en Viña del Mar con mi esposa por 5 días en el mes de febrero (desde el 3 hasta el 6). Quisiera alquilar un carro para esos mismos días y espero que me haga el favor de alquilar uno.

Le ruego que me confirme la reserva a su más pronta conveniencia.

En anticipación de su pronta atención, le quedo agradecido.

Stephen McAteer

18. ¿ Cuándo llegan los McAteer a Viña del Mar?

1. el 4 de agosto
2. .. el dos de enero
3. el 7 de octubre
4. el 3 de febrero

PART 4 WRITING (30%)

Part 4 Directions: Choose two of the three writing tasks provided below. Your answer to each of the two questions should be written entirely in Spanish and should contain a minimum of **30 words**.

Place names and brand names written in Spanish count as one word. Contractions are counted as one word. Salutations, closings and commonly used abbreviations are included in the word count. Numbers, unless written as words, and names of people do not count as words.
Be sure that you have satisfied the purpose of the task. The sentence structure and /or expressions used should be connected logically and demonstrate a wide range of vocabulary with minimal repetition.

4a. Your pen pal is seeking information on the means of transportation people use to travel to the largest town or city in your geographic area. In your written response you may wish to include:

- The name of the largest city or town in your geographic region
- Why this city or town is important
- What means of transportation people use to arrive there
- How long it takes to arrive there
- What is the cost of the fare, if applicable
- What you consider to be the best means of transportation from your community

4b. You and your family are going to take a trip to a Spanish-speaking country. You wish to reserve a room by e-mail. In your message you may wish to include:

- The name of the city or region where you will be
- When you are going to be in the above named city
- Who will be with you
- When you plan to arrive
- How long you plan to stay
- A description of the room you would like to have
- Questions you may have on the facilities

4c. During a recent trip to another country, you were impressed by a particular worker in the travel/transportation industry. Write a letter of commendation to the local Spanish newspaper or company for which that person worked. In your letter you may wish to include:

- A (made-up) first and last name for that employee
- The occupation that person held in the travel/ transportation field
- Where during your trip you met this person
- What this person did that impressed you

ANSWER SHEET

Nombre y Apellido ________________________________ Fecha _______________

Part I **Speaking** __________ (30%)
Part 2 **Listening (30%)**

2a.	2b.	2c.
1._____	4._____	7._____
2._____	5._____	8._____
3._____	6._____	9._____
		10._____

PART 3: READING (20%)

3a.(8%)	3b.(12%)
11._____	15._____
12._____	16._____
13._____	17._____
14._____	18._____

Part 4 **Writing (20%) 20 words** **Write 2 paragraphs** **4a , 4b or 4c**

1____

2____

TRAVEL 2

HANDBOOK 3

Thirteen Proficiency Tests by topic

PERSONAL IDENTIFICATION

PERSONAL IDENTIFICATION 3

TEACHER'S SCRIPT FOR THE EXAM, PART II (Listening, 30%)

Part 2a Directions: For each question, you will hear some background information in English. Then you will hear a passage in Spanish twice, followed by a question in English. Listen carefully. After you have heard the question, read the question and the four suggested answers. Choose the best answer and write its number in the appropriate space on your answer sheet. (9%)

1. Your aunt is telephoning the school to say that her son will be absent that day. You hear her say:

   ¿Cómo se llama mi hijo? Mi hijo se llama Alberto Romero...¡No! No se llama Roberto... ¡Se llama Alberto!........... ¡Si! Su nombre es Alberto Romero.

   What didn't the secretary understand? (2)

2. Your friend is speaking to you about his father. He says:

   Mi padre es muy bueno e inteligente. El es alto y muy gordo. .

   What physical characteristics does your friend tell you about his father? (3)

3. Luisa is telling you about her relatives in Colombia. She says:

   Yo tengo ocho primos en Colombia. Cinco primos viven en la ciudad de Bogotá y tres primos viven en Maracaibo. Carlos es mi primo favorito. El vive en Maracaibo con su familia.

   How many cousins does Luisa have living in Colombia? (1)

Part 2b Directions: For each question, you will hear some background information in English. Then you will hear a passage in Spanish twice, followed by a question in Spanish. Listen carefully. After you hear the question, read the question and the four suggested answers. Choose the best answer and write its number in the appropriate space on your answer sheet. (9%)

4. You are speaking by phone to your Mexican pen pal. You are describing yourself. You say:

   Yo soy bajo y flaco. Tengo el pelo largo y rubio. Tengo los ojos azules.

   ¿De qué color son tus ojos? (4)

5. Teresa, your pen pal from Venezuela, is describing her English teacher. She says:

   Mi profesor de inglés se llama Señor Brown. No es un hombre simpático. El no tiene paciencia. Es muy malo.

   ¿Cómo es el profesor de inglés? (3)

6. While on a plane to Florida, you overhear a conversation between a South American gentleman and the young stewardess. You hear the stewardess say:

   Yo soy norteamericana. Nací en el estado de California en la ciudad de Sacramento. Ahora vivo en San Francisco. Es una ciudad muy grande.

   ¿De dónde es la señorita? (2)

Part 2c Directions: For each question, you will hear some background information in English. Then you will hear a passage in Spanish twice, followed by a question in English. Listen carefully. After you have heard the question, read the question and look at the four pictures on your test. Choose the picture that best answers the question and write its number in the appropriate space on your answer sheet. (12%)

7. Your brother has asked you to verify some information. You say to him:

   ¡ No! mañana no es el treinta y uno. La fecha de hoy es el treinta de abril. Mañana es sábado, el primero de mayo.

   Where did you get this information from? (3)

8. Your friend is showing you photographs she has just picked up at the photographer´s. She says of the first photo

   Es mi primo, Juanito. Es el día de su cumpleaños. El tiene dos años. Es muy simpático, ¿verdad?

   Which photograph does she show you? (2)

9. It's a snowy Saturday morning and your mother comes to your room to tell you that your friends are at the doorstep with shovels. You say to her.

   No, no quiero salir con ellos. Es sábado por la mañana. Prefiero dormir ahora..

   What do you want to do? (4)

10. You are telling your friend about your married sister and her baby. You say:

    Mi hermana se llama Teresa. Ella tiene el pelo largo. Ella es rubia. Su hijo se llama Ricardo. El es rubio también.

    Which of the following is your sister? (1)

Listening Comprehension answers:
For all chapters, the answers are indicated in parentheses following each question.

Reading Comprehension:

3a. (8%)	11. __2__	12. __4__	13. __3__	14. __2__
3b. (12%)	15. __3__	16. __3__	17. __4__	18. __1__

Nombre ______________________________ Fecha __________________________

EXAMINATION

Part 1 SPEAKING (30%)
Part 2 LISTENING (30%)

Part 2a Directions: For each question, you will hear some background information in English. Then you will hear a passage in Spanish twice, followed by a question in English. Listen carefully. After you have heard the question, read the question and the four suggested answers. Choose the best answer and write its number in the appropriate space on your answer sheet. (9%)

1. What didn't the secretary understand?

   1. the telephone number
   2. the child's name
   3. the zip code
   4. the teacher's name

2. What physical characteristics does your friend tell you about his father?

   1. that he is strict.
   2. that he is extremely thin.
   3. that he is tall and rather fat.
   4. that he has red hair.

3. How many cousins does Luisa have living in Colombia?

   1. eight
   2. seven
   3. two
   4. five

Part 2b Directions: For each question, you will hear some background information in English. Then you will hear a passage in Spanish twice, followed by a question in Spanish. Listen carefully. After you hear the question, read the question and the four suggested answers. Choose the best answer and write its number in the appropriate space on your answer sheet. (9%)

4. ¿De qué color son tus ojos?

   1. verdes
   2. de color café
   3. negros
   4. azules

5. ¿Cómo es el profesor de inglés?

   1. pelirrojo
   2. alto
   3. antipático
   4. guapo

6. ¿De dónde es el muchacho?

   1. Italia
   2. Puerto Rico
   3. la ciudad de San Francisco
   4. el estado de Nuevo México

PERSONAL IDENTIFICATION 3

Part 2c Directions: For each question, you will hear some background information in English. Then you will hear a passage in Spanish twice, followed by a question in English. Listen carefully. After you have heard the question, read the question and look at the four pictures on your test. Choose the picture that best answers the question and write its number in the appropriate space on your answer sheet. (12%)

7. Where did you get this information from?

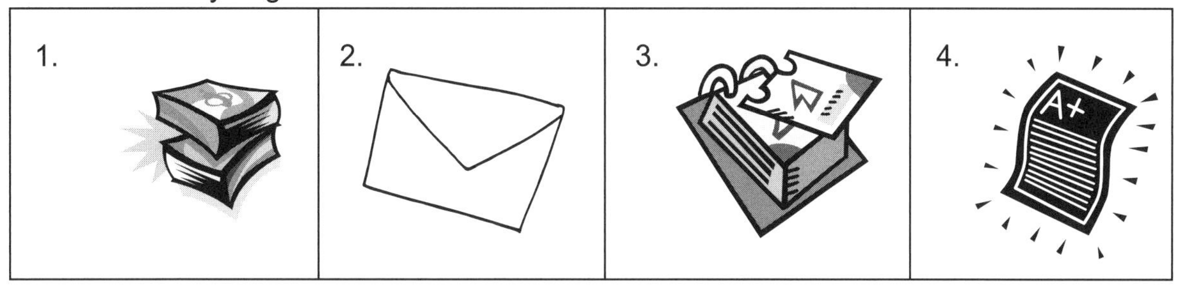

8. Which photograph does she show you?

9. What do you want to do?

10. Which of the following is your sister?

Part 3a Directions: Answer the question in English based on the reading selection in Spanish. Choose the best answer to each question. Base your choice on the content of the reading selection. Write the number of your answer in the appropriate space on your answer sheet. (8%)

SEMANA DEL 2 DE SEPTIEMBRE

L 2 *cita con dentista 2 pm*
M 3 *partido de golf 10 am*
M 4 *lección de inglés*
J 5 *visita a mi prima Consuelo*
V 6 *exhibición de arte*
S 7 *ópera Rigoletto 2 pm*
D 8 *matrimonio de Juan y Ana*

11. According to the above calendar, when is this person seeing a doctor?
    1. Sunday
    2. Monday
    3. Tuesday
    4. Saturday

12. What is this person doing on Tuesday ?
    1. visiting a relative
    2. seeing an art show
    3. learning a foreign language
    4. playing a sport

SOLICITUD DE EMPLEO Fecha de hoy _______

A. Nombre y Apellido __________
B. Dirección ___________________
C. Ciudad ____________________
D. Fecha de nacimiento _________
E. País de nacimiento ___________
F. Actividades ____________________

13. On what line do you write your birthdate?
    1. (B) 2. (C) 3. (D) 4. (F)

De: operafan2@gahoo.com
A: jmwt6@juno.com
Fecha: viernes, el 12 de junio de 2002 18:26:29 -0400
Objeto: mi actividad favorita

Querido Hector,

¿Mi actividad favorita? A mi familia le gusta mucho la música. Mi madre es pianista. Mi padre es guitarrista y mi hermano es violonista. ¿Y yo? Me gusta mucho cantar. Me gusta mucho escuchar las óperas de Mozart.

Saludos,
Cristina

14. What kind of television program might Cristina enjoy?

1. a college basketball game
2. a panel discussion on politics
3. a philharmonic symphony
4. a show on French cooking

Part 3b Directions: Answer the question in Spanish based on the reading selection in Spanish. Choose the best answer to each question. Base your choice on the content of the reading selection. Write the number of your answer in the appropriate space on your answer sheet (12%).

Juan Sánchez
1554 Broadway
Toledo, Ohio 43608
USA

Señor Pablo Montero
Avenida Génova, 755
Puerto Vallarta, Jalisco 48310
México

15. ¿En qué país vive Pablo Montero?

1. en los Estados Unidos
2. en México
3. en Avenida Génova
4. en Toledo

16. ¿Cuál es el código postal de Puerto Vallarta?

1. 48310
2. 1554 Broadway
3. Jalisco
4. en el estado de Ohio

DOCUMENTO DE INMIGRACIÓN

Nombre..Edad.................. Sexo M F
Dirección ....
Ciudad .... Provincia ....
País ....
Yo viajo con :
Esposo/a ....Edad..................Sexo M F
Hijos ....Edad............................M F
....Edad .... M F
....Edad .... M F
Destino
....
¿Por qué? ....

17. ¿Cuántos años tiene el padre de esta familia?
1. cuarenta años
2. quince años
3. trece años
4. treinta y siete años

18. ¿ En qué ciudad vive la familia?
1. Orlando
2. Villa Angela
3. Argentina
4. Chaco

Part 4 Writing (20%)

Part 4 Directions: Choose two of the three writing tasks provided. Your answer for each of the two questions should be written entirely in Spanish and should contain a minimum of **30 words.**

Place names and brand names written in Spanish count as one word. Contractions are counted as one word. Salutations, closings and commonly used abbreviations are included in the word count. Numbers, unless written as words, and names of people do not count as words.

Be sure that you have satisfied the purpose of the task. The sentence structure and /or expressions used should be connected logically and demonstrate a wide range of vocabulary with minimal repetition.

4a. Your younger sibling will be attending your school in the fall. You discover that he/she will be having the same Spanish language teacher as you had the previous year. Describe the teacher to him/her. You may want to include:

- The teacher's physical characteristics, including color of eyes and hair.
- The teacher's personality attributes.
- The teacher's likes and dislikes.

4b. A pen-pal with whom you have been corresponding by e-mail has requested that you mail him by post a book about American sports. You send him/her an e-mail to get the correct mailing address. In your e-mail you may wish to ask:

- for his/her first and last name
- his/her address
- for the name of his town and country
- for his correct postal code

4c. You wish to have a pen pal in a Spanish speaking country. You decide to advertise for one in a Spanish language magazine. Write out an ad describing yourself. In the ad you may wish to include

- Your name
- Your age
- Your interests and preferences for leisure activities
- A brief physical description of yourself
- Your address

PERSONAL IDENTIFICATION 3

Nombre y Apellido ______________________________ Fecha ______________

Part I **Speaking** __________ (30%)
Part 2 **Listening (30%)**

2a.	2b.	2c.
1._____	4._____	7._____
2._____	5._____	8._____
3._____	6._____	9._____
		10._____

PART 3: READING (20%)

3a.(8%)	3b.(12%)
11._____	15._____
12._____	16._____
13._____	17._____
14._____	18._____

Part 4 **Writing (20%) 20 words** **Write 2 paragraphs** **4a , 4b or 4c**

1 ____

2 ____

FAMILY

FAMILY LIFE 3

TEACHER'S SCRIPT FOR THE EXAM, PART II (Listening, 30%)

Part 2a Directions: For each question, you will hear some background information in English. Then you will hear a passage in Spanish twice, followed by a question in English. Listen carefully. After you have heard the question, read the question and the four suggested answers. Choose the best answer and write its number in the appropriate space on your answer sheet. (9%)

1. You meet your friend Hector in a gift shop. He says to you:

   Este domingo, el nueve de mayo, mi familia tiene dos celebraciones. Vamos a celebrar el cumpleaños de mi hermano y el Día de las Madres. Mayo es mi mes favorito.

   When is Hector's brother's birthday? (1)

2. Your friend Juan is telling you that he is going to be a godfather to his cousin's daughter. He says to you

   Mi prima va a dar a su hija el nombre de María del Carmen. Es un nombre muy popular en mi familia. Mi bisabuela se llamaba María del Carmen. Mi abuela, mi prima y la madre de mi prima se llaman María del Carmen también.

   What did Juan tell you about his goddaughter? (1)

3. Isabel is talking about her brother. She says:

   Mi hermano se acuesta a las nueve porque se levanta a las seis de la mañana. El trabaja en la capital.

   At what time does Isabel's brother go to bed?

Part 2b Directions: For each question, you will hear some background information in English. Then you will hear a passage in Spanish twice, followed by a question in Spanish. Listen carefully. After you have heard the question, read the question and the four suggested answers. Choose the best answer and write its number in the appropriate space on your answer sheet (9%).

4. A classmate is speaking to you about a relative. He says:

   A mi tío le gusta jugar a los deportes. Cuando él no está mirando un partido de béisbol a la televisión, él está jugando a basquetbol con sus hijos. Cada sábado, mi tío y mi padre van a jugar al tenis.

   ¿Cómo es el tío de Tomás? (3)

5. Your friend Maria is talking to you about her aunt. She says to you:

   Mi madre tiene una hermana muy joven. Tía Juanita tiene solo dieciocho años. Ella asiste a una universidad en la capital. Es muy inteligente.

   ¿Cuántos años tiene la tía de María? (3)

6. Consuelo is showing you a recent family portrait.

   En mi familia todos nosotros tenemos los ojos verdes. Todos los miembros de mi familia son pelirrojos: mi padre, mi madre, mi hermano mayor, mi hermano menor. Pero, yo soy la única persona que tiene el pelo negro.

   ¿De qué color es el pelo de Consuelo? (1)

Part 2c Directions: For each question, you will hear some background information in English. Then you will hear a passage in Spanish twice, followed by a question in English. Listen carefully. After you have heard the question, read the question and look at the four pictures on your test. Choose the picture that best answers the question and write its number in the appropriate space on your answer sheet. (12%)

7. You are listening to the radio. The announcer is promoting his radio show. He says:

   La esposa toda en blanco es muy bonita. Su esposo alto y delgado es muy guapo. ¿Y la música? La música es romántica. Las personas románticas escuchan siempre nuestro programa. ¿Por qué no escucha Ud. también?

   What background scene does the announcer describe to advertise his radio show? (1)

8. Adelina is speaking to her friend on the telephone. She says:

   En mi escuela hay tres profesores con los apellidos de Mesalunga:
   Señor Mesalunga es profesor de inglés. Su mujer es la Señora Mesalunga. Ella es profesora de español. Le hija mayor es también una profesora. La Señorita Mesalunga enseña la clase de arte.

   Which is the Mesalunga family? (3)

9. Rosa is telling you about her daily routines. She says:

   Todos los días me despierto a las seis y media. Me levanto pronto. Me ducho y después me visto. Yo como el cereal. Salgo de la casa a las siete y media.

   What might this person do next? (4)

10. You are at your neighbor's house. Her cousin is visiting and she says

> Yo tengo treinta y dos años. Nací en Colombia el dos de enero de mil novecientos .... * Ahora yo vivo en Nueva York con mi esposo, Juan y mi hijo,Tomás.
>
> Who is your neighbor´s cousin? (3)

* substract "32" from whatever the current year is to get the year in question...

Listening Comprehension Answers:
For all chapters, the answers are indicated in parentheses following each question. (See questions 1-10 on the previous pages.)

Reading Comprehension answers:

3a. (8%)   11. __2__   12. __2__   13. __3__   14. __1__

3b. (12%)   15. __4__   16. __3__   17. __ 2__   18. __3__

FAMILY LIFE 3

Nombre ______________________________ Fecha ____________________________

EXAMINATION

Part 1 SPEAKING (30%)
Part 2 LISTENING (30%)

Part 2a Directions: For each question, you will hear some background information in English. Then you will hear a passage in Spanish twice, followed by a question in English. Listen carefully. After you have heard the question, read the question and the four suggested answers. Choose the best answer and write its number in the appropriate space on your answer sheet. (9%)

1. When is Hector's brother's birthday?

   1. Sunday, May 9th
   2. Sunday, August 29
   3. Friday, March 10th
   4. Monday, December 25th

2. What did Juan tell you about his goddaughter?

   1. her name
   2. where she was born
   3. the child's birthdate
   4. how many siblings she has

3. At what time does Isabel's brother go to bed?

   1. at midnight
   2. at six
   3. at nine
   4. at four-thirty

Part 2b Directions: For each question, you will hear some background information in English. Then you will hear a passage in Spanish twice, followed by a question in Spanish. Listen carefully. After you have heard the question, read the question and the four suggested answers. Choose the best answer and write its number in the appropriate space on your answer sheet (9%).

4. ¿Cómo es el tío de Tomás?

   1. es débil
   2. es muy gordo
   3. es tonto
   4. es atlético

5. ¿Cuántos años tiene la tía de María?

   1. cuarenta años
   2. treinta y seis años
   3. dieciocho años
   4. cincuenta años

6. ¿De qué color es el pelo de Consuelo?

   1. negro
   2. verde
   3. rojo
   4. blanco

FAMILY LIFE 3

Part 2c Directions: For each question, you will hear some background information in English. Then you will hear a passage in Spanish twice, followed by a question in English. Listen carefully. After you have heard the question, read the question and look at the four pictures on your test. Choose the picture that best answers the question and write its number in the appropriate space on your answer sheet. (12%)

7. What background scene does the announcer describe?

10. Which is the Mesalunga family?

9. What might this person do next?

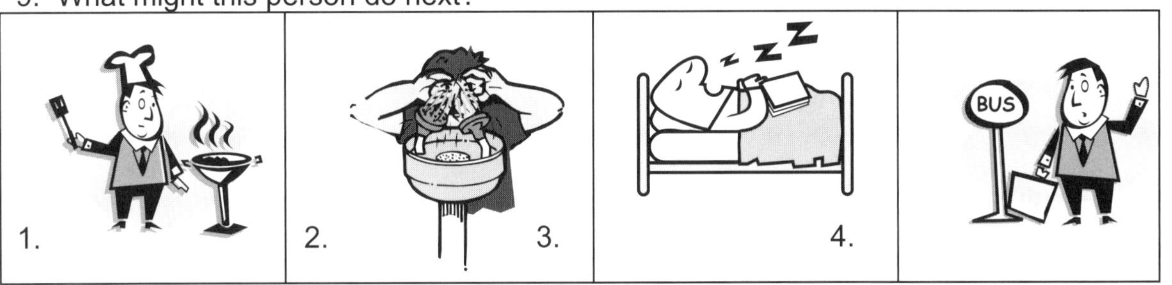

10. Who is your neighbor's cousin?

Part 3a Directions: Answer the question in English based on the reading selection in Spanish. Choose the best answer to each question. Base your choice on the content of the reading selection. Write the number of your answer in the appropriate space on your answer sheet. (8%)

el Sr. Carlos Nieves Rosado
y
la Sra. Clara Pinto Baéz de Nieves

el Sr. Victor Ruíz Cordero
y
la Sra. Ana María Soler Abri de Ruíz

invitan cordialmente al matrimonio de sus hijos

Juana Yolanda y Pedro Roberto

11. What is Juana Yolanda's full maiden name?

1. Juana Yolanda Ruíz Cordero
2. Juana Yolanda Nieves Pinto
3. Juana Yolanda Soler Abri
4. Juana Yolanda Rosado Nieves

Vengan a Celebrar Nuestra Familia

Ocasión Reunión de la Familia Quiñones
Cuando Domingo, el 4 de junio
Donde Restaurante El Zorro Rojo
35, Avenida General Belgrano
Buenos Aires

12. What is this announcement for?

1. a baptism
2. a family reunion
3. a wedding
4. a religious occasion

MI *MADRASTRA*
VIENE DEL PLANETA
JÚPITER

la nueva esposa del padre de Bobby tiene un secreto grande. ......
y Bobby es la sola persona que lo sabe.............................

una película cómica de ciencia-ficción
con los talentos de Josefa Ruíz, Nelson Primo y Juanito Fuentes

13. What secret does Bobby know?
    1. that his father is an undercover agent
    2. that his uncle is a spy
    3. that his stepmother is an alien
    4. the arrival of an impending disaster

EL DÍA DE LOS ABUELOS

El 28 de agosto es el día de los padres de nuestros padres: los abuelos. Hay abuelos jóvenes, pero la mayoría de los abuelos son viejos. Nuestros abuelos nos dan amor y consejos, juegan con nosotros y nos enseñan de la vida. Nosotros somos la continuación de sus vidas.

14. Who should we remember on August 28th according to the above announcement?

1. our grandparents	3. our fathers
2. our nephews and nieces	4. our uncles

FAMILY LIFE 3

Part 3b Directions: Answer the question in Spanish based on the reading selection in Spanish. Choose the best answer to each question. Base your choice on the content of the reading selection. Write the number of your answer in the appropriate space on your answer sheet. (12%)

El cowboy y cantante norteamericano más popular en los años cincuenta era Roy Rogers. El nació el 5 de noviembre de 1911 en la ciudad de Cincinnati en el estado de Ohio. En 1937 el Studio Republic que buscaba un cowboy cantante lo descubrió. La carrera de Rogers empezó inmediatamente. Su película más popular fue, en 1944, "The Cowboy and the Señorita" junto con Dale Evans, la actriz que se convirtió en su esposa. Roy Rogers y Dale Evans eran los padres de nueve hijos (de los cuales cinco eran adoptados). Roy Rogers murió en California en 1997 a la edad de 86 años.

15. ¿En qué año nació Roy Rogers?

1. 1937
2. 1997
3. 1944
4. 1911

16. ¿Cuántos hijos tenían Roy Rogers y Dale Evans.

1. 8
2. 3
3. 9
4. 12

FAMILY LIFE 3

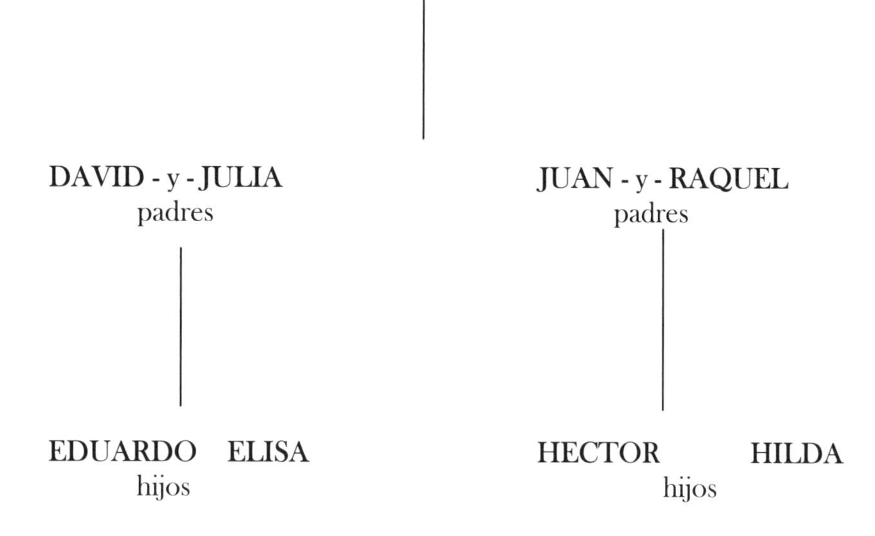

17. Según el árbol de familia, ¿quién es el hermano de Hilda ?

1. Juan	3. Eduardo
2. Hector	4. Carlos

18. Según el árbol de familia, ¿cómo se llama la tía de Eduardo?

1. Hilda	3. Raquel
2. Carmen	4. Elisa

Part 4 Writing (20%)
Part 4 Directions: Choose two of the following writing tasks below. Your answer to each of the two questions should be written entirely in Spanish and should contain a minimum of **30 words.**

Place names and brand names written in Spanish count as one word. Contractions are counted as one word. Salutations, closings and commonly used abbreviations are included in the word count. Numbers, unless written as words, and names of people do not count as words.

Be sure that you have satisfied the purpose of the task. The sentence structure and /or expressions used should be connected logically and demonstrate a wide range of vocabulary with minimal repetition.

4a. People say that you are very similar to one of your relatives. Choose a member of your family and describe, in your opinion, how you are similar and different. You may wish to include:
- What that relatives name is and the relationship.
- What your physical characteristics are and how ´he-she is the same and different.
- What your personality is like and how it is similar or different to this relative..
- What your favorite activities are and if your relative has similar interests

4b. Your pen pal in Argentina wants to know what your family and relatives do when they get together. In Spanish, write a note to your pen pal describing a family gathering. You may wish to include:

- What holiday or event your family and relatives get together.
- Who these members were
- If these members bring something to this event .
- What kind of activities does the family do, such as singing, dancing, preparing a meal, watching TV or playing a game.

4c. You have recently seen a TV program or film about a particular family. Write a summary about the characters in this production. You may wish to include:

- The name of the production
- Who the characters are and their relationship to each other
- Give a description of the various family members
- Mention their physical characteristics
- Mention what the family members do, such as their occupations, favorite activities.

FAMILY LIFE 3

Nombre y Apellido ______________________________ Fecha ______________

Part I **Speaking** __________ (30%)
Part 2 **Listening (30%)**

PART 3: READING (20%)

2a.	2b.	2c.	3a.(8%)	3b.(12%)
1._____	4._____	7._____	11._____	15._____
2._____	5._____	8._____	12._____	16._____
3._____	6._____	9._____	13._____	17._____
		10._____	14._____	18._____

Part 4 **Writing (20%) 20 words** **Write 2 paragraphs** **4a , 4b or 4c**

1 ____

____

____

____

____

____

____

____

____

2 ____

____

____

____

____

____

____

____

____

____

____

____

FAMILY LIFE 3

House and Home

HOUSE AND HOME 3

TEACHER'S SCRIPT FOR THE EXAM, PART II (Listening, 30%)

Part 2a Directions: For each question, you will hear some background information in English. Then you will hear a passage in Spanish twice, followed by a question in English. Listen carefully. After you have heard the question, read the question and the four suggested answers. Choose the best answer and write its number in the appropriate space on your answer sheet (9%).

1. Your brother is looking for the portable phone. You say:

   Creo que el teléfono está en el cuarto de nuestra hermana. Tú sabes que ella siempre habla por teléfono con sus amigos. Mira en el tocador.

   Where do you suggest that the phone might be? (2)

2. You are moving into a new house. The movers speak only Spanish so you explain to them where you want certain pieces of furniture. You say:

   Quisiera la mesa de metal en la cocina y la mesa de madera en el comedor. Ponga el sillón rojo en la sala y ponga el espejo en el cuarto a la derecha.

   Where do you tell the movers to put the red armchair? (1)

3. You are in a carpet store. You hear a mother talking to her daughter. The mother says:

   Yo sé que el blanco es tu color favorito, pero con este color tú vas a pasar la aspiradora cada día. ¿Por qué no compras una alfombra oriental? Es bonito y hay muchos colores.

   What does this mother suggest to her daughter? (4)

Part 2b Directions: For each question, you will hear some background information in English. Then you will hear a passage in Spanish twice, followed by a question in Spanish. Listen carefully. After you have heard the question, read the question and the four suggested answers. Choose the best answer and write its number in the appropriate space on your answer sheet (9%).

4. Your friend Thomas spent the summer at his pen pal´s house in Colombia. He tells you:

   Mi amigo vive en una casa grande. Hay tres pisos. En el primer piso hay la cocina, la sala, un baño y el comedor. En el segundo piso hay cuatro dormitorios y un baño. En el tercer piso, hay una biblioteca y un pequeño dormitorio dónde yo dormí..

¿Dónde está la cocina? (1)

5. A gentleman in a car stops and asks you for directions. You say:

 ¿La casa de los López? Está allí. Es la casa gris y verde con un garaje para dos coches.

 ¿De qué color es la casa de los López? (3)

6. Teresa is telling you what chores people in her family have. She says

 A mí no me gusta trabajar en casa. En el verano mi abuela viene a visitarnos. Mi abuela es una mujer fuerte y muy activa. Le gusta ayudar a mi madre en casa. Entonces, es mi abuela que limpia el baño, lava los platos y hace las camas.

 ¿Cómo es la abuela de Teresa? (2)

Part 2c Directions: For each question, you will hear some background information in English. Then you will hear a passage in Spanish twice, followed by a question in English. Listen carefully. After you have heard the question, read the question and look at the 4 pictures on your test. Choose the picture that best answers the question and write its number in the appropriate space on your answer sheet. (12%)

7. . Your Uncle Raúl is showing you his new apartment. He says:

 Mi apartamento es pequeño, pero es muy conveniente. Yo soy profesor en una escuela local y yo puedo caminar al trabajo.

 How does Uncle Raúl get to work? (3)

8. Your friend´s father tells you why he likes his house. He says

 Me gusta mucho esta casa porque es muy grande. Hay cuatro pisos. A mis hijos les gusta la música mucho. Pedro toca la guitarra y Juan toca el saxofón. Cuando ellos quieren tocar la música, ellos van al ático y yo voy en el sótano.

 What does your friend and his brother like to do? (1)

9. You and your friend Mariana are in a department store. She says to you

 Yo necesito un escritorio nuevo. Lo que tengo es más pequeño. Este escritorio es bastante grande y largo. Yo puedo escribir y hacer mi tarea aquí a la derecha y a la izquierda yo puedo tener la computadora, el monitor, la lámpara y los libros..

What is Mariana thinking of buying? (2)

10. Your mother is speaking to you by phone. She says:

    Estoy aquí delante del fregadero. Estoy lavando los platos y no tengo tiempo para hablar. El rosbif está en el horno y la sopa está en la estufa. Todo sera listo en diez minutos. Ven a casa y hablaremos.

    Where is your mother? (4)

Listening Comprehension Answers:
For all chapters, the answers are indicated in parentheses following each question. (See questions 1-10 on the previous pages.

Reading Comprehension answers:

3a. (8%)	11. __2__	12. __3__	13. __3__	14. __4__
3b (12%)	15. __1__	16. __3__	17. __2__	18. __1__

HOUSE AND HOME 3

Nombre ___________________________ Fecha _______________

EXAMINATION

Part 1 SPEAKING (30%)
Part 2 LISTENING (30%)

Part 2a Directions: For each question, you will hear some background information in English. Then you will hear a passage in Spanish twice, followed by a question in English. Listen carefully. After you have heard the question, read the question and the four suggested answers. Choose the best answer and write its number in the appropriate space on your answer sheet (9%).

1. Where do you suggest that the phone might be?

    1. in the kitchen
    2. in a bedroom
    3. in the bathroom
    4. in the garage

2. Where do you tell the movers to put the red armchair?

    1. in the living room
    2. in the attic
    3. in your grandfather´s bedroom
    4. in the garage

3. What does this mother suggest to her daughter?

    1. that she get wall-to-wall carpeting.
    2. that she get three or four throw rugs.
    3. that the kitchen be painted first
    4. that she buy an Oriental rug.

Part 2b Directions: For each question, you will hear some background information in English. Then you will hear a passage in Spanish twice, followed by a question in Spanish. Listen carefully. After you have heard the question, read the question and the four suggested answers. Choose the best answer and write its number in the appropriate space on your answer sheet (9 %).

4. ¿Dónde está la cocina?

    1. en el primer piso.
    2. en el segundo piso.
    3. en el tercer piso
    4. en el sótano.

5. ¿De qué color es la casa de los López?

    1. blanca
    2. blanca y parda
    3. gris y verde.
    4. azul

6. ¿Cómo es la abuela de Teresa?
   1. antipática
   2. débil
   3. perezosa e inpaciente
   4. activa y simpática

Part 2c Directions: For each question, you will hear some background information in English. Then you will hear a passage in Spanish twice, followed by a question in English. Listen carefully. After you have heard the question, read the question and look at the 4 pictures on your test. Choose the picture that best answers the question and write its number in the appropriate space on your answer sheet. (12%)

7. How does uncle Raúl get to work?

9. What does your friend and his brother like to do?

8. What is Mariana thinking of buying?

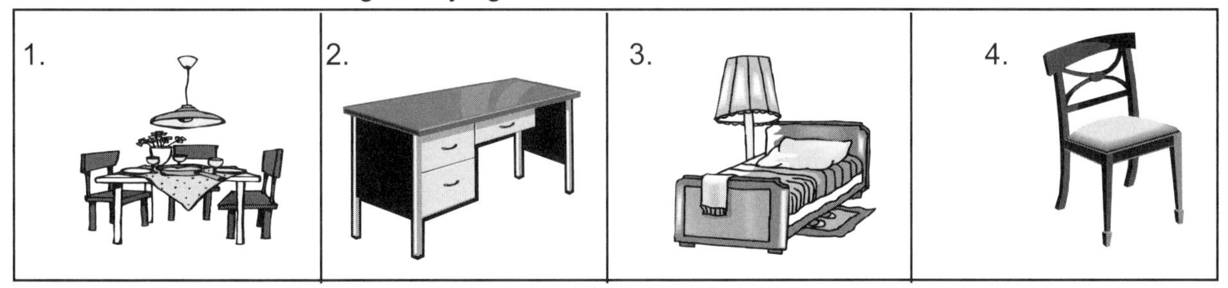

10. Where is your mother?

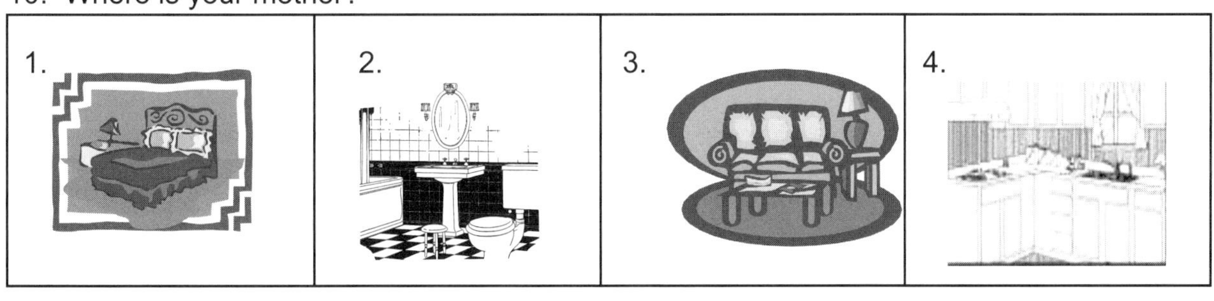

Part 3 READING (20%)

Part 3a Directions: Answer the questions in English based on the reading selections in Spanish. Choose the best answer to each question. Base your choice on the content of the reading selection. Write the number of your answer in the appropriate space on your answer sheet (8%).

Página Web:

Reparación repuestos lavaplatos neveras hornos microondas lavadoras secadoras estufas
reparación de electrodomésticos
www.ayudoelec.com/repuestos/servicio_tecnico.htm

11. One would access the above web page if they
    1. were looking for a house cleaning service
    2. needed to have an electric appliance repaired
    3. wanted to buy bedroom furniture
    4. were doing a biology report on microbes

CLASIFICADOS

A. BARILOCHE
Julio y agosto
Apartamento bonito con 1 dormitorio, amueblado, baño, cocina, sala, chiminea. Primer piso. Ideal para las vacaciones de invierno. A 300 metros de las pistas . de esquí. Tel. 545-764-456

B. BAHÍA BLANCA
¡Maravilloso!
Alquilo apartamento con 2 dormitorios, cocina y baño, terraza magnífica. Parking incluído, muy bonito. 4º piso
Enero y febrero.
Tel. 655-398-196

C. ROSARIO
¡Perfecto! Vendo casa tres pisos, 5 dormitorios, 3 baños, cocina completa, sala, garaje para 2 coches, sótano, jardín y piscina.
Tel. 555-101-884

D. BUENOS AIRES
¡ Véalo ! Vendo casa
2 dormitorios, comedor, cocina, sala, baño, garaje
Aire acondicionado central.
Tel. 955-760-507

12. Which listing advertises a swimming pool?
    1. A 2. B 3. C 4. D

13. In which city can one rent an apartment near a ski slope?
    1. Bahía Blanca 3. Bariloche
    2. Rosario 4. Buenos Aires

TITO LOQUITO
¡ Mis precios son los más bajos !

Videocaseteras
Radios y Televisores
Instrumentos musicales eléctricos
Juegos electrónicos
Discos compactos y casetes
Equipos de sonido y estéreos
Teléfonos decorativos

Abierto lunes - viernes 10AM - 10PM
sábado 9:30AM - 10PM
domingo 11AM - 5PM

765, Avenida Santa Cruz, Monterey

14. According to the announcement

1. the store opens at 10 AM on Saturday
2. the store closes at 10PM on Sunday
3. one can buy linens and bedspreads here
4. one can buy entertainment equipment here

Part 3b Directions: Answer the question in Spanish based on the reading selection in Spanish. Choose the best answer to each question. Base your choice on the content of the reading selection. Write the number of your answer in the appropriate space on your answer sheet (12%).

CINCO HERMANAS Y UNA ESCOBA MÁGICA

servicio profesional de limpieza con Adela, Bárbara, Celia, Dora y Ester
¡ En 3 horas ponemos su casa en orden ! tel. 665-7849

Adela va a lavar la ropa, sacar la basura y lavar los platos
Bárbara va a pasar la aspiradora, sacudir y lustrar los muebles
Celia va a cortar el césped, barrer el patio y limpiar el jardín
Dora va a limpiar el baño y lavar las ventanas
Ester va a hacer las camas y arreglar los cuartos

Sí, limpiamos también el garaje..

Servicio simple $ 150
Servicio delujo $ 200

Cada hora adicional: $70 - $80

15. ¿Qué servicio **no** ofrece esta compañía de limpieza?

1. no lava los coches
2. no limpia los muebles
3. no lava la ropa
4. no hace la cama

16. ¿Cuánto cuesta el servicio simple?

1. doscientos dólares
3. cien cincuenta dólares
3. trescientos dólares
4. quinientos treinta dólares

17. ¿Quién va a limpiar el inodoro y el lavabo?

1. Ester
2. Dora
3. Bárbara
4. Celia

La Casa:

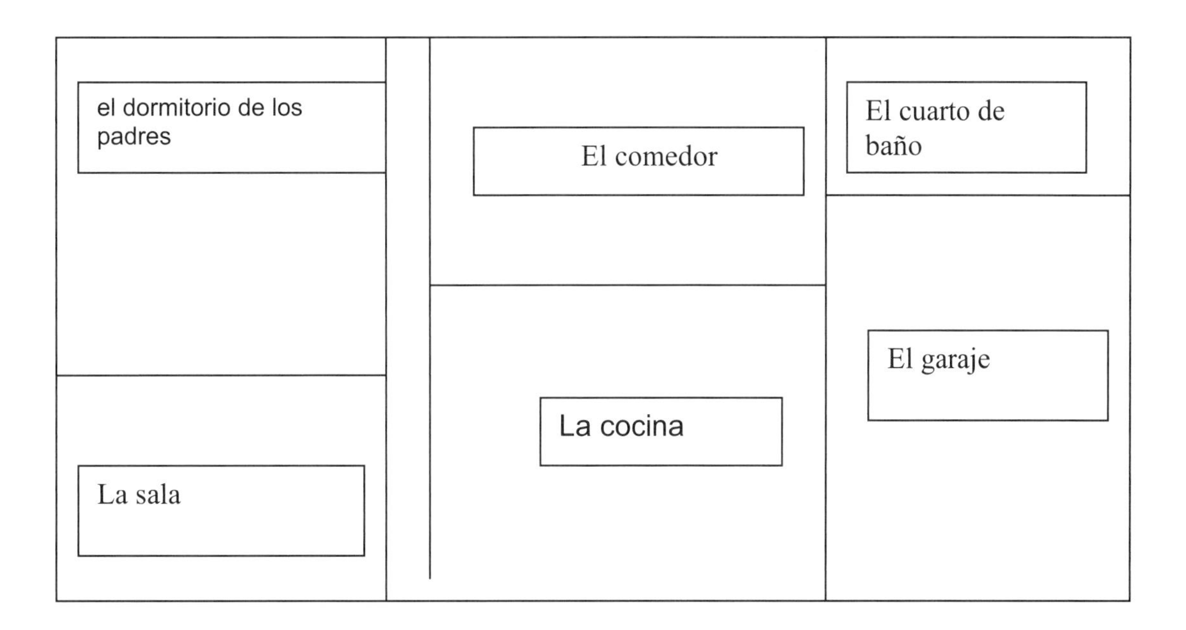

18. ¿Dónde está el comedor?

1. entre el dormitorio y el baño
2. en el baño
3 cerca de la sala.
4. entre el garaje y la sala

Part 4 Writing (20%)

Part 4 Directions: Choose two of the three writing tasks provided below. Your answer to each of the two questions should be written entirely in Spanish and should contain a minimum of **30 words**.

Place names and brand names written in Spanish count as one word. Contractions are counted as one word. Salutations, closings and commonly used abbreviations are included in the word count. Numbers, unless written as words, and names of people do not count as words.

Be sure that you have satisfied the purpose of the task. The sentence structure and /or expressions used should be connected logically and demonstrate a wide range of vocabulary with minimal repetition.

4a. The Spanish club in your school needs to raise money. Your club has decided to offer some sort of cleaning service. Write an advertisement that you will place in the local Spanish language newspaper: In your advertisement you may wish to include:

- What kind of service you are offering: car washing/ waxing, garage cleaning/ gardening
- What this service will include
- The days and hours when this service will be given
- The charge for this service
- Why your club is offering this service

4b. You are on vacation at a country house in a Spanish-speaking nation. Write a letter to your friend about the house where you are staying. In your letter you may wish to include:

- Where this country house is located
- Who is with you in this housed
- The size of the house and number of rooms and floors
- What kind of furnishings the house has
- What additional facilities there are: a laundry room, garage, swimming pool, garden, patio

4c. You are selling some old, but fine furniture that you are selling. You wish to advertise the furniture in a newspaper. Write an ad. In your ad you many wish to include:

- What pieces of furniture you are selling.
- A description of the furniture, such as its size, shape, color, origin
- What the furniture is made of (plastic, wood, metal)
- For what room this piece of furniture would be ideal
- What the selling price is
- The telephone number that a person needs to all for additional information

HOUSE AND HOME 3

Nombre y Apellido ______________________________ Fecha ______________

Part I **Speaking** __________ (30%)
Part 2 **Listening (30%)** **PART 3: READING** (20%)

2a.	2b.	2c.	3a.(8%)	3b.(12%)
1._____	4._____	7._____	11._____	15._____
2._____	5._____	8._____	12._____	16._____
3._____	6._____	9._____	13._____	17._____
		10._____	14._____	18._____

Part 4 **Writing (20%) 20 words** **Write 2 paragraphs** **4a , 4b or 4c**

1____

____

____

____

____

____

____

____

____

2____

____

____

____

____

____

____

____

____

____

____

____

____

EDUCATION

EDUCATION 3

EDUCATION 3

TEACHER'S SCRIPT FOR THE EXAM, PART II (Listening, 30%)

Part 2a Directions: For each question, you will hear some background information in English. Then you will hear a passage in Spanish twice, followed by a question in English. Listen carefully. After you have heard the question, read the question and the four suggested answers. Choose the best answer and write its number in the appropriate space on your answer sheet (9%).

1. Kevin is talking to you about school. He says:

   El español es una materia muy fácil para mí. Los padres de mi madre vienen de Argentina. Mi papá viene del Uruguay. En casa, siempre hablamos en español. Un día espero ser profesor de español.

   What foreign language is Kevin studying? (3)

2. You are in a stationery store with your friend. You say:

   En la clase del Señor Rodríguez estamos estudiando triángulos y círculos. Yo tengo ya una calculadora, pero yo necesito comprar una regla.

   What does Señor Rodríguez teach? (2)

3. You are in Spanish class. The teacher says to you:

   Levántate y ve a la pizarra. Escribe la respuesta al problema número 30. Aquí tienes la tiza.

   What do you do next? (2)

Part 2b Directions: For each question, you will hear some background information in English. Then you will hear a passage in Spanish twice, followed by a question in Spanish. Listen carefully. After you have heard the question, read the question and the four suggested answers. Choose the best answer and write its number in the appropriate space on your answer sheet. (9%)

4. You and your classmate Luisa are going to your next period together. You say to her:

   Me gusta mucho esta clase. Yo soy muy artistico. Me gustar dibujar y pintar con los colores. Un día quiero ser un artista como Pablo Picasso.

   ¿Cuál es tu clase favorita ? (3)

5. Pablo is showing you his report card. He says:

   No me gusta estudiar o tomar apuntes. Soy afortunado que me gustan mucho los deportes. El señor Perez es el profesor de esta clase y él dice que soy muy atlético. El me quiere en el equipo de béisbol de la escuela.

   ¿Qué enseña el señor Pérez? (4)

6. Graciela is talking to her friend about her schedule. She says:

   Al mediodía yo como el almuerzo en la cafetería. Después del almuerzo, tengo la clase de matemáticas en el segundo piso. A la una y treinta tengo mi clase favorita. Es la clase de español. Saco siempre buenas notas en esta clase.

   ¿Cuándo tiene Graciela su clase favorita? (1)

   1, por la tarde
   2. en el período dos
   3. por la mañana
   4. en el período uno

Part 2c Directions: For each question, you will hear some background information in English. Then you will hear a passage in Spanish twice, followed by a question in English. Listen carefully. After you have heard the question, read the question and look at the 4 pictures on your test. Choose the picture that best answers the question and write its number in the appropriate space on your answer sheet. (12%)

7. Hector is looking through his bookbag. Then he turns to you and says:
   No tengo mi libro. ¿Tienes tú el libro? Quiero ver un problema en la página doscientos.

   What does Hector want to borrow from you? (3)

8. La señora Cuevas is talking to her fourth grade class. She picks up an item from her desk and says to the class:

   Brasil es el país más grande de la América del Sur. Brasil toca todos los países del continente excepto Chile y Ecuador.

   What item is the teacher holding? (3)

9. You are in Señor Hurtado´s class. He has asked the class to turn to page 200 in their textbook. Then he says:

   Miren el mapa. En los Estados Unidos hay cincuenta estados. Hay ocho estados con nombres españoles y cuatro de estos tocan el país de México. El estado de Florida está aquí, cerca de la isla de Cuba.

   What picture is the class looking at? (1)

10. You will be taking a district-wide mathematics test tomorrow. The teacher is explaining the procedure. She says:

    Mañana, para el examen Uds. no pueden escribir las respuestas en tinta. Entonces, no necesitan bolígrafo. Vamos a usar el lápiz. Uds. necesitan una calculadora y una regla también

    What item will you need tomorrow? (4)

Listening Comprehension Answers:
For all chapters, the answers are indicated in parentheses following each question. (See question 1-10 on the previous pages.)

Reading Comprehension answers:

3a (8%) 11. __2__ 12. __3__ 13. __3__ 14. __2__

3b (12%) 15. __1__ 16. __4__ 17. __3__ 18. __2__

EDUCATION 3

Nombre ______________________ Fecha ______________

EXAMINATION

Part 1 SPEAKING (30%)
Part 2 LISTENING (30%)

Part 2a Directions: For each question, you will hear some background information in English. Then you will hear a passage in Spanish twice, followed by a question in English. Listen carefully. After you have heard the question, read the question and the four suggested answers. Choose the best answer and write its number in the appropriate space on your answer sheet (9%).

1. What foreign language is Kevin studying?

   1. Italian
   2. French
   3. Spanish
   4. Russian

2. What does Señor Rodríguez teach?

   1. Language Arts
   2. Mathematics
   3. Chemistry
   4. History

3. What do you do next?

   1. Look for your pen.
   2. Go to the board.
   3. Open your geography book.
   4. Leave the classroom.

Part 2b Directions: For each question, you will hear some background information in English. Then you will hear a passage in Spanish twice, followed by a question in Spanish. Listen carefully. After you have heard the question, read the question and the four suggested answers. Choose the best answer and write its number in the appropriate space on your answer sheet. (9%)

4. ¿Cuál es tu clase favorita?

   1. la clase de español
   2. la clase de historia
   3. la clase de arte
   4. la clase de educación física

5. ¿Qué enseña el señor Pérez?

   1. geografía
   2. matemáticas
   3. ciencia
   4. educación física

6. ¿Cuándo tiene Graciela su clase favorita?

1, por la tarde	3. por la mañana
2. en el período dos	4. en el período cuatro

Part 2c. Directions: For each question, you will hear some background information in English. Then you will hear a passage in Spanish twice, followed by the question in English. Listen carefully. After you have heard the question, read the question and look at the four pictures on your test paper. Choose the picture that best answers the question and write its number in the appropriate space on your answer sheet.

7. What does Hector want to borrow from you?

8. What item is the teacher holding?

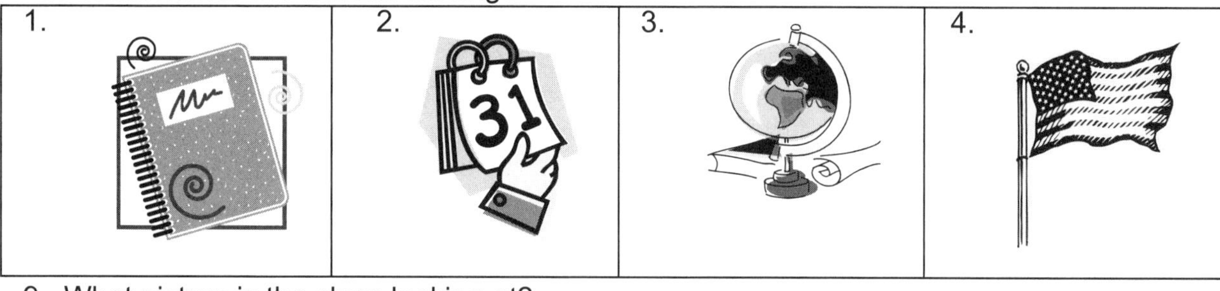

9. What picture is the class looking at?

10. What item will you need to have for the test?

Part 3 READING (20%)

Part 3a Directions: Answer the question in English based on the reading selection in Spanish. Choose the best answer to each question. Base your choice on the content of the reading selection. Write the number of your answer in the appropriate space on your answer sheet (8%).

el 9 de septiembre

Querida Señora Davalos,

Yo no estoy contenta con mi horario. Mi primera clase está en el cuarto piso. Para mi segunda clase, yo tengo que bajar la escalera hasta el primer piso. Para la clase de música (período tres) yo tengo que subir al cuarto piso. Después, para la clase de francés (período 4) yo estoy de nuevo en el primer piso. Para período 5 yo estoy en el cuarto piso y período 6 yo estoy en la cafetería en el sótano. A la una y media yo tengo la clase de matemáticas en el tercer piso . Yo termino el día escolar en el sótano con mi clase de arte.
Quisiera un cambio de algunas clases, por favor. ¿Puede ayudarme?

Patricia Lorca

11. What is Patricia writing to her counselor about?

    1. a conflict with a classmate
    2. the location of her classes
    3. the food service in the cafeteria
    4. one of her class projects

12. According to her letter, when most likely might Patricia have her art class?

    1. the period just before lunchtime
    2. 1:30 PM
    3. at 2:15 PM
    4. Period 1

SACAPUNTOS

Descuentos de 20 % Desde el 1 de Septiembre hasta el 14 de Septiembre

A **Artículos para la escuela**	*B* **Artículos para la oficina**	*C* **Productos de limpieza**	*D* **Electrónicos**
pizarras y tiza	acesorios de escritorios	aspiradoras	acesorios para computadoras
papel	carpetas	escobas y palas	impresoras
cuadernos	calendarios	jabón de limpiadores	computadoras y monitores
diccionarios	boligrafos	limpiadores de piso y alfombras	cámaras y escanares
pupitres y sillas	lápices	esponjas	papel láser
mapas	marcadores		
reglas	sobres		
colores			

13. Under what listing would a janitor look for floor or carpet cleaners?

1. A 2. B 3. C 4. D

14. Who primarily would be interested in buying the products from List A?

1. those in the medical field
2. those in the educational field
3. those in the restaurant business
4. those in the musical profession

Part 3b Directions: Answer the question in Spanish based on the reading selection in Spanish. Choose the best answer to each question. Base your choice on the content of the reading selection. Write the number of your answer in the appropriate space on your answer sheet (12%).

ESCUELA DE BRUJERIA
123, Calle 31 de Octubre

Nombre y apellido ......Marcol Malhechos...............

MATERIA	NOTA	PROFESOR
Astrología	....	H. Potter
Encantaciónes	....	E. Price
Espiritualismo	....	A. Nolove
Magia	....	L. Oscuro
Poderes psíquicos	....	W. de Oz

15. ¿Cómo se llama el alumno?

1. Marcos Malhechos
2. Hector Potter
3. L. Oscuro
4. E. Price

16. ¿En qué asignatura es más débil el alumno?

1. magía
2. encantaciones
3. espiritualismo
4. astrología

ESCUELA PERUANA DE IDIOMAS

Aprenda facilmente a hablar

inglés	francés	ruso	alemán
japonés	portugués	italiano	árabe
griego	coreano	turco	chino

lecciones privadas o en grupo
lunes - jueves 9 AM - 7 PM
viernes: solo lecciones privadas
sábado: clases de inglés y portugués
9AM, 11 AM, 1 PM

17. Una persona va a asistir a esta escuela .....

1. para aprender a cocinar
2. para ser dentista
3. para trabajar en una companía internacional
4. para reparar coches

18. ¿Cuándo no hay clases?

1. lunes y jueves
2. domingo
3. sábado y miércoles
4. viernes

Part 4 WRITING (20%)
Part 4 Directions: Choose two of the three writing tasks provided below. Your answer to each one of the two questions should be written entirely in Spanish and should contain a minimum of **30 words**.

Place names and brand names written in Spanish count as one word. Contractions are counted as one word. Salutations, closings and commonly used abbreviations are included in the word count. Numbers, unless written as words, and names of people do not count as words.

Be sure that you have satisfied the purpose of the task. The sentence structure and /or expressions used should be connected logically and demonstrate a wide range of vocabulary with minimal repetition.

4a. You had lived with a host family in Mexico and attended the local school. Your Spanish club newspaper has asked you to write about your observations about the Mexican school there. In your article you may wish to include:

- How many days a week students attend school
- The number of periods there is in a school day
- What the students and teachers wear
- How the students and teachers address each other
- How the lessons are conducted
- Which subjects are taught in the school
- How students are graded
- Whether there is a library, a gymnasium, lab rooms

4b. You are about to begin your school year. Your pen pal in Spain would like to know what items students are required to have. In your reply, you may wish to include

- What general items you buy for all your classes.
- What additional items are purchased for specialized classes. (calculator for math, sneakers for gym class, crayons for art etc.)
- What items are found or provided in specific classes (maps and globe in geography rooms).
- Whether there is a library or laboratories in your school.

4c. Your school participates in a student-exchange cultural program with a district in Uruguay. You have been asked to write a letter to a possible exchange-student candidate for information. In your letter, you may wish to ask:

- Where the student lives.
- The name of his / her school.
- How the student gets to school.
- What classes the student takes
- When the school day begins and ends.
- Which is his/ her favorite class.
- What clubs or activities are available after school

EDUCATION 3

Nombre y Apellido ______________________________ Fecha ______________

Part I **Speaking** __________ (30%)
Part 2 **Listening (30%)**

2a.	2b.	2c.
1.______	4.______	7.______
2.______	5.______	8.______
3.______	6.______	9.______
		10.______

PART 3: READING (20%)

3a.(8%)	3b.(12%)
11.______	15.______
12.______	16.______
13.______	17.______
14.______	18.______

Part 4 **Writing (20%) 20 words** **Write 2 paragraphs** **4a , 4b or 4c**

1____
____
____
____
____
____
____
____
____

2____
____
____
____
____
____
____
____
____
____
____
____

Community and Neighborhood

COMMUNITY AND NEIGHBORHOOD 3

COMMUNITY AND NEIGHBORHOOD 3

TEACHER'S SCRIPT FOR THE EXAM, PART II (Listening, 30%)

Part 2a Directions: For each question, you will hear some background information in English. Then you will hear a passage in Spanish twice, followed by a question in English. Listen carefully. After you have heard the question, read the question and the four suggested answers. Choose the best answer and write its number in the appropriate space on your answer sheet. (9%)

1. You ask the hotel manager for driving directions to the Art Museum. He replies:

   No use el coche. El museo está en el centro de la ciudad, pero está prohibido estacionarse el coche allí. Si Ud. toma el metro, tiene que caminar muchas cuadras. El museo está lejos de la estación. Le recomiendo tomar el autobús número 22. La parada del autobús está enfrente del museo. Es muy conveniente.

   What does the hotel manager recommend? (2)

2. Your teacher is giving instructions to her students about a class trip. She says:

   Cuando llegamos al cine, ustedes tienen que estar juntos. La película está completamente en español, pero con subtítulos en inglés. Escuchen bien. Es una película muy divertida..

   What will you be seeing on this class trip? (4)

3. You are visiting Acapulco, Mexico for the first time. It's lunchtime and you ask a passerby to recommend a good restaurant. He replies:

   Hay cinco buenos restaurantes en este pueblo. ¿Qué tipo de comida quiere comer? Hay un restaurante alemán, un restaurante español y una pizzería italiana. Hay también un restaurante mexicano y un café francés. Todos los cinco son excelentes. Y todos están en la plaza central. La plaza está muy cerca de aquí. Ud. puede ir a pie.

   What will you do next? (1)

Part 2b Directions: For each question, you will hear some background information in English. Then you will hear a passage in Spanish twice, followed by a question in Spanish. Listen carefully. After you have heard the question, read the question and the four suggested answers. Choose the best answer and write its number in the appropriate space on your answer sheet. (9%)

4. Your family is visiting relatives in Puerto Rico. Your cousin is talking to his older sister. He says:

No quiero ir a la playa hoy porque hace mal tiempo. Vamos a la piscina interior de la universidad. Es una piscina grande y está debajo de un techo.

¿Qué quieren hacer tus primos? (4)

5. Your brother is going to the store. He says:

Yo voy ahora a la Tienda Miraldi porque esta semana hay muchas ofertas especiales. Yo necesito comprar cuadernos, bolígrafos y lápices para mi clase de ingés. ¿Por qué no vienes conmigo.

¿Para qué vas de compras? (3)

6. You are traveling with your family. You hear your mother say to your father

Mira. Hay una gasolinera en la esquina de esta cuadra. Mira, hay también una heladería a la derecha. ¡Qué bueno! Mientras que tú hablas con el mecánico, los niños y yo vamos a comprar un refresco en la heladería

¿Cómo viaja tu familia? (4)

Part 2c Directions: For each question, you will hear some background information in English. Then you will hear a passage in Spanish twice, followed by a question in English. Listen carefully. After you have heard the question, read the question and look at the four pictures on your test. Choose the picture that best answers the question and write its number in the appropriate space on your answer sheet. (12%)

7. You are at a hotel in Madrid, Spain. You hear this announcement on the television.

La Casa del Libro es una famosa librería en la Gran Vía de Madrid. Se venden libros, revistas y periódicos de todo el mundo. La librería tiene un medio millón de títulos. Es la más grande en lengua española..

What is the announcer describing? (3)

8. You are staying with a host family in Venezuela. The host father wants to take you to a museum. He says

Hay una exposición especial en el Museo del Transporte. Vamos a ver muchos coches clásicos y viejos. Mi coche favorito es la Ferrari. Vamos a ver también trenes y autobuses. El museo es muy grande y muy interesante.

What will you see at this museum? (2)

9. You telephone your friend Veronica. Her sister answers and says:

   Verónica trabaja ahora en ese restaurante nuevo cerca de la biblioteca. Ella prepara las comidas en la cocina. Lo siento pero yo no sé cuando regresará del trabajo..

   What is Veronica doing now? (4)

10. David is talking to Dorothy on the phone. He says to her:

    Tengo que escribir un informe sobre los grandes gatos. ¿Tú sabes....los tigres, los leones, los jaguares? ¿Quieres ir al parque zoológico conmigo?

    Where does David want to go? (1)

Listening Comprehension Answers:
For all chapters, the answers are indicated in parentheses following each question. (See questions 1-10 on the previous pages.)

Reading Comprehension answers:

3a (8%) 11. __1__ 12. __1__ 13. __2__ 14. __1__

3b (12%) 15. __3__ 16. __4__ 17. __4__ 18. __2__

Nombre ______________________________ Fecha _________________________

EXAMINATION

Part I SPEAKING (30%)
Part 2 LISTENING (30%)

Part 2a Directions: For each question, you will hear some background information in English. Then you will hear a passage in Spanish twice, followed by a question in English. Listen carefully. After you have heard the question, read the question and the four suggested answers. Choose the best answer and write its number in the appropriate space on your answer sheet. (9%)

1. What does the hotel manager recommend?

   1. that you walk to the museum
   2. that you go by bus
   3. that you visit the amusement park
   4. that you go on another day

2. What will you be seeing on this class trip?

   1. a flamenco dance
   2. a concert
   3. penguins and aquatic animals
   4. a funny movie

3. What will you do next?

   1. Ask him for directions to the town square
   2. Take the train to the next town.
   3. Order a meal from him
   4. Buy some souvenirs.

Part 2b Directions: For each question, you will hear some background information in English. Then you will hear a passage in Spanish twice, followed by a question in Spanish. Listen carefully. After you have heard the question, read the question and the four suggested answers. Choose the best answer and write its number in the appropriate space on your answer sheet (9%).

4. ¿Qué quieren hacer tus primos?
   1. jugar al tenís
   2. asistir a una clase de arte
   3. esquiar
   4. nadar

5. ¿Para qué vas de compras?

   1. para una fiesta
   3. para un viaje
   3. para la escuela
   4. para un bautizo .

6. ¿Cómo viaja tu familia?
   1. en tren
   2. en avión
   3. en bote
   4. en coche

Part 2c Directions: For each question, you will hear some background information in English. Then you will hear a passage in Spanish twice, followed by a question in English. Listen carefully. After you have heard the question, read the question and look at the 4 pictures on your test. Choose the picture that best answers the question and write its number in the appropriate space on your answer sheet. (12%)

7. What is the announcer describing?

8. What will you see at this museum?

9. What is Veronica doing now?

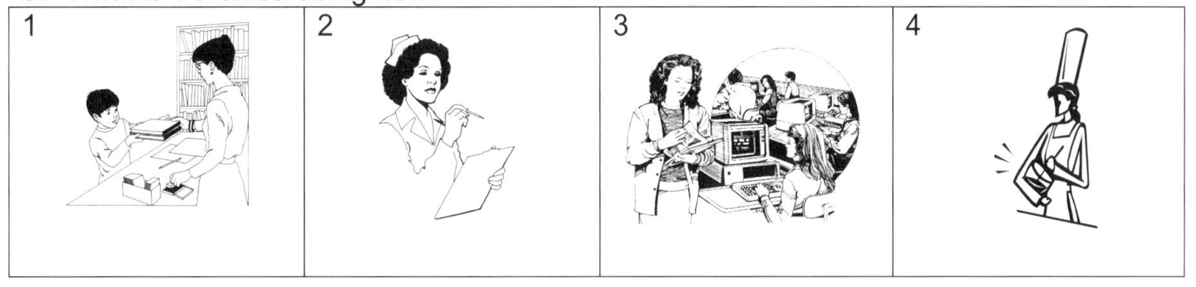

10. Where does David want to go?

COMMUNITY AND NEIGHBORHOOD 3

Part 3a Directions: Answer the question in English based on the reading selection in Spanish. Choose the best answer to each question. Base your choice on the content of the reading selection. Write the number of your answer in the appropriate space on your answer sheet.

CUPON DE DESCUENTO
Oferta Especial del ***Hotel Alhambra***
Avenida Pizarro, # 12

Use este cupón para obtener un descuento de 15% en nuestro restaurante **El Sultan** y en nuestro bar **El Bazar**. y en las tiendas siguientes: La Frutería Hmos. Vallario ***La Heladería del Payaso***, **La Pastelería Casa Dulce**, **La Panadería Dorado** y La Tienda "Guitarra Gitana."

El Sultan
Avenida Pizarro, #12

La Heladería de Payaso
Calle Pizarro, # 290

La Frutería Hmos. Vallario
Calle Gerona, #30

La Panadería Dorado
Calle Colón, #10

11. According to the hotel discount coupon, where is the participating ice cream store located?

1. Calle Pizarro. # 290
2. Calle Colon, # 10
3. Avenida Pizarro, #12
4. Calle Gerona. # 30

12. Where might one buy bread and rolls?

1. La Panadería Dorado
2. La Tienda Guitarra Gitana
3. La Heladería del Payaso
4. El Bazar

SUPERMERCADO PARA NUESTROS ABUELOS SE ABRE EN VILLA GRIS

Hay un nuevo supermercado en nuestra ciudad que es verdaderamente extraordinario. Es único en el mundo. ¿Por qué? Porque hay un mini-tren en el supermercado que viaja alrededor de la tienda. Ud. puede subir o bajar en cada sección del supermercado: la frutería, la carnicería, la lechería, la panadería, la pastelería, etc. ¿Dónde está este supemercado? Está en Villa Gris - el barrio de nuestro pueblo reservado a la gente anciana.

13. What is unusual about this supermarket?

    1. Everything can be bought for under a dollar.
    2. There is a train inside the store
    3. They don´t sell dairy products
    4. It's over 100 years old.

14. What is true about the Villa Gris neighborhood?

    1. Most of the residents are elderly people.
    2. It is a fishing community
    3. There are a lot of elementary schools
    4. Bicycle riding is forbidden.

COMMUNITY AND NEIGHBORHOOD 3

Part 3b Directions: Answer the question in Spanish based on the reading selection in Spanish. Choose the best answer to each question. Base your choice on the content of the reading selection. Write the number of your answer in the appropriate space on your answer sheet. (8%)

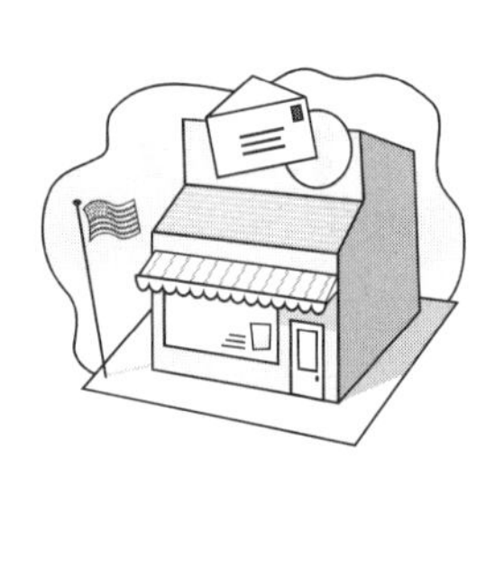

15. La casa de correos está a la izquierda de ___

    1. una gasolinera
    2. un parque
    3. una iglesia
    4. un hospital

16. ¿Dónde está el hospital?

    1. entre la gasolinera y el cine
    2. a la derecha del parque
    3. a la derecha de la gasolinra
    4. entre el cine y la iglesia

EXPOSICIÓN HOMENAJE
a
Germán Cabrera (1903-33)
el escultor más famoso del Uruguay
en el centenario de su nacimiento

la semana del 3 de agosto en la Rotonda
del Banco Central de Uruguay
¡Venga a ver sus creaciones artísticas!

17. ¿Qué pasa la semana del 3 de agosto?

    1. un espectáculo de teatro
    2. una corrida de toros
    3. un partido de béisbol
    4. una exposición de arte

18. ¿Por qué es famoso Germán Cabrera?

    1. Es actor
    2. Es una persona artística
    3. Es un jugador de fútbol
    4. Es jugador de golf

Part 4 Writing (20%)

Part 4 Directions: Choose two of the three writing tasks provided below. Your answer to each of the two questions should be written entirely in Spanish and should contain a minimum of **30 words**.

Place names and brand names written in Spanish count as one word. Contractions are counted as one word. Salutations, closings and commonly used abbreviations are included in the word count. Numbers, unless written as words, and names of people do not count as words.

Be sure that you have satisfied the purpose of the task. The sentence structure and /or expressions used should be connected logically and demonstrate a wide range of vocabulary with minimal repetition.

4a. Many people from your community make use of a very large park in the area. Your Spanish-speaking pen pal wants to know how people from your area make use of it. Write a description of this park. In your reply you may wish to include

- The name of the park and where it is located
- How people might travel to this park
- The kinds of facilities or attractions that this park has (zoo, theater, restaurant etc.)
- What activities people can do in this park
- Whether you like or dislike this park and why

4b. A pen pal from Bolivia lives in a very rural town. She is curious about traffic in the your "downtown" area of your community. Write out a response that you will send her. In your message you may wish to include:

- The location of the downtown area (name the street intersections)
- What buildings are found at this intersection
- Whether there is a lot of traffic in the downtown area and why
- What vehicles one can see in this area
- Whether vehicles can stop or park in this area

4c. Your pen pal from Venezuela is curious about shopping malls in your community. He / she has asked you to describe your favorite shopping mall. Write a letter. In your letter you may wish to include:

- The name of your favorite shopping mall
- In what town it is located
- What kind of stores are located there
- When these stores are open
- Why you like this shopping mall

COMMUNITY AND NEIGHBORHOOD 3

Nombre y Apellido ______________________________ Fecha ______________

Part I **Speaking** __________ (30%)
Part 2 **Listening (30%)** **PART 3: READING** (20%)

2a.	2b.	2c.	3a.(8%)	3b.(12%)
1._____	4._____	7._____	11._____	15._____
2._____	5._____	8._____	12._____	16._____
3._____	6._____	9._____	13._____	17._____
		10._____	14._____	18._____

Part 4 **Writing (20%) 20 words** **Write 2 paragraphs** **4a , 4b or 4c**

1____

____

____

____

____

____

____

____

____

2____

____

____

____

____

____

____

____

____

____

____

____

Food and Meal Taking

TEACHER'S SCRIPT FOR THE EXAM, PART II (Listening, 30%)

Part 2a Directions: For each question, you will hear some background information in English. Then you will hear a passage in Spanish twice, followed by a question in English. Listen carefully. After you have heard the question, read the question and the four suggested answers. Choose the best answer and write its number in the appropriate space on your answer sheet. (9%)

1. You are traveling in Mexico with your parents It is lunchtime and you are hungry. Your father says:

   Vamos a comer en el restaurante de nuestro hotel para el almuerzo hay platos especiales de la región. Me gustaría comer un burrito o una enchilada con nachos. Además, el restaurante tiene aire acondicionado.

   Where does your father want to go? (3)

2. You meet Carolina on your way home after school. She says to you:

   Para la merienda, no como ni queso ni pasteles. Yo prefiero comer una fruta. Tú sabes el proverbio "Una manzana por día te tiene lejos de la enfermería."

   What would Carolina choose for a snack? (1)

3. You over hear a conversation between the cashier and your neighbor, Rosita. The cashier says to her:

   En el estado de Nueva York la edad legal para comprar cerveza es veinte y un años. Lo siento, señorita, pero Ud. es muy joven y yo necesito ver su tarjeta de identidad.

   Why couldn't Rosita make the purchase? (4)

Part 2b Directions: For each question, you will hear some background information in English. Then you will hear a passage in Spanish twice, followed by a question in Spanish. Listen carefully. After you have heard the question, read the question and the four suggested answers. Choose the best answer and write its number in the appropriate space on your answer sheet. (9%)

4. You have invited your friend Bárbara to have lunch at your house. You say to her:

   Vamos a comer en el patio. Hace buen tiempo. Yo traigo los platos y los vasos. Tú traes el mantel y las servilletas.

   1. ¿Qué van a hacer tú y Bárbara? (1)

5. You are living with a host family in Chile. Your host mother is asking you questions about your home life. You say:

   Generalmente, yo traigo mi almuerzo a la escuela. Traigo algo preparado de mi mamá. Es siempre un sándwich. Puede ser un sándwich de jamón y queso, o un sándwich de crema de mani y jalea. Otro día puede ser de pollo o de pavo. Bebo leche y como galletas también.

   ¿De qué comida habla David? (1)

6. You are out shopping with your friend Luisa. You suggest that you stop at a snack bar. Your friend says:

   No tengo hambre. Pero tengo sed. Pienso pedir un vaso de limonada o un vaso de jugo de naranja.

   ¿Qué va a pedir tu amiga, Luisa? (3)

Part 2c Directions: For each question, you will hear some background information in English. Then you will hear a passage in Spanish twice, followed by a question in English. Listen carefully. After you have heard the question, read the question and look at the 4 pictures on your test. Choose the picture that best answers the question and write its number in the appropriate space on your answer sheet. (12%)

7. On the way to the picnic grounds, you meet up with your friends. Graciela says to you.

   Juan tiene el hielo. Mariela tiene el jugo de manzana. Yo tengo una botella grande de Coca Cola. Pedro tiene la limonada. Tenemos todo, pero, hay un problema. Nos faltan los vasos. ¿Cómo vamos a beber los refrescos?

   What did your friends forget? (2)

8. You are in a Venezuelan restaurant. The waiter tells you what the specials of the day are. He says:

   Hoy tenemos tres platos del día. el jamón con piña, el salmón a la parilla y carne de ternera con legumbres. Con todos los platos especiales del día, servimos una ensalada verde.

   What is served with the dish of the day? (3)

9. You are watching television in Chile. The announcer comes on and says:

   El mejor café del mundo viene de Colombia. Y el mejor café se llama Café Tía Juana. Ud. puede beber este café por la mañana, por la tarde, por la noche. Café Tía Juana, negro o con leche...siempre el mejor.

   What is being advertised? (2)

10. You and your Spanish language class are having a meal in a Spanish restaurant. Your teacher tells the class:

    Les recomiendo el gazpacho. Es una sopa hecha con tomates y cebollas y otras legumbres. Es muy diferente. La sopa es fria, no caliente. Es una sopa muy típica de España.

    What does the teacher suggest you try? (4)

Listening Comprehension answer:
For all chapters, the answers are indicated in parentheses following each question. (See questions 1-10 on the previous pages.)

Reading Comprehension answers:

3a (8%) 11. __4__ 12. __1__ 13. __1__ 14. __2__

3b (12%) 15. __1__ 16. __3__ 17. __2__ 18. __4__

MEAL TAKING / FOOD / DRINK 3

Nombre ____________________________ Fecha ______________________________

EXAMINATION

Part 1 SPEAKING (30%)
Part 2 LISTENING (30%)

Part 2a Directions: For each question, you will hear some background information in English. Then you will hear a passage in Spanish twice, followed by a question in English. Listen carefully. After you have heard the question, read the question and the four suggested answers. Choose the best answer and write its number in the appropriate space on your answer sheet. (9%)

1. Where does your father want to go?

   1. to the local supermarket
   2. to an outdoor snack bar
   3. back to the hotel
   4. to the beach

2. What would Carolina choose for a snack?

   1. raisins
   2. oatmeal cookies
   3. chocolate ice cream
   4. tea biscuits

3. Why couldn't Rosita make the purchase?

   1. The customer was short 21 cents.
   2. She had forgotten her credit card.
   3. She didn't have proper ID
   4. The store was out of stock on the merchandise

Part 2b Directions: For each question, you will hear some background information in English. Then you will hear a passage in Spanish twice, followed by a question in Spanish. Listen carefully. After you have heard the question, read the question and the four suggested answers. Choose the best answer and write its number in the appropriate space on your answer sheet.

4. 1. ¿Qué van a hacer tú y Bárbara?

   1. poner la mesa
   2. hacer la cama
   3. lavar el coche
   4. plantar las legumbres

5. ¿De qué comida habla David? (1)

   1. el desayuno
   2. el almuerzo
   3. la cena
   4. la merienda

6. ¿Qué va a pedir tu amiga, Luisa? (3)

1. un sándwich de jamón
2. un helado de chocolate
3. jugo de fruta
4. una ensalada

Part 2c Directions: For each question, you will hear some background information in English. Then you will hear a passage in Spanish twice, followed by a question in English. Listen carefully. After you have heard the question, read the question and look at the 4pictures on your test. Choose the picture that best answers the question and write its number in the appropriate space on your answer sheet. (12%)

7. What did your friends forget?

8. What is served with the dish of the day?

9. What is being advertised?

11. What does the teacher suggest you try?

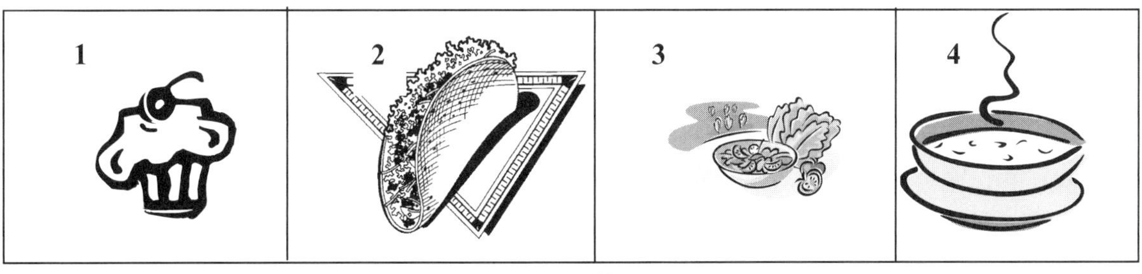

PART 3: READING (20%) **Part 3a Directions:** Answer the question in English based on the reading selection in Spanish. Choose the best answer to each question. Base your choice on the content of the reading selection. Write the number of your answer in the appropriate space on your answer sheet (8%)

Señora Vélez,

Los niños tienen que hacer la tarea antes de la cena.
Mi hijo Carlos tiene que practicar el piano por media hora antes de la cena. La cena está en la estufa. Para postre, hay helado en la nevera. Laura pone la mesa y Teresa la quita. Carlos lava los platos esta noche.

Ellos no pueden salir de la casa. Pueden mirar la televisión.
Limite el uso del teléfono, por favor. Ninguna llamada después de las diez. Regresamos a las dos.
En caso de emergencia, llámenos al 555-8792.

11. Who wrote this note?
    1. Carlos
    2. the teacher
    3. a babysitter
    4. a parent

12. What are the children **not** permitted to do
    1. they are not allowed to go out with their friends
    2. They may not use the telephone
    3. They cannot watch television
    4. They may not have dessert.

BATIDO DE CREMA DE GUAYABA (sirve 6 personas)

2 tazas de pulpa de guayaba
2 tazas de bananas
1 huevo
1/2 taza de azúcar
3 vasos de leche
1 cucharada de jugo de limón
1/2 vaso de agua

Mezcle en la licuadora

13. What ingredient is **not** called for in this recipe?

1. apple juice
2. eggs
3. sugar
4. milk

LA SOPERA

116/ Avenida Rey Carlos de Borbón

Estamos enfrente de la estación de ferrocarril a la derecha del cine

Gazpacho andaluz ......3,00 euros
Sopa de legumbres......2,75 euros
Sopa de pescado....... .5,00 euros
Sopa de pollo.............4,00 euros

Ensalada de espinacas..............4 euros
Ensalada mixta ....3 euros
Ensalada de frijoles................ 4 euros
Ensalada griega........................7 euros

Nosotros servimos sólamente quesos españoles: mahón - manchego - majorero
cabrales - zamorano

Cada plato de queso 5 euros

Abierto todos los días excepto los jueves
lunes - miércoles 10.00 - 4.00
viernes - domingo 9.30 - 3.30

14. What is zamorano?

1. a kind of Spanish soup
2. a type of cheese
3. a specialized salad
4. a vegetable

Part 3b Directions: Answer the question in Spanish based on the reading selection in Spanish. Choose the best answer to each question. Base your choice on the content of the reading selection. Write the number of your answer in the appropriate space on your answer sheet.

Mi Fiesta Favorita

El Día del Pavo es muy especial en mi casa. Este es un día nacional en los Estados Unidos...y también en Puerto Rico, donde yo nací.

Esta fiesta siempre cae el tercer jueves de noviembre. Todos en mi familia nos levantamos muy temprano para ayudar a mi madre con la comida.

Mi hermana menor lava las legumbres: judías verdes, papas y guisantes.

Mi hermana mayor hace la sopa de cebolla a la francesa. Mi padre hace el pastel de calabaza y yo hago la salsa de arándano agrio. Y mi mamá cocina el pavo en el horno. Me gusta mucho cuando llegan mis abuelos. Ellos traen siempre tortas, vino italiano y dulces. Es mi fiesta favorita.

Nelson Ortega

15. Esta fiesta se celebra ....

1. el jueves
2. en la primavera
3. el 31 de octubre
4. el Día de la Madre

16. ¿Dónde nació Nelson?

1. en Italia
2. en Francia
3. en Puerto Rico
4. en los Estados Unidos

En el mundo hispano las legumbres y las frutas tienen una variedad de nombres. Por ejemplo, en Argentina el plátano se llama *la banana*, y la piña se llama *el ananás*. En Puerto Rico la naranja se llama *la china*. En España - la madre tierra de la lengua española - hay también una confusión. Lo que los habitantes de Madrid llaman judías verdes, en la ciudad de Córdoba se llaman habichuelas verdes, y en Orihuela se llaman bajocas y en Sevilla se llaman chícharos…Y para contribuir a la confusión lo que se llaman guisantes en España, se llaman chícharos en el país de México.

17. ¿Qué es el ananás?

1. es una legumbre
2. es una fruta
3. es un país
4. es un chícharo

18. Este artículo habla _______

1. de la agricultura en China
2. de la geografía entre España y Argentina
3. de los bailes típicos del mundo hispano
4. del vocabulario de un idioma

Part 4 WRITING (20%)

Part 4 Directions: Choose two of the three writing tasks provided below. Your answer to each of the two questions should be written entirely in Spanish and should contain a minimum of 30 words.

Place names and brand names written in Spanish count as one word. Contractions are counted as one word. Salutations, closings and commonly used abbreviations are included in the word count. Numbers, unless written as words, and names of people do not count as words.

Be sure that you have satisfied the purpose of the task. The sentence structure and /or expressions used should be connected logically and demonstrate a wide range of vocabulary with minimal repetition.

4a. Your brother attends college in a Spanish speaking country. He has been asked to host a luncheon and writes to you for suggestions on how to set the table properly. Write a letter to him. In your letter you may wish to include:
- What items to put on the table
- What is the correct placement of the silverware and dishes
- What kind of a menu he should serve
- What the order of courses should be

4b. You have had a meal in a Spanish restaurant and were pleased with the service. Write a letter to the management. You may include:

- The day and time you went to the restaurant
- Why you liked the atmosphere in this restaurant (decor, music, air conditioning)
- What meal you had and why you liked it
- The name of your waiter / waitress and why you are complimenting this person
- A brief description of that person
- What you will do to show your appreciation (recommendations)

4c. You are staying with a host family in a Spanish-speaking country. Write a letter about a meal that you had there. In your letter you may wish to include:

- What meal you had
- At what time they serve this meal
- Who prepares this meal
- Whether this meal is different or similar from one served in your country
- Whether you liked the meal or not

MEAL TAKING / FOOD / DRINK 3

Nombre y Apellido ______________________________ Fecha ______________

Part I **Speaking** __________ (30%)
Part 2 **Listening (30%)**

2a.	2b.	2c.
1._____	4._____	7._____
2._____	5._____	8._____
3._____	6._____	9._____
		10._____

PART 3: READING (20%)

3a.(8%)	3b.(12%)
11._____	15._____
12._____	16._____
13._____	17._____
14._____	18._____

Part 4 **Writing (20%) 20 words** **Write 2 paragraphs** **4a , 4b or 4c**

1____

2____

Shopping

SHOPPING 3

SHOPPING 3

TEACHER'S SCRIPT FOR THE EXAM, PART II (Listening, 30%)

Part 2a Directions: For each question, you will hear some background information in English. Then you will hear a passage in Spanish twice, followed by a question in English. Listen carefully. After you have heard the question, read the question and the four suggested answers. Choose the best answer and write its number in the appropriate space on your answer sheet. (9%)

1. You and your younger brother are getting ready to go skiing today. He says to you:

   ¡Ay de mí! Estos pantalones para esquiar no me quedan bien.ahora. Son más cortos. Son los pantalones que me compró la abuela el invierno pasado.

   What is the problem? (1)

2. You and your friend Manuela are out shopping for Christmas gifts. Manuela says:

   ¡Qué divertido es ir de compras! A mi hermano le voy a comprar un videojuego. A mi hermana menor le doy un disco compacto de música. A mi padre le doy un libro de su autor favorito. A mi mamá quiero comprarle aretes y un collar.

   What does Manuela want to buy her father? (1)

3. You are in the department store with your friend Carmen. She says to the saleslady:

   Busco una blusa para mi prima. Sus colores favoritos son el verde y el amarillo. Tiene Ud. algo en esos colores?

   What is your friend looking for? (2)

Part 2b Directions: For each question, you will hear some background information in English. Then you will hear a passage in Spanish twice, followed by a question in Spanish. Listen carefully. After you have heard the question, read the question and the four suggested answers. Choose the best answer and write its number in the appropriate space on your answer sheet. (9%)

4. You are with your cousin Elena in a clothing store. She is going to pay for something she is holding. She says to you

   Compro esta falda para llevar a mi escuela. Yo voy a una escuela privada. No tenemos que usar un uniforme. Sólo, tenemos usar la ropa con los colores de la escuela. Los colores de mi escuela son azul y rojo.

   ¿Qué está comprando tu prima? (3)

5. Your friend is showing you his new leather jacket. You say to him

   ¡No me digas! ¡Qué ganga! ¿Tú pagaste solo ochenta dólares por esto? Yo necesito una chaqueta nueva también. ¿Dónde la compraste?

   ¿Qué quieres saber tú? (2)

6. You and your friend Alicia are window shopping at a local mall. Alicia says to you:

   Los precios en esta joyería son siempre bajos y razonables. Me gusta mucho el collar de oro. Pero lo quiero de plata. Entremos. Quiero comprar aretes de plata también.

   ¿Qué quiere comprar Alicia? (2)

Part 2c Directions: For each question, you will hear some background information in English. Then you will hear a passage in Spanish twice, followed by a question in English. Listen carefully. After you have heard the question, read the question and look at the 4 pictures on your test. Choose the picture that best answers the question and write its number in the appropriate space on your answer sheet. (12%)

7. Your parents are getting ready to go out with friends. Your father says to your mother:

   ¿Dónde está mi corbata nueva? Es rosada y gris. La compraste ayer. Estaba en mi cama. La corbata queda bien con mi traje.

   What is your father looking for? (4)

8. You are talking to your friend Lisa in the kitchen. She says:

   Yo quiero hacer un flan para el postre. Tengo el azúcar, y la leche y la vainilla. Pero no tengo huevos. Voy al supermercado para comprarlos.

   What does Luisa need? (1)

9. You are with your father. He is talking to a woman at a desk. He says to her:

   Voy a viajar en España el próximo mes. Tengo una tarjeta de crédito, pero quiero también traer cheques de viajero conmigo. ¿Vende este banco cheques de viajero en euros?

   Where is your father? (2)

10. You are in a store and hear this announcement.

    Buenos días, clientes. Hoy hay una venta fantástica en el departamento de ropa para hombres. Tenemos trajes italianos en venta por doscientos dólares. ¡Qué ganga!

    What is on sale today? (3)

Listening Comprehension Answers:
For all chapters, the answers are indicated in parentheses following each question. (See questions 1-10 on the previous pages.)

Reading Comprehension answers:

3a. (8%) 11. __3__ 12. __2__ 13. __3__ 14. __4__

3b (12%) 15. __1__ 16. __4__ 17. __1__ 18. __3__

SHOPPING 3

Nombre ______________________________ Fecha _________________________

EXAMINATION

Part I SPEAKING (30%)
Part II LISTENING (30%)

Part 2a Directions: For each question, you will hear some background information in English. Then you will hear a passage in Spanish twice, followed by a question in English. Listen carefully. After you have heard the question, read the question and the four suggested answers. Choose the best answer and write its number in the appropriate space on your
answer sheet (9%)

1. What is the problem?
   1. Your brother grew taller
   2. There is a blizzard
   3. Your grandmother is coming for a visit
   4. You can't find the car keys

2. What does Manuela want to buy her father?
   1. something to read
   2. a cassette tape
   3. an article of clothing
   4. some jewelry

3. What is your friend looking for?
   1. A blue and red skirt
   2. A green and yellow blouse
   3. A black and white tie
   4. A yellow dress

Part 2b Directions: For each question, you will hear some background information in English. Then you will hear a passage in Spanish twice, followed by a question in Spanish. Listen carefully. After you have heard the question, read the question and the four suggested answers. Choose the best answer and write its number in the appropriate space on your answer sheet. (9%)

4. ¿Qué está comprando tu prima?
   1. una blusa amarilla
   2. una blusa negra
   3. una falda azul
   4. un uniforme gris y verde

5. ¿Qué quieres saber tú?
   1. el color de sus ojos
   2. el nombre de la tienda
   3. la fecha de su nacimiento
   4. el precio de los pantalones

6. ¿Qué quiere comprar Alicia?
   1. zapatos
   2. joyas
   3. un vestido
   4. un cuaderno

SHOPPING 3

Part 2c Directions: For each question, you will hear some background information in English. Then you will hear a passage in Spanish twice, followed by a question in English. Listen carefully. After you have heard the question, read the question and look at the 4 pictures on your test. Choose the picture that best answers the question and write its number in the appropriate space on your answer sheet. (12%)

7. What is your father looking for?

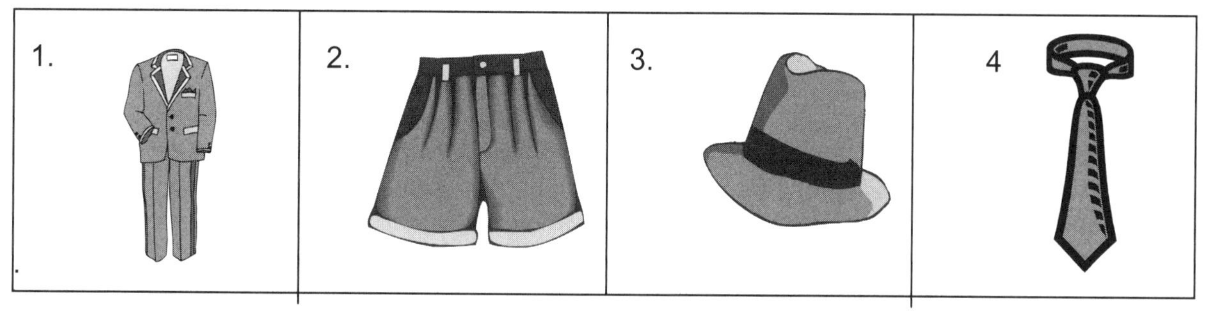

8. What does Luisa need?

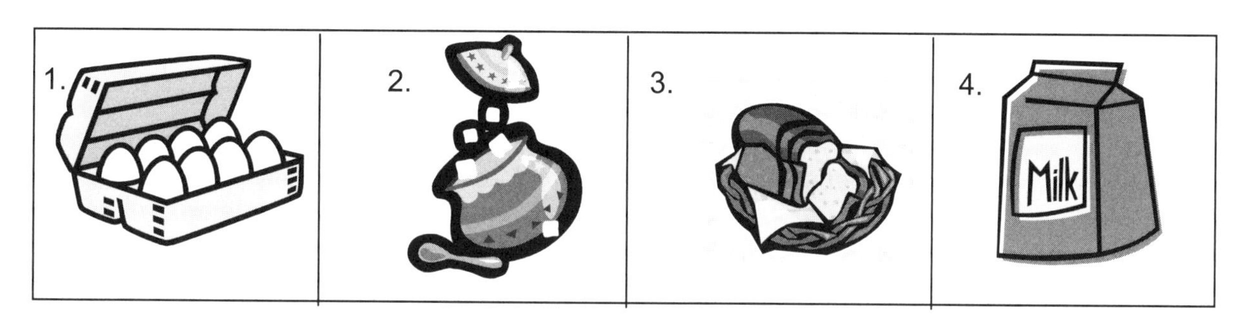

9. Where is your father?

10. What is on sale today?

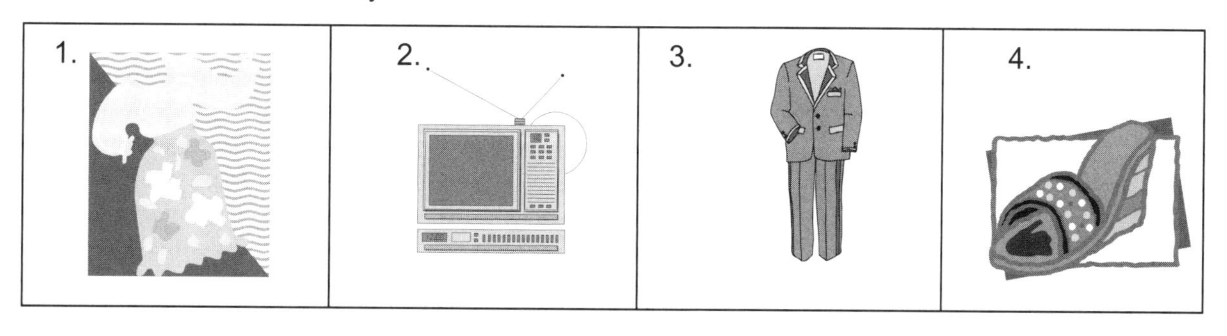

Part 3a Directions: Answer the question in English based on the reading selection in Spanish. Choose the best answer to each question. Base your choice on the content of the reading selection. Write the number of your answer in the appropriate space on your answer sheet (8%).

EL PAIS *el principal periódico europeo en español*

Madrid (el 31 de julio) - Esta semana muchos turistas en Madrid pueden pasar por El Corte Inglés, un almacén bien conocido, para ver ropa usada por ochenta personas famosas de la historia. Por ejemplo, en la primera planta se puede ver los calcetines blancos de Michael Jackson y la corbata que el presidente John F. Kennedy llevó durante la segunda guerra mundial. En la segunda planta se puede observar el camisón de Lucille Ball y treinta pares de tacones de Imelda Marcos. En la tercera planta están los pantalones de Frida Kahlo, el sombrero de Diego Rivera y los guantes militares de Napoleon. Es una exposición muy única. Vale la pena visitar esta tienda.

---

11. What is this newspaper article about?

   1. the opening of a wax museum
   2. the life of a famous designer
   3. an unusual display of clothing
   4. a fire at a famous store

12. What can be said about El Corte Inglés?

   1. They serve excellent food.
   2. It's a landmark department store
   3. It's a well known travel agency.
   4. Famous people slept there.

PESCADERÍA y FRUTERÍA HERMANOS BAUER

Calle Pacífico, 455 **tel. 667-9076**

Abierto todos los días 6 AM - 10 PM
Aceptamos tarjetas de crédito

Se venden frutas exóticas de todo el mundo
Día de pescado, miércoles y viernes

---

13. On what days of the week, do the fishing boats deliver fresh fish?

    1. Sundays and Mondays
    2. Mondays and Wednesdays
    3. Wednesdays and Fridays
    4. Every day, except Friday.

14. According to the advertisement, customers **cannot** expect ....

    1. to buy strawberries, kiwis, or bananas here.
    2. to telephone the store during busy hours
    3. to pay by major credit cards
    4. to buy imported ham or fresh lamb.

Part 3b Directions: Answer the questions in Spanish based on the reading selection in Spanish. Choose the best answer to each question. Base your choice on the content of the reading selection. Write the number of your answer in the appropriate space on your answer sheet.

BAG-a-BONDO

Nuestra compañía fabrica bolsas personalizadas de alta calidad para su tienda. Mire los ejemplos aquí.

A
bolsa de papel

TIOVIVO
pasteles, tortas
galletas de alta
calidad
tel. 643.775

B
bolsa de mercancía

FARMACIA REX
abierto todos los días
desde las 9 hasta las 9
tel. 754.990
fax 886.990

C
bolsa de papel con asa de nylon

Mesamax
servilletas y
manteles
plata labrada
platos y vasos

D
bolsa de plástico

ZAPATERÍA FIORELLI
MADRID LIMA
GRANADA QUITO

15. La persona que compra postres va a llevar bolsa _____

1. A
2. B
3. C
4. D

16. ¿Dónde se puede comprar botas?

1. Tiovivo
2. Mesamax
3. Farmacia Rex
4. Zapatería Fiorelli

PANADERÍA HERMANOS RODRÍGUEZ

NUESTRA TIENDA ESTÁ ABIERTA 24 HORAS AL DÍA

¡PAN FRESCO CUANDO UD. LO QUIERE!

17. Según el anuncio ¿a qué hora va el músico a esta tienda?

 1. al mediodía
 2. a las cinco de la tarde
 3. a la una menos cuarto de la tarde
 4. a las diez y diez de la mañana

18. Según el anuncio, ¿quién va a la panadería a las cinco y cinco?

 1. el trabajador
 2. el artista
 3. la profesora
 4. el detective

SHOPPING 3

Part 4 WRITING (20%)

Part 4 Directions: Choose two of the three writing tasks provided below. Your answer to each of the two questions should be written entirely in Spanish and should contain a minimum of **30 words**.

Place names and brand names written in Spanish count as one word. Contractions are counted as one word. Salutations, closing, and commonly used abbreviations are included in the word count. Numbers, unless written as words, and names of people do not count as words.

Be sure that you have satisfied the purpose of the task. The sentence structure and-or expressions used should be connected logically and demonstrate a wide range of vocabulary with minimal repetition.

4a. Your pen pal would like to purchase gifts from the United States for his relatives. You are having a mail-order catalogue sent to him/ her and are writing a letter alerting him / her of that fact. In your letter you may wish to include:

- The name of the company catalogue that he / she is going to receive
- A general description of the type of products this company sells (clothing, foods, jewelry etc.)
- An item that you may have purchased and whether you liked or disliked it.
- A recommendation of an item and specify for whom in his/ her family it would be perfect

4b. Your Spanish club is having a sale on donated items to earn money for a trip. You have volunteered to write an article for the local Spanish newspaper. In your article you may wish to include:

- The date and time when the Spanish club is having the sale and where in the school building it is taking place.
- What type of items are being sold
- The quantity of items being offered
- What item you recommend and why
- Whether refreshments will be offered and what the cost will be, if any

4c. Your pen pal in Ecuador would like to know about the main shopping street in your town. Write him a letter. In your letter you may wish to include:

- The name of the street.
- The types of stores found there
- Which is your favorite store and why
- What items are sold in that store
- Whether there are any other types of buildings on this street (museum, theater, library)
- A general description of that street (tranquil, busy, clean)

SHOPPING 3

Nombre y Apellido ______________________________ Fecha _____________

Part I **Speaking** __________ (30%)
Part 2 **Listening (30%)**

PART 3: READING (20%)

2a.	2b.	2c.	3a.(8%)	3b.(12%)
1.____	4.____	7.____	11.____	15.____
2.____	5.____	8.____	12.____	16.____
3.____	6.____	9.____	13.____	17.____
		10.____	14.____	18.____

Part 4 **Writing (20%) 20 words** **Write 2 paragraphs** **4a , 4b or 4c**

1____

____

____

____

____

____

____

____

____

2____

____

____

____

____

____

____

____

____

____

____

____

Health and Welfare

TEACHER'S SCRIPT FOR THE EXAM, Part 2 (LISTENING 30%)

Part 2a Directions: For each question, you will hear some background information in English. Then you will hear a passage in Spanish twice, followed by a question in English. Listen carefully. After you have heard the question, read the question and the four suggested answers. Choose the best answer and write its number in the appropriate space on your answer sheet. (9%)

1. Dorotea is telling you about her job at the local hospital. She says:

   Es verdad que yo trabajo en un hospital, pero no trabajo ni con los medicos ni con las enfermeras. Yo trabajo cinco días por semana.Yo tengo que limpiar el hospital. Paso la aspiradora en todos los cuartos, lavo los pisos y los baños.

   What does Dorotea do at the hospital? (3)

2. Your gym teacher is talking to his class. He says:

   Mi hermano mayor es dentista. El me dice siempre que es más importante beber leche y comer queso. Ayuda a tener los dientes fuertes. A mi yo prefiero tomar el helado para postre.

   What is your teacher talking about?

3. You work in the school nurse's office. You hear the nurse speaking to a mother on the phone. The nurse says:

   La profesora de tu hijo dice que tu hijo no puede ver bien la pizarra. Él se sienta en al frente de la clase. Quizás, él necesita anteojos. ¿Por qué no le lleva a un oculista para un examen de visión?

   What advice does the nurse give?

Part 2b Directions: For each question, you will hear some background information in English. Then you will hear a passage in Spanish twice, followed by a question in Spanish. Listen carefully. After you have heard the question, read the question and the four suggested answers. Choose the best answer and write its number in the appropriate space on your answer sheet. (9%)

4. You are watching a soap opera. The scene is taking place in a doctor's office. The doctor is speaking to the patient. He says:

   Lo siento, señora, peró cuando Ud. se cayó en la calle esta mañana Ud. se rompió el brazo derecho. Mire la radiografía. La fractura está aquí.

   ¿Qué tiene la paciente? (3)

5. You host mother is calling the school about her daughter. She says:

   Mi hija Catalina no asiste a la escuela hoy. Tiene la rubeola. El doctor dice que ella debe quedarse en cama por algunos días. ¿Puede enviar el trabajo de la escuela a casa con su hermano Felipe? No quiero que a mi hija le falten las lecciones y la tarea.

   ¿Dónde está Catalina ahora ? (1)

6. You are at the pharmacy. A woman is speaking to the pharmacist. She says:

   Mi hijo tiene tres años. Él tiene un resfriado terrible. Necesito algo para él, pero no quiero ni pildoras ni pastillas. Quiero una jarabe que puedo mezclar con leche o jugo de naranja. Es más fácil beber para él.

   ¿Qué quiere la madre para su hijo pequeño?

Part 2c Directions: For each question, you will hear some background information in English. Then you will hear a passage in Spanish twice, followed by a question in English. Listen carefully. After you have heard the question, read the question and look at the four pictures on your test. Choose the picture that best answers the question and write its number in the appropriate space on your answer sheet. (12%)

7. You are listening to the radio. You hear this announcement:

   Si Ud. es un atleta serio, Ud. necesita zapatos de deportes serios. En nuestra zapatería tenemos zapatos para cada actividad y deporte. Si le gusta a Ud. jugar al tenis, o jugar al golf...si le gusta a Ud bailar o caminar, venga a nuestra tienda: Amigo del Pie en la esquina de la Calle Coronado y Avenida Rosario. Abierta todos los días desde las nueve a las siete.

   What can one expect to buy in this store? (2)

8. Your family is getting ready to leave for an outing, Your sister says:

   Hoy hace mucho calor. Si vamos a la playa necesito el parasol y el bronceador. Mi piel es delicada. Creo que la loción anti-solar está en el baño debajo del lavabo (1)

   What does you sister need? (1)

9. Laura has just returned from a trip to Spain where she met her pen pal Teresa. She is now describing this person to her friend Bernardo. :

   Mi amiga de correspondencia es una muchacha baja. Es muy gorda. Tiene pelo negro corto. Es una muchacha simpática, inteligente y amable. Mi amiga se llama Teresa.

   Which person is Teresa? (4)

10. The TV sports reporter is interviewing a figure skater from Argentina.. You hear the skater say:

    Patino desde 1997. No estoy patinando ahora porque me caí el mes pasado y me lastimé el hombro. No puedo levantar el brazo cuando hago circulos. Espero regresar al patinario en la próxima estación.

    What did this skater injure? (4)

Listening Comprehension answers:
For all chapters, the answers are indicated in parentheses following each question. (See questions 1-10 on the previous pages.)

Reading Comprehension answers:

3a (8%) 11. __1__ 12. __2__ 13. __3__ 14. __4__

3b (12%) 15. __1__ 16.__3__ 17. __4__ 18. __4__

HEALTH AND WELFARE 3

Nombre ______________________________ Fecha __________________________

EXAMINATION

Part 1 SPEAKING (30%)
Part 2 LISTENING (30%)

Part 2a Directions: For each question, you will hear some background information in English. Then you will hear a passage in Spanish twice, followed by a question in English. Listen carefully. After you have heard the question, read the question and the four suggested answers. Choose the best answer and write its number in the appropriate space on your answer sheet. (9%)

1 What does Dorotea do at the hospital? (3)

1. She answers the telephone
2. She works in the billing department
3. She keeps the rooms clean
4. She takes X-rays

2. What is your teacher talking about?

1. how to do sit-ups
2. the importance of walking
3. different swimming techniques
4. one way to have healthy teeth

3. What advice does the nurse give?

1. that her son exercise
2. that her son go to bed early
3. that her son visit an eye doctor
4. that her son visit the dentist

Part 2b Directions: For each question, you will hear some background information in English. Then you will hear a passage in Spanish twice, followed by a question in Spanish. Listen carefully. After you have heard the question, read the question and the four suggested answers. Choose the best answer and write its number in the appropriate space on your answer sheet. (9%)

4. ¿Qué tiene la paciente?

1. un resfriado
2. el sarampión
3. un brazo roto
4. indigestión

5. ¿Dónde está Catalina ahora ?

1. en su casa
2. en la escuela
3. en la consulta del dentista
4. en la farmacia

6. ¿Qué quiere la madre para su hijo pequeño?

1. dulces duras
2. un número de teléfono
3. aseguro médico
4. medicina en forma de líquido

HEALTH AND WELFARE 3

Part 2c. Directions: For each question, you will hear some background information in English. Then you will hear a passage in Spanish twice, followed by the question in Spanish. Listen carefully. After you have heard the question, read the question and look at the four pictures on your test paper. Choose the picture that best answers the question and write its number in the appropriate space on your answer sheet.

1. What can one expect to buy in this store?

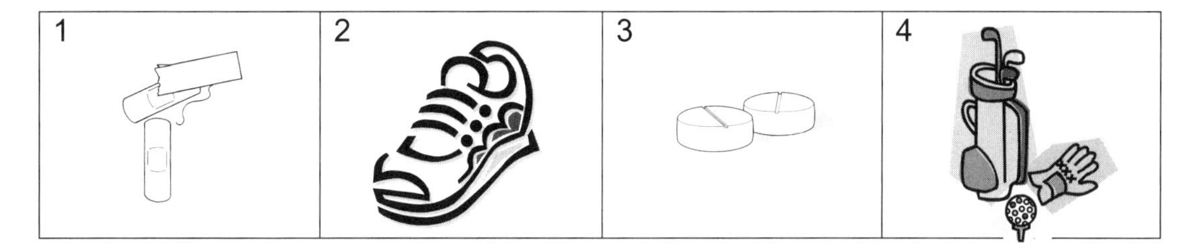

8. What does your sister need?

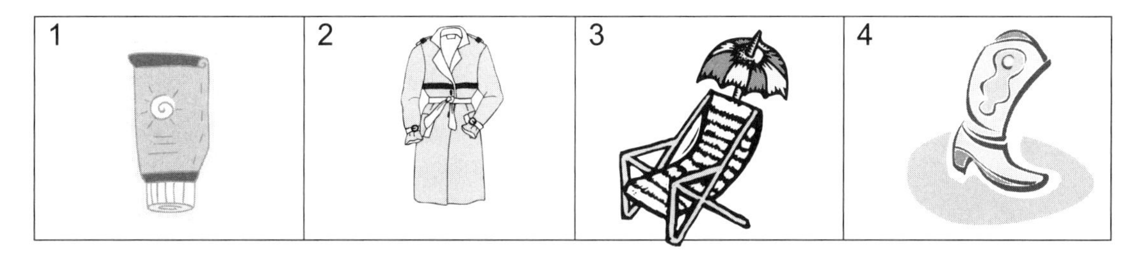

9. Which person is Teresa?

10. What did this skater injure?

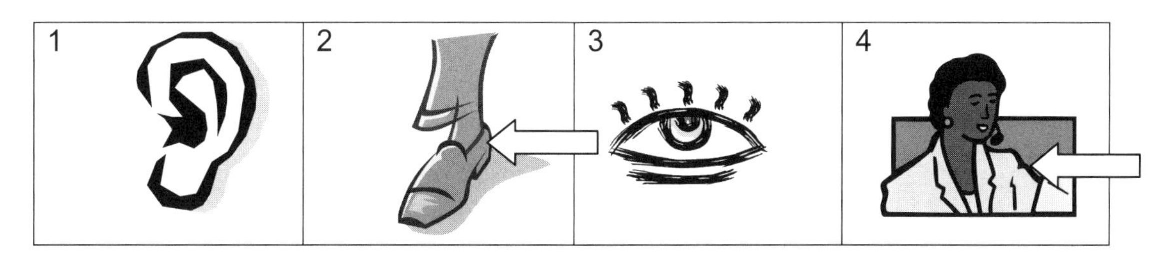

Part 3a Directions: Answer the question in English based on the reading selection in Spanish. Choose the best answer to each question. Base your choice on the content of the reading selection. Write the number of your answer in the appropriate space on your answer sheet. (8%)

Grupo Médico Caritas

con oficinas en <u>cuatro</u> comunidades

Dr. Armando González, especialista en tratornos de la piel
Dr. Luis Tamburro, oftalmólogo para trastornos y cirugía del ojo
Dr. Tomás Francho, especialista en: trastornos de oídos, nariz y garganta
Dr. Hector Wolff, Urólogo
Dra. Rosa Gunther de Wolff, especialista en trastornos metabólicos y hormonales

Ciudad Pando
Avenida Castillo, 677
tel. 55.75.90

lunes - miercoles - viernes
10 am - 1 pm
3 pm - 7 pm

Cobija
Calle La Paz, 77
tel. 55.80.91

martes - jueves
10 am - 1 pm

Belmar
Plaza Mayor, 3
tel. 55.80.24
3 pm - 5 pm

Santa Rosa
Calle LaReina, 99
tel. 56.10.45

sábado
10 am - 1pm

11. Who would you see if you had a problem with your eyes?

1. Dr. Tamburro
2. Dr. Francho
3. Dr. Wolff
4. Dr. Gunther

12. Why would you make an appointment with Dr. Gonzales?

1. You have a cold
2. You have a skin rash
3. You have a sore throat
4. You have a respiratory problem

13. Which office would you need to visit for a Monday morning appointment?

1. Cobija
2. Santa Rosa
3. Ciudad Pando
4. Belmar

14. What is **true** about this medical group?

1. They are located in a hospital
2. They are open 7 days a week
3. They are closed on Wednesdays
4. They have offices in several locations

Part 3b Directions: Answer the question in Spanish based on the reading selection in Spanish. Choose the best answer to each question. Base your choice on the content of the reading selection. Write the number of your answer in the appropriate space on your answer sheet (12%)

Dra. Consuelo Navarra Ybáñez
Calle Puerto Nuevo, 66
Caracas 88,86,05

PACIENTE: APELLIDO Sandovar NOMBRE Miguel
DIRECCION 20 Calle Rosa
Caracas
TELEFONO 88, 92, 45 EDAD 6
SINTOMAS la tos y fiebre

INSTRUCCIONES toma el jarabe para la tos 2 veces al día
toma mucha agua
duerme mucho
toma Tylenol 2 veces al día

15. ¿Cuántos años tiene el paciente?

1. menos de 10 años
2. entre diez y treinta años
3. más de cincuenta años
4. entre treinta y cincuenta años

16. ¿Cuántas veces tiene que tomar la medicina por día?

1. cuatro veces
2. tres veces
3. dos veces
4. una vez

Nuesto Pueblocito en las Noticias

por Patricia Zarzuga

Si Usted visita nuestro parque local durante los meses del verano, Ud. va a ver a un joven artista sentado debajo de un árbol dibujando a los niños que están jugando. El artista se llama Alonso Pastibi y a él le gusta dibujar a los chiquitos. Pero hay algo diferente con los dibujos de Alonso. Sus dibujos son abstractos y los colores no son normales. Por ejemplo, a él le gusta dar colores diferentes a los partes diferentes del cuerpo. Entonces, se puede ver a los ninos con un nariz anaranjado o azul o verde, con una oreja roja y otra de color de salmón, con una mano azul, y la otra de violeta, un brazo derecho gris y un brazo izquierdo marrón. Pero, todos los niños tienen una cosa en común - el pelo blanco. ¿Por qué? Porque el artista él mismo tiene el pelo blanco, el resultado de un defecto congenital. En el invierno Alonso va a vivir en el Sur cerca del océano donde dibuja a los niños en el mar.

17. ¿Qué es el sujeto de los dibujos de Alonso Pastibi?

1. edificios
2. el océano
3. parques
4. los niños

18. ¿De qué color es el pelo de Alonso?

1. azul
2. verde
3. violeta
4. blanco

Part 4 WRITING (20%)

Part 4 Directions: Choose two of the three writing tasks provided below. Your answer to each of the two questions should be written entirely in Spanish and should contain a minimum of 30 words.

Place names and brand names written in Spanish count as one word. Contractions are counted as one word. Salutations, closings and commonly used abbreviations are included in the word count. Numbers, unless written as words, and names of people do not count as words.

Be sure that you have satisfied the purpose of the task. The sentence structure and /or expressions used should be connected logically and demonstrate a wide range of vocabulary with minimal repetition.

4a. You have recently been very ill and haven´t been in contact with your e-mail buddy for some time. Write an e-mail message to your friend. In your message you may wish to include:

- What illness you had
- What were the symptoms
- How the illness affected your daily activities
- Whether you visited the doctor
- What medication you took

4b. You have a favorite celebrity whom your pen pal in Spain has never seen or heard of. Describe this person to your pen pal. In your written description you may wish to:

- Name this person and give his or her profession
- Give a physical description of this person
- Describe this person's personality
- Give personal information about this celebrity such as age, date of birth
- Explain why this person is your favorite celebrity

4c. Your local health club has asked you to write an article for its Spanish language newsletter on how to stay fit physically. In your article you may wish to include:

- What one should eat and not eat
- What one should drink and not drink
- What exercises one should do and why
- What one can do to prevent vision and hearing problems
- How overexertion in a particular sport can cause injury to a particular part of the body (e.g. skating/ankles, tennis/elbow)

HEALTH AND WELFARE 3

Nombre y Apellido ______________________________ Fecha ______________

Part I **Speaking** __________ (30%)
Part 2 **Listening (30%)**

2a.	2b.	2c.
1._____	4._____	7._____
2._____	5._____	8._____
3._____	6._____	9._____
		10._____

PART 3: READING (20%)

3a.(8%)	3b.(12%)
11._____	15._____
12._____	16._____
13._____	17._____
14._____	18._____

Part 4 **Writing (20%) 20 words** **Write 2 paragraphs** **4a , 4b or 4c**

1 ____

____

____

____

____

____

____

____

____

2 ____

____

____

____

____

____

____

____

____

____

____

____

PHYSICAL ENVIRONMENT

PHYSICAL ENVIRONMENT 3

PHYSICAL ENVIRONMENT 3

TEACHER´S SCRIPT FOR THE EXAM, PART II (Listening, 30%)

Part 2a Directions: For each question, you will hear some background information in English. Then you will hear a passage in Spanish twice, followed by a question in English. Listen carefully. After you have heard the question, read the question and the four suggested answers. Choose the best answer and write its number in the appropriate space on your answer sheet. (9%)

1. Your Mexican pen pal Alicia tells you what her favorite month is. She says:

   Mi mes favorito es noviembre. Primero, mi cumpleaños es el quince de noviembre. El veinte es el aniversario de matrimonio de mis padres. En la primera semana del mes hay dos fiestas importantes para los mexicanos: el Día de Todos los Santos y el Día de los Muertos. Pues, el treinta de este mes es el cumpleaños de mi hermano Mario.

   Why is November Alicia´s favorite month? (3)

2. Susana is explaining to her friends why she doesn´t like her grandparents' summer home. She says:

   Quiero mucho a mis abuelos, pero no me gusta donde queda su casa de verano. Mis abuelos viven en una isla pequeña. La isla está en el medio de un lago. No hay otras casas y no hay mucho que hacer. No hay puente. Para ir de compras o visitar a unos amigos tengo que tomar un bote.

   Where is this summer house located? (3)

3. Roberto and his family are on vacation. In the morning, Roberto says to his family:

   No quiero ir al museo hoy. Hace buen tiempo ahora. ¿Por qué no vamos al lago para pescar? Nosotros podemos ir al museo en un día cuando llueve.

   What would Roberto like to go today? (2)

PHYSICAL ENVIRONMENT 3

Part 2b Directions: For each question, you will hear some background information in English. Then you will hear a passage in Spanish twice, followed by a question in Spanish. Listen carefully. After you have heard the question, read the question and the four suggested answers. Choose the best answer and write its number in the appropriate space on your answer sheet.

4. Your brother has called you on his cell phone from the local park. At one point he says to you

   Tengo que irme. Está comenzando a llover y no tengo ni paraguas ni impermeable. Tengo que correr. Chao. .

   ¿Qué tiempo hace? (1)

5. An exchange student from Chile is telling you about her home town. She says:

   Yo vengo de un pueblo muy pequeño en Chile. Donde yo vivo no hay ni edificios altos ni tiendas. No hay ni escuela ni iglesia. En mi pueblo hay solo una gasolinera y catorce casas. Yo vivo en la casa roja al lado de un parque.

   ¿Qué puedes ver en este pueblo? (2)

6. Your family is driving through a forest. Your father says :

   Miren las montañas que están delante de nosotros. Miren los colores de los árboles. Las hojas están rojas, anaranjadas, amarillas y pardas. Me encanta mucho esta estación cuando todo es hermoso y hace fresco.

   ¿En qué estación estamos? (4)

Part 2c Directions: For each question, you will hear some background information in English. Then you will hear a passage in Spanish twice, followed by a question in English. Listen carefully. After you have heard the question, read the question and look at the four pictures on your test. Choose the picture that best answers the question and write its number in the appropriate space on your answer sheet.

7. Your friend calls you on the telephone. He says:

   No vamos al estadio mañana. Está la posibilidad de nieve. La radio dice que va a nevar desde el mediodía hasta las once de la noche. ¿Por qué no vienes a mi casa mañana? Podemos jugar a videojuegos.

   What kind of weather is expected tomorrow? (1)

PHYSICAL ENVIRONMENT 3

8. Maria is telling her friends about her trip to New Jersey. She says:

   Cuando yo voy a visitar a mis primos en Atlantic City, la primera cosa que quiero ver es el océano. Yo vivo en Las Vegas una ciudad grande en el estado de Nevada. La ciudad está en un desierto. Aquí yo puedo ver un río o un lago, pero el océano está mas lejos de mi ciudad..

   What does Maria look forward to seeing when she visits her cousins´s home? (3)

9. Ramona González is speaking to a fifth grade class in Bogotá about her work. She says:

   Trabajo en las calles de una ciudad grande. En esta ciudad hay muchos carros, taxis y autobuses. Yo dirigo el tráfico. Trabajo cuando hace mal tiempo y cuando hace buen tiempo.

   Where does Ramona Gonzalez work? (2)

10. Pedro is talking about his summer vacation plans. He says:

    Quiero ser veterinario porque me gustan mucho los animales. Este verano voy a prepararme trabajando en una granja grande en el campo. Solo con la experiencia puedo aprender mucho.

    Where does Pedro plan to spend his summer? (1)

Listening Comprehension Answers:
For all chapters, the answers are indicated in parentheses following each question.
(See questions 1-10 on the previous pages.)

Reading Comprehension answers:

3a. (8%) 11. __3__ 12. __4__ 13. __3__ 14. __4__

3b (12%) 15. __1__ 16. __4__ 17. __4__ 18. __2__

PHYSICAL ENVIRONMENT 3

Nombre ______________________________ Fecha ________________________

EXAMINATION

Part 1 SPEAKING (30%)
Part 2 LISTENING (30%)

Part 2a Directions: For each question, you will hear some background information in English. Then you will hear a passage in Spanish twice, followed by a question in English. Listen carefully. After you have heard the question, read the question and the four suggested answers. Choose the best answer and write its number in the appropriate space on your answer sheet. (9%)

1. Why is November Alicia´s favorite month?

   1. She likes the weather
   2. She gets to take a trip
   3. She gets to celebrate a lot of holidays
   4. Her grandmother always visits then

2. Where is this summer house located?

   1. next to a shopping mall
   2. in a desert
   3. on a small island in a lake
   4. underneath a bridge

3. What would Roberto like to go today?

   1. see an adventure movie
   2. go fishing
   3. visit his cousins.
   4. stay at home

Part 2b Directions: For each question, you will hear some background information in English. Then you will hear a passage in Spanish twice, followed by a question in Spanish. Listen carefully. After you have heard the question, read the question and the four suggested answers. Choose the best answer and write its number in the appropriate space on your answer sheet. (9%)

4. ¿Qué tiempo hace?

   1. Está lloviendo
   2. Hace sol.
   3. Está nevando.
   4. Hace buen tiempo.

5. ¿Qué puedes ver en este pueblo?

   1. una universidad
   2. una gasolinera
   3. un rascacielos
   4. un almacen.

PHYSICAL ENVIRONMENT 3

6. ¿En qué estación estamos?

1. el invierno
2. la primavera
3. el verano
4. el otoño

Part 2c Directions: For each question, you will hear some background information in English. Then you will hear a passage in Spanish twice, followed by a question in English. Listen carefully. After you have heard the question, read the question and look at the four pictures on your test. Choose the picture that best answers the question and write its number in the appropriate space on your answer sheet. (12%)

7. What kind of weather is expected tomorrow?

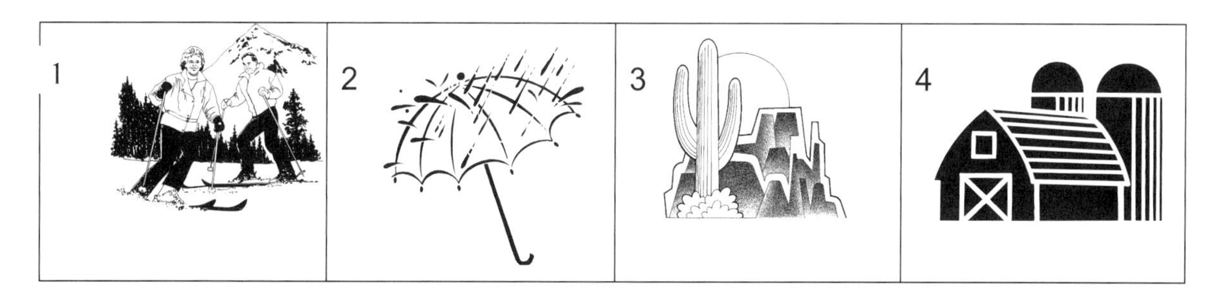

8. What does Maria look forward to seeing when she visits her cousin's home?

9. Where does Ramón Gonzalez work?

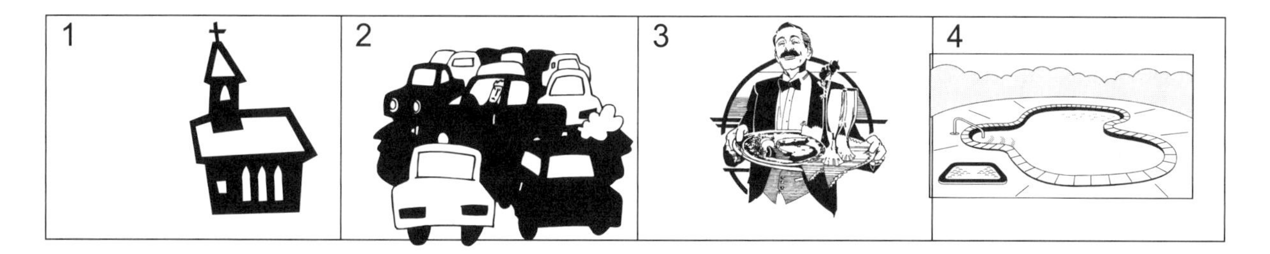

10. Where does Pedro plan to spend his summer?

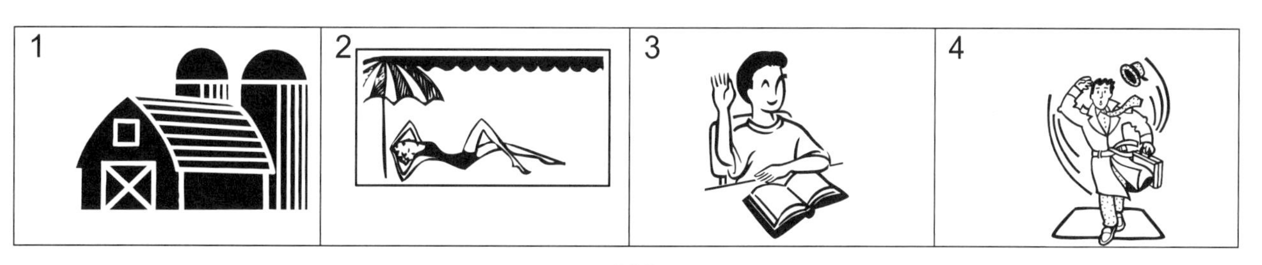

Part 3a Directions: Answer the question in English based on the reading selection in Spanish. Choose the best answer to each question. Base your choice on the content of the reading selection. Write the number of your answer in the appropriate space on your answer sheet. (8%)

El Milagro de un Desierto Florido

El desierto de Atacama está considerado el más seco y árido del mundo. Una vez cada quince años, el desierto de Atacama irrumpe en un fenómeno multicolor.

No llueve mucho en la región del desierto y cuando lo hace, las aguas de las lluvias despiertan las semillas que durante los años "dormían" entre riscos y arenas. Después de las abundantes lluvias que caen en el desierto de Atacama se ven muchas flores multicolores. La belleza de este desierto atrae a muchos vistantes, especialmente a los científicos.

11. This article is about ...

1. a fishing trip
2. a volcano
3. a desert
4. a forest

12. Why do tourists come to this region?

1. to buy clay pots
2. to go swimming
3. to see the glaciers
4. to marvel at the flowers

España

España está en el suroeste del continente de Europa. En área, el país es menos grande que el estado de Texas, pero más grande que el estado de California. Los cuarenta millones de españoles viven en una gran península separada de Francia al norte por los Pirineos. Portugal, un país independiente, ocupa la parte occidental de la misma peninísula. España es limitaba en los otros lados por el Océano Atlántico y el Mar Mediterráneo.

En topografía, España se parece mucho a California en que hay muchas montañas y pocos ríos navegables. El único río navegable de España es el Guadalquivir que desemboca en el Océano Atlántico. El clima de las ciudades españolas del sur es muy parecido al clima del estado de Arizona en la primavera, el verano y el otoño. En el noroeste de España llueve mucho como en Colorado. En el centro hace mucho calor en el verano y mucho frío en el invierno

13. What two geographic areas are being compared?

1. Spain and Portugal
2. Spain and France
3. Spain and the United States
4. Portugal and France

14. What is the Guadalquivir?

1. a state
2. a mountain
3. a desert
4. a river

Part 3b Directions: Answer the question in Spanish based on the reading selection in Spanish. Choose the best answer to each question. Base your choice on the content of the reading selection. Write the number of your answer in the appropriate space on your answer sheet. (12%)

el Puerto de Malabo

el 14 de septiembre

Querido Carlos,

Hace una semana que estoy aquí en Malabó, la capital de Guinea Ecuatorial. Aquí hace siempre mucho calor. La temperatura es 39 C Es como un horno y la escuela donde trabajo no tiene aire acondicionado. Enseño el inglés y la historia global. Los estudiantes son muy simpáticos. Espero regresar para la Navidad.

Tu primo.
Hector

al Señor Carlos Montero
55, Calle Segovia
Madrid,
España.

15. ¿Dónde está Hector?

1. en Guinea Ecuatorial
2. en Australia
3. en Alaska
4. en Finlandia

16. ¿Cómo es el clima?

1. Hace siempre frío
2. Nieva mucho
3. Hace viento
4. Hace mucho calor

17. ¿Por qué está Hector allá?

1. Él está de vacaciones
2. Él canta en un concierto
3. Él es doctor
4. Él trabaja en una escuela

18. ¿Quién es Carlos?

1. Es su mujer
2. Es un pariente
3. Es un chico de 5 años
4. Es su padre

PHYSICAL ENVIRONMENT 3

Part 4 WRITING (20%)

Part 4 Directions: Choose two of the three writing tasks provided below. Your answer to each of the two questions should be written entirely in Spanish and should contain a minimum of **30 words**.

Place names and brand names written in Spanish count as one word. Contractions are counted as one word. Salutations, closings and commonly used abbreviations are included in the word count. Numbers, unless written as words, and names of people do not count as words.

Be sure that you have satisfied the purpose of the task. The sentence structure and /or expressions used should be connected logically and demonstrate a wide range of vocabulary with minimal repetition.

4a. Your Spanish-speaking pen pal would like to know about the region where you live. Choose a political jurisdiction (city, county, state, province or country) where you live and write a letter about it. You may wish to include:

- The name of the town, country, state, province, or country in which you live
- A description of the topography of your region by giving the names of local rivers, lakes, mountains, deserts etc.
- A list of the important landmarks in your region
- A list of some of the important industries in your region
- Activities you can do.

4b. You are writing a letter to your friend in Chile inviting that person to spend winter recess in your country. In your letter you may wish to include:

- Where you will be going on winter recess
- What kind of weather he or she might expect
- What kind of clothing to bring
- What means of transportation you will be taking to get there
- What kind of activities you can do there

4c. Your class has visited a museum of natural history,- where you were able to observe animals in a showcase. Write a letter to a pen pal describing one of these animals. In your letter you may wish to include:

- Where and when you visited this museum
- What animal you saw
- A description of the animal
- The location of the habitat where the animal can be found: mountains, ocean,
- The climate that is typical in this habitat
- Whether you liked or disliked the showcase display and why

PHYSICAL ENVIRONMENT 3

Nombre y Apellido ______________________________ Fecha ____________

Part I **Speaking** __________ (30%)
Part 2 **Listening (30%)**

PART 3: READING (20%)

2a.	2b.	2c.	3a.(8%)	3b.(12%)
1._____	4._____	7._____	11._____	15._____
2._____	5._____	8._____	12._____	16._____
3._____	6._____	9._____	13._____	17._____
		10._____	14._____	18._____

Part 4 **Writing (20%) 20 words** **Write 2 paragraphs** **4a , 4b or 4c**

1____

2____

PHYSICAL ENVIRONMENT 3

EARNING A LIVING

EARNING A LIVING 3

TEACHER'S SCRIPT FOR THE EXAM, Part 2 (LISTENING 30%)

Part 2a Directions: For each question, you will hear some background information in English. Then you will hear a passage in Spanish twice, followed by a question in English. Listen carefully. After you have heard the question, read the question and the four suggested answers. Choose the best answer and write its number in the appropriate space on your answer sheet. (9%)

1. Edgar is telling his guidance counselor about his future aspirations. He says:

   Soy editor del periódico escolar. Me gusta mucho escribir. Saco buenas notas en mi clase de literatura. Quiero ser reportero. Entonces, cuando voy a la universidad, quiero estudiar el periodismo.

   What would Edgar like to study in college? (1)

2. Cristina is reading a want ad in a Spanish-language newspaper. She reads:

   Esta compañía de teatro busca a una modista o a un sastre con experiencia para diseñar y crear trajes y vestidos para actores y actrices. Llame para una entrevista.

   A person applying for this job should know how to .....(2)

3. Pedro is talking to you about his older sister Margarita. He says:

   Mi hermana trabaja en un restaurante argentino como cocinera. Ella me dice que los camareros reciben propinas generosas de los clientes y que ellos ganan más dinero que ella por semana. Mientras que ella prepara las comidas en una cocina caliente, los camareros sirven a los clientes en una sala con aire acondicionado.

   What does Pedro's sister do at her workplace? (1)

Part 2b Directions: For each question, you will hear some background information in English. Then you will hear a passage in Spanish twice, followed by a question in Spanish. Listen carefully. After you have heard the question, read the question and the four suggested answers. Choose the best answer and write its number in the appropriate space on your answer sheet. (9%)

4. Your friend Francsico calls you on the phone. He says:

   Yo no puedo ir al parque ahora contigo. Tengo un dolor de muelas terrible y tengo que ir ahora al dentista. Si me siento bien, podemos ir al parque mañana.

   ¿Adónde tiene que ir tu amigo? (4)

5. Your sister Teresa is looking for employment. You offer her a suggestion. You say:

   ¿Por qué no vas a trabajar en un almacén en el centro comercial. Tú eres muy amable y simpática. Pues, tú trabajabas en esa tienda de ropa en la esquina. Tú tienes experiencia como vendedora. ¿Qué piensas?

   ¿Qué clase de empleo sugieres tú? (1)

6. Mario is talking to his cousin about his future. He says:

   Me interesa mucho como se construyen las casas y los edificios. Soy muy creativo y artístico. Y soy muy bueno en las matemáticas y en el diseño.

   ¿Qué quiere ser Marío? (4)

Part 2c Directions: For each question, you will hear some background information in English. Then you will hear a passage in Spanish twice, followed by a question in English. Listen carefully. After you have heard the question, read the question and look at the four pictures on your test. Choose the picture that best answers the question and write its number in the appropriate space on your answer sheet. (12%)

7. Your friend is showing you photographs in his family album. He says to you:

   El hombre de pelo negro en el traje blanco es mi tío. No lo vemos mucho porque es doctor en un hospital grande. Trabaja en la sala de emergencia. .

   Where does your friend´s uncle work? (1)

8. You are going shopping with your friend Juan. You want to know what he will buy. He says

   Mi tío es peluquero y quiero comprarle un regalo que él pueda usar en el trabajo. Muchos de sus clientes son personas famosas. Una vez, él cortó el pelo de Julio Iglesias, el cantante español.

   What might Juan buy his uncle?

9. Your friend´s neighbor tells you about her work. She says

Enseño en una escuela muy moderna. Mis estudiantes son muy responsables y ambiciosos. Hacen siempre la tarea y prestan atención.

Where does this woman work? (2)

10. Your friend is talking on the cell phone to his sister. You overhear him say:

¿Dónde estás? ....¿con el mecánico? ....¡Ohhh!....¡con ell médico!... ¡tú estás con el médico! ¿Oh, tú te caíste? ¿Tienes dolor de brazo? .... Oh, comprendo. Tienes dolor de espalda. ¡Qué lástima!

Where is your friend´s sister? (3)

Listening Comprehension Answers:
For all chapters, the answers are indicated in parentheses following each question. (See questions 1-10 on the previous pages.)

Reading Comprehension answers:

3a (8%) 11. __1__ 12. __2_ 13. __3__ 14. __1__

3b (12%) 15. __2__ 16. __1__ 17. __3_ 18. __1__

EARNING A LIVING 3

Nombre ______________________________ Fecha __________________________

EXAMINATION

Part 1 SPEAKING (30%)
Part 2 LISTENING (30%)

Part 2a Directions: For each question, you will hear some background information in English. Then you will hear a passage in Spanish twice, followed by a question in English. Listen carefully. After you have heard the question, read the question and the four suggested answers. Choose the best answer and write its number in the appropriate space on your answer sheet. (9%)

1. What would Edgar like to study in college?

   1. jounalism
   2. science
   3. oceanography
   4. mathematics

2. A person applying for this job should know how to .....

   1. repair cars
   2. sew clothes
   3. teach a foreign language
   4. sing

3. What does Pedro's sister do at her workplace?

   1. She seats the customers
   2. She checks hats and coats
   3. She cooks the meals
   4. She works the cash register

Part 2b Directions: For each question, you will hear some background information in English. Then you will hear a passage in Spanish twice, followed by a question in Spanish. Listen carefully. After you have heard the question, read the question and the four suggested answers. Choose the best answer and write its number in the appropriate space on your answer sheet. (9%)

4. ¿Adónde tienes que ir tu amigo?

   1. a una fiesta
   2. a la biblioteca
   3. a una escuela
   4. al dentista

5. ¿Qué clase de empleo sugieres tú?

   1. una enfermera
   2. un contadora
   3. una vededora
   4. una criada

6. ¿Qué quiere ser Marío?

   1. profesor de alemán
   2. criado
   3. jugardor de fútbol
   4. arquitecto

Part 2c Directions: For each question, you will hear some background information in English. Then you will hear a passage in Spanish twice, followed by a question in English. Listen carefully. After you have heard the question, read the question and look at the four pictures on your test. Choose the picture that best answers the question and write its number in the appropriate space on your answer sheet. (12%)

7. Where does your friend's uncle work?

8. What might Juan buy his uncle?

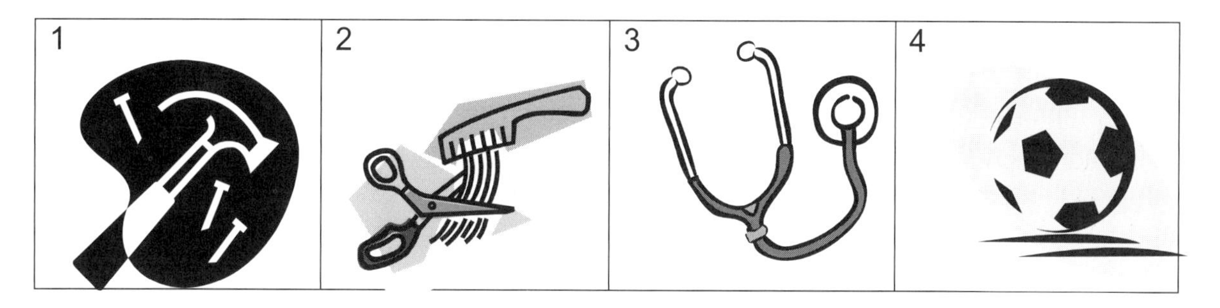

9. Where does this woman work?

10. Where is your friend's sister?

Part 3a Directions: Answer the question in English based on the reading selection in Spanish. Choose the best answer to each question. Base your choice on the content of the reading selection. Write the number of your answer in the appropriate space on your answer sheet. (8%)

SHERLOCK HOLMES DE BAKER STREET

Bienvenidos al sitio Web dedicado al detective más celebre del mundo. Aquí Ud. puede leer todo - en español - sobre este detective maravilloso y su amigo inseparable el Doctor Watson. Ud. puede también cambiar mensajes con otros aficionados de los libros de Conan Alfred Doyle.

Aquí tienen los "casos" para el mes de agosto:

Primera semana: La aventura de los bailarines
Segunda semana: La aventura de la Liga de los Pelirrojos
Tercera semana: La aventura del dedo pulgar del ingeniero
Cuarta semana: La aventura de los tres estudiantes
Quinta semana: La aventura de la ciclista solitaria

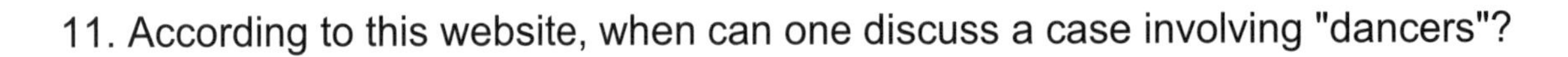

11. According to this website, when can one discuss a case involving "dancers"?

1. First week
2. Second week
3. Third week
4. Fourth week

SANTIAGO, Chile -- El jueves los bomberos que lucharon contra los fuegos en el sur de Chile creían que la nieve y la lluvia que estaban cayendo en las zonas montañosas les ayudaban en su lucha contra el fiego. Pero las precipitaciones también añadieron un nuevo peligro - el riesgo de avalanchas de tierra en las regiones que han quedado destruídas por el paso del incendio.

12. This article is about ...

1. how detectives solved a mystery
2. how firefighters were helped
3. a new mountain resort in Chile
4. a farming community

TABLÓN DE ANUNCIOS DE EMPLEO

A122. Se necesita abogado para trabajo de media jornada desde su propia casa. El trabajo consiste en realizar una serie de informes sobre diferentes ramas de Derecho internacional.

B255. Se necesitan interpretes para la Unión Europea: español-griego, español-polaco, español-frances, español- maltés, español- italiano. Empleo inmediato.

C378. Te ofrecemos puesto de camarera para los meses de julio y agosto en un restaurante de la Costa del Sol. Incluye alojamiento y comida.

D885. Se necesita peluquero de caballeros para trabajar en un vapor transatlántico entre Barcelona - Nueva York

13. Which ad is only for summer employment?

1. A122
2. B255
3. C378
4. D885

14. Which job allows the employee to work from home?

1. A122
2. B255
3. C378
4. D885

LA PRENSA el 3 de octubre

NOTICIAS DEL TEATRO

por Diego Herrera

Ayer fui al Teatro Nacional donde se presentaba la primera de cinco óperas italianas para el mes de octubre con un cuadro de cantantes internacionales. El Barbero de Sevilla por Gioacchino Rossini es una de las óperas más cómicas. El primer acto es mi favorito y termina con un argumento turbulento entre el Doctor Bartolo y el Conde Almaviva, que se hace el papel de un soldado borracho. Don Basillo (profesor de música) y Berta (la criada) tratan de contener al doctor mientras que Figaro (el barbero) y Rosina (la novia del conde) tratan de separar a Almaviva.

Fue una presentación excelente y divertida. El tenor francés Pierre LaMothe hace el papel de Figaro. La soprano argentina Luisa Macchio hace el papel de Rosina. Hans Hoffenret, tenor alemán, se hace pasar el papel del Conde Almaviva.

15. ¿Cuál es la profesión de Diego Herrera

1. barbero
2. reportero
3. cantante
4. profesor

16. Diego Herrera dice que la ópera es....

1. muy cómica	3. muy seria
2. aburrida	4. muy violenta

17. ¿Cuál es la profesión de Fernando Quiñones?

1. músico	3. abogado
2. atleta	4. policía

18. ¿A quién le interesa este anuncio?

1. a una persona que fue arrestatda	3. a una persona que quiere casarse
2. a una persona que quiere ser actor	4. a una persona que escribe novelas

EARNING A LIVING 3

Part 4 WRITING (20%)

Part 4 Directions: Choose two of the three writing tasks provided below. Your answer to each of the two questions should be written entirely in Spanish and should contain a minimum of 30 words.

Place names and brand names written in Spanish count as one word. Contractions are counted as one word. Salutations, closings and commonly used abbreviations are included in the word count. Numbers, unless written as words, and names of people do not count as words.

Be sure that you have satisfied the purpose of the task. The sentence structure and /or expressions used should be connected logically and demonstrate a wide range of vocabulary with minimal repetition.

4a. You recently visited a village restoration museum - a way of life that once was. Write a letter to a Spanish-speaking pen pal about your visit. You may wish to include:

- The name and location of this village museum
- The period of time in history (pre-colonial, colonial, early 1900) this village represented
- What buildings and shops you saw
- The kinds of occupations that were represented
- Whether these occupations are now obsolete and why

4b. You are applying for a job at a vacation resort in South America through a Spanish - language employment agency. In your letter you may wish to include:

- Personal information about yourself
- What foreign languages you speak
- What skills or talents you have such as singing, cooking, swimming etc.
- What jobs you have held before
- Why you would want to work in South America

4c. Your local newspaper would like to honor a merchant or professional person in your community. Write a letter to the editor about your nomination. You may wish to include:

- The name of this person and his or her profession
- Where this person works in your community
- What this person does in the community
- Why you are nominating this person

EARNING A LIVING 3

Nombre y Apellido ______________________________ Fecha ______________

Part I **Speaking** __________ (30%)
Part 2 **Listening (30%)** **PART 3: READING** (20%)

2a.	2b.	2c.	3a.(8%)	3b.(12%)
1._____	4._____	7._____	11._____	15._____
2._____	5._____	8._____	12._____	16._____
3._____	6._____	9._____	13._____	17._____
		10._____	14._____	18._____

Part 4 **Writing (20%) 20 words** **Write 2 paragraphs** **4a , 4b or 4c**

1____

2____

LEISURE

LEISURE 3

TEACHER´S SCRIPT FOR THE EXAM, PART II (Listening, 30%)

Part 2a Directions: For each question, you will hear some background information in English. Then you will hear a passage in Spanish twice, followed by a question in English. Listen carefully. After you have heard the question, read the question and the four suggested answers. Choose the best answer and write its number in the appropriate space on your answer sheet. (9%)

1. It´s Friday and Leonardo is at the shopping mall with his mother. He says to her:

   Necesito un traje de baño nuevo. Mañana mis amigos y yo vamos a la piscina municipal para practicar la natación

   What does Leonardo want to buy? (1)

2. You and your friend Rosalia are looking through the newspaper: Rosalia points out an advertisement and says to you:

   Mira. El sábado, dan una presentación especial en el Teatro Ramírez. Es el drama *Don Quijote de La Mancha* de Cervantes. Empieza.a las siete. ¿Quieres ir?

   What is the ad about? (2)

3. Your mother drops you off at the library. After looking at your watch, you say to her:

   Son las ocho y cuarto. La biblioteca se cierra en cuarenta y cinco minutos. Tengo que sacar uno o dos libros sobre el arte de Picasso. Ven en media hora, por favor. Voy a esperarte en la esquina.

   How long will you be in the library? (3)

Part 2b Directions: For each question, you will hear some background information in English. Then you will hear a passage in Spanish twice, followed by a question in Spanish. Listen carefully. After you have heard the question, read the question and the four suggested answers. Choose the best answer and write its number in the appropriate space on your answer sheet. (9%)

4. You and your cousin Juan are deciding on what to do. He says:

   Está lloviendo ahora. Nos quedamos en casa. Tengo unos nuevos videojuegos. Podemos jugar en la sala.

   ¿Dónde quiere jugar tu primo Juan? (4)

5. Your friend gets off his cell phone and says to you.

   Era mi primo Juan. Él dice que hay un concierto de rock en el Estadio Municipal a las seis. Nos invita. ¿Quieres ir? El grupo "Las Notas Altas" va a cantar.

   ¿Por qué llamó Juan? (3)

6. You are telling your friend about your mother´s part-time job. You say:

   Mi madre trabaja dos días por semana en la universidad donde enseña la natación. El Centro Atlético de la universidad tiene dos piscinas olímpicas. A toda mi familia le encanta mucho este deporte, pero yo prefiero nadar en el mar.

   ¿Qué lleva tu madre cuando trabaja? (1)

Part 2c Directions: For each question, you will hear some background information in English. Then you will hear a passage in Spanish twice, followed by a question in English. Listen carefully. After you have heard the question, read the question and look at the 4 pictures on your test. Choose the picture that best answers the question and write its number in the appropriate space on your answer sheet. (12%)

7. Juanita's mother calls her daughter to the phone. Juanita replies:

   Mamí, tú sabes que estoy mirando mi telenovela favorita. No hablo con nadie desde las tres hasta las cuatro.

   What is Juanita doing? (3)

8. You meet your neighbor Hector in a sporting goods store. He says:

   Tengo que comprar un guante nuevo y un par de calcetines blancos. Yo juego para el equipo de mi escuela. La gorra y el uniforme que llevo son rojos y blancos. Son los colores de mi escuela.

   What sport does Hector play? (2)

9. Luisa is telling her friend Roberto about an event at the local convention center. Roberto replies:

   No, gracias. No quiero ir contigo. Para mí, los juegos de mesa son aburridos. No me gusta el ajedrez. Solo dos personas pueden jugar al ajedrez. Prefiero ver un partido de deporte con muchos jugadores. Hay mucha acción

   Which of the following activities would **NOT** be of interest to Roberto? (3)

10. You are at a travel agency where you hear an elderly Spanish couple talking at the next desk. The husband says to his wife:

    Cuando yo voy de vacaciones, no quiero ni correr de un museo a otro ni ir de compras en todas las tiendas del pueblo. Cuando voy de vacaciones, quiero hacer una cosa solamente: descansar...Sí, quiero descansar en el hotel por la mañana, en la playa por la tarde y en la plaza por la noche.

    Where will this husband spend most of his vacation time. (4)

Listening Comprehension Answers:
For all chapters, the answers are indicated in parentheses following each question. (See questions 1-10 on the previous pages.)

Reading Comprehension answers:

3a. (8%) 11. __2__ 12. __2__ 13. __1__ 14. __4__

3b (12%) 15. __3__ 16. __4__ 17. __2__ 18. __3__

LEISURE 3

Nombre ______________________________ Fecha __________________________

EXAMINATION

Part 1 SPEAKING (30%)
Part 2 LISTENING (30%)

Part 2a Directions: For each question, you will hear some background information in English. Then you will hear a passage in Spanish twice, followed by a question in English. Listen carefully. After you have heard the question, read the question and the four suggested answers. Choose the best answer and write its number in the appropriate space on your answer sheet. (9%)

1. What does Leonardo want to buy?

   1. a bathing suit
   2. a helmet
   3. a baseball glove
   4. sneakers

2. What is the ad about?

   1. a sports event
   2. a theatrical production
   3. a museum exhibition
   4. a poetry reading

3. How long will you be in the library?

   1. one hour
   2. several hours
   3. thirty minutes
   4. about two and a half hours

Part 2b Directions: For each question, you will hear some background information in English. Then you will hear a passage in Spanish twice, followed by a question in Spanish. Listen carefully. After you have heard the question, read the question and the four suggested answers. Choose the best answer and write its number in the appropriate space on your answer sheet. (9%)

4. ¿Dónde quiere jugar tu primo Juan?

   1. en un parque
   2. en el estadio
   3. en la piscina
   4. en tu casa

5. ¿Por qué llamó Juan?

   1. Quiere jugar al basquétbol
   2. Quiere ver una película
   3. Invitó a su primo a un concierto
   4. Necesita información.

6. ¿Qué lleva tu madre cuando trabaja?

   1. un traje de baño
   2. un uniforme azul
   3. un vestido blanco
   4. un sombrero de cocinero

Part 2c Directions: For each question, you will hear some background information in English. Then you will hear a passage in Spanish twice, followed by a question in English. Listen carefully. After you have heard the question, read the question and look at the 4 pictures on your test. Choose the picture that best answers the question and write its number in the appropriate space on your answer sheet. (12%)

7. What is Juanita doing?

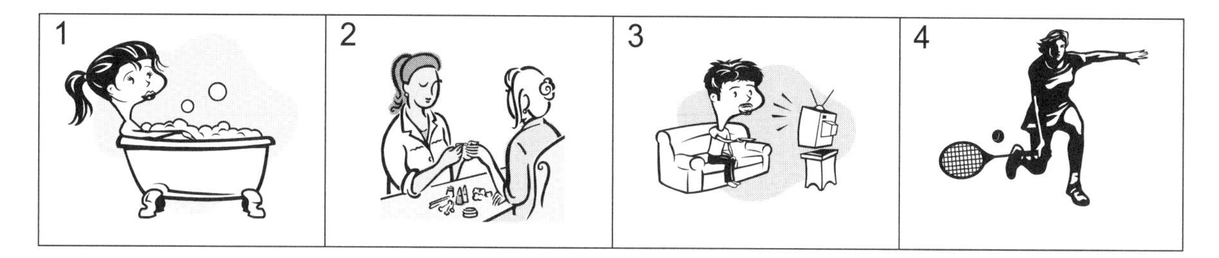

8. What sport does Hector play?

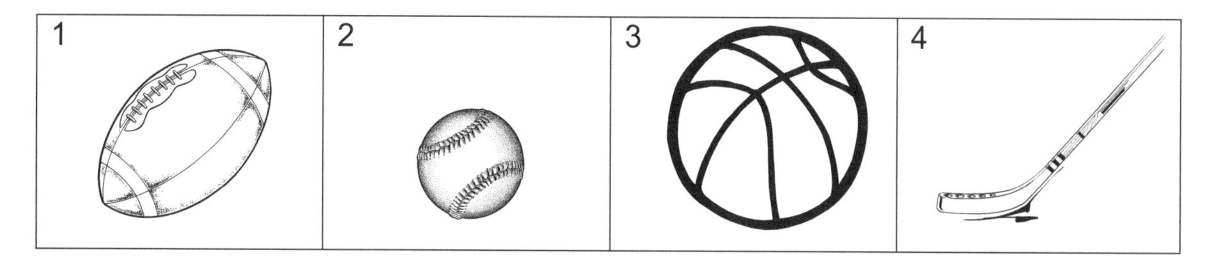

9. Which of the following activities would **NOT** be of interest to Roberto?

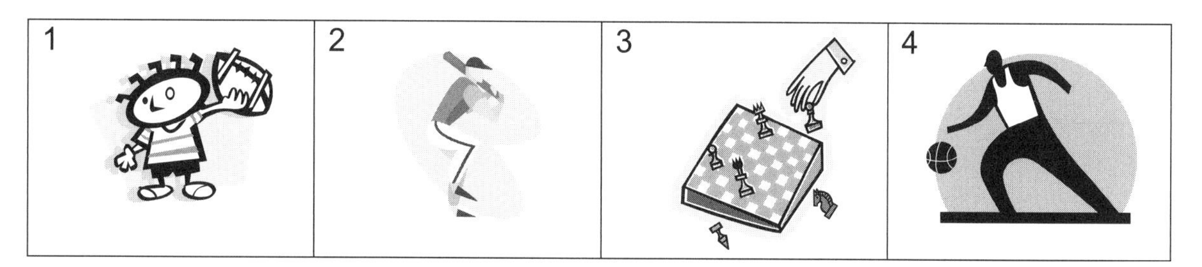

10. Where will this husband spend most of his vacation time?

Part 3a Directions: Answer the question in English based on the reading selection in Spanish. Choose the best answer to each question. Base your choice on the content of the reading selection. Write the number of your answer in the appropriate space on your answer sheet.
(8%)

Me llamo Juan Ortiz. Tengo quince años. Me gustan mucho los deportes de invierno: el esquí, el patinaje sobre hielo, el hockey sobre hielo. Busco a un amigo de correspondencia con los mismos interéses.

Me llamo Antonio Rivera y tengo dieciséis años. Soy atlético y soy muy inteligente también. Me gusta pensar, y por eso, prefiero los juegos de mesa. Me gustan el ajedrez y jugar a las cartas.

Me llama Ursula Dupont. Tengo dieciocho años. Prefiero deportes individuales como la natación, el patinaje, el ciclismo y el golf. Busco amigos con intereses similares

Me llamo Yolanda Tedesco. Tengo dieciséis años. Me encantan mucho los deportes acuáticos. Soy capitán del equipo de natación de mi escuela. Me gusta también el esquí acuático.

11. Which statement is **false**?
    1. Ursula is older than Juan
    2. Ursula belongs to a swimming team.
    3. Ursula knows how to skate
    4. Ursula can ride a bike.

12. Who would most likely enjoy playing chess or checkers with you?
    1. Juan Ortiz
    2. Antonio Rivera
    3. Yolanda Tedesco
    4. Ursula Dupont

13. What is probably Juan's favorite season?
    1. winter
    2. spring
    3. summer
    4. fall

Programas del TV - Jueves

4.00 Los Días Mágicos (telenovela argentina)
4.30 Babar y sus amigos (programa para los niños)
5.00 Las Llamas de Chile (documentario)
6.00 Las Noticias a las Seis
6.30 Meteo-boletín - El tiempo de mañana
6.35 La Rueda de la Fortuna (programa de juego)
6.45 Los Tres Tenores en Madrid (concierto especial)
7.30 Tele-película "Invasión del Extraterrestre de Júpiter"

14. What would you watch at 6:30?
    1. a children's program
    2. a soap opera
    3. a movie
    4. the weather

Part 3b Directions: Answer the question in Spanish based on the reading selection in Spanish. Choose the best answer to each question. Base your choice on the content of the reading selection. Write the number of your answer in the appropriate space on your answer sheet. (12%)

CAMPEONATO DE RODEO Y ESPECTÁCULO DEL VIEJO OESTE

Semana del 12 de agosto

ESTADIO RIO GRANDE

a solo 15 minutos de la frontera mexicana

Muestra de Ganadería - todos los días
Espectáculo de Billy Goat Wild West Show
jueves y viernes por la noche

Seis eventos cada día: montar en pelo, tumbar un novillo, lazar en equipo, jinetear el caballo bronco, lazar un becerro y jinetear un toro.

15. ¿Qué puedes ver en este estadio durante la semana del 12 de agosto?
    1. un partido de béisbol
    2. un juego de bolos
    3. vaqueros y animales
    4. una exhibición de arte

CALENDARIO DE LA UNIVERSIDAD DE PUERTO RICO

El Cine-Club presentará de sus archivos la celebre película mexicana "Simon Bolivar" para celebrar la Semana Panamericana. El precio de entrada es dos dólares. En la película Julián Soler hace el papel del liberatador, Simón Bolivar. La película - en español con subtítulos en inglés - se presentará en el Pequeño Teatro el trece de abril a las tres de la tarde. Julián Soler es miembro de una famosa familia mexicana de actores. Sus hermanos se llaman Andrés, Fernando y Domingo.

16. El Cine-Club presenterá esta película para celebrar ...

1. una fiesta religiosa
2. el nacimiento de un actor
3. una familia puertorriqueña
4. una ocasión internacional

17. ¿A qué hora dan la película?

1. a las dos de la tarde
2. a las tres de la tarde
3. a las cuatro de la mañana
4. a la una de la mañana

18. ¿Quién es Julián Soler?

1. miembro del Cine-Club
2. autor inglés
3. estrella del cine mexicano
4. estudiante de la universidad

Part 4 WRITING (20%)

Part 4 Directions: Choose two of the three writing tasks provided below. Your answer to each of the two questions should be written entirely in Spanish and should contain a minimum of **30 words.**

Place names and brand names written in Spanish count as one word. Contractions are counted as one word. Salutations, closings and commonly used abbreviations are included in the word count. Numbers, unless written as words, and names of people do not count as words.

Be sure that you have satisfied the purpose of the task. The sentence structure and /or expressions used should be connected logically and demonstrate a wide range of vocabulary with minimal repetition.

4a. In a note in the target language to your pen pal, write him or her about the type of recreational activities your community sponsors. You may wish to include:

- The name of your town or community
- The type of activities your community sponsors
- For which groups of people these activities are (senior citizens, youth etc.)
- Where these activities take place
- Whether you or members of your family participate in these activities

4b. You belong to a hiking and outdoors club. Write a letter to your pen pal. In your letter you may wish to include:

- The type of outdoor activities they offer
- Which one of these activities is your favorite and why
- The season in which you participate in your favorite outdoor activity
- Where you would go to participate in this activity
- What kind of clothing and equipment you need to participate in this outdoor activity

4c. You have just returned from a musical event. In a note in Spanish write about one or more of the performers you observed. You may wish to include:

- The name or names of the performers
- What kind of music was performed
- What equipment or musical instrument was used
- A description of the clothing worn by the performer or performers
- Where you went to see this performance
- Who went with you
- Your feelings about the performance

LEISURE 3

Nombre y Apellido ______________________________ Fecha ______________

Part I **Speaking** __________ (30%)
Part 2 **Listening (30%)**

2a.	2b.	2c.
1._____	4._____	7._____
2._____	5._____	8._____
3._____	6._____	9._____
		10._____

PART 3: READING (20%)

3a.(8%)	3b.(12%)
11._____	15._____
12._____	16._____
13._____	17._____
14._____	18._____

Part 4 **Writing (20%) 20 words** **Write 2 paragraphs** **4a , 4b or 4c**

1____

2____

Public and Private Services

TEACHER'S SCRIPT FOR THE EXAM, PART II (Listening, 30%)

Part 2a Directions: For each question, you will hear some background information in English. Then you will hear a passage in Spanish twice, followed by a question in English. Listen carefully. After you have heard the question, read the question and the four suggested answers. Choose the best answer and write its number in the appropriate space on your answer sheet (9%).

1. Your uncle is treating you to lunch at a fancy restaurant near where he works. He says to you:

   Este restaurante es caro pero la comida es excelente. Cada día se sirve comida de un país diferente del mundo hispano. Lo que me gusta más es que sobre cada mesa hay un periódico de uno de estos países. Cuando vengo aquí yo como y yo leo las noticias en español.

   What can be found on the tables in this restaurant? (3)

2. You are in a hotel. You overhear the hotel manager speaking to a guest. He says:

   Las cabinas del teléfono están a la izquierda de los ascensores. Pero, Ud. puede hacer una llamada desde su cuarto. Hay una guía telefónica sobre la mesa de lámpara entre las dos camas.

   What does this hotel guest want to do? (1)

3. Your mother is at the post office. You hear the postal clerk say to her:

   Esta carta va a una gran ciudad. Si Ud. quiere que la carte se reciba pronto, le recomiendo que Ud. ponga el codigo postal. ¿Lo sabe Ud.?

   What is missing on the envelope? (3)

Part 2b Directions: For each question, you will hear some background information in English. Then you will hear a passage in Spanish twice, followed by a question in Spanish. Listen carefully. After you have heard the question, read the question and the four suggested answers. Choose the best answer and write its number in the appropriate space on your answer sheet (9%).

4. You are an exchange student in Argentina. The teacher is speaking. She says:

   Tu carta debe incluir todas las cinco partes: la fecha, los saludos, el cuerpo de la carta, la despedida y la firma. Por favor, escribe la carta con tu mejor caligrafía.

   ¿Qué está enseñando la profesora? (2)

5. You are in a library in Caracas, Venezuela. The reference librarian says to you:

   Para usar una computadora aquí tengo que ver una tarjeta de identificacion. ¿Tiene algo con su fotografía? (1)

   ¿Qué tienes que dar a la bibliotecaria ?

6. You are in Puerto Rico. You want to mail a package to your grandmother at the post office. You ask the cashier in the drugstore next to your hotel for directions. She says:

   Deme el paquete. Yo veo que este paquete es pequeño y pesa menos de tres libras. Entonces Ud. puede enviar el paquete desde aquí. Tenemos el servicio postal aquí en esta farmacia.

   ¿Cuánto pesa el paquete? (4)

Part 2c Directions: For each question, you will hear some background information in English. Then you will hear a passage in Spanish twice, followed by a question in English. Listen carefully. After you have heard the question, read the question and look at the 4 pictures on your test. Choose the picture that best answers the question and write its number in the appropriate space on your answer sheet. (12%)

7. You are in a store in Bogotá with your host father. The sales lady is speaking to him. She says:

   ¿Ud. necesita sobres grandes? Tenemos hoy una venta especial. Compre dos cajas de sobres grandes y recibe un abrecartas gratis. Los sobres están en el primer pasillo con otros objetos de escritorio.

   What is your host father buying? (3)

8. Your mother is speaking to someone at the door. You hear a gentleman speaking. He says:

   Tengo su correo aquí. Tengo también una carta registrada para Usted. Por favor, firme este papel. Gracias, señora. Y aqui tiene el correo.

   What is this person at the door delivering? (4)

9. A visitor from Colombia is telling you about the community where he lives. He says:

   Tengo más de 80 años. No camino bien. No puedo subir el autobus. Mi comunidad ofrece un autobús especial para a la gente incapacitada. Cuando tengo que ir al médico o ir de compras, puedo llamar un número especial. El autobús viene a mi casa y me lleva donde quiero ir. Por eso, me gusta mi comunidad.

   Who is the visitor? (3)

10. Rodolfo is walking with his grandfather. He says:

    Abuelo, tú necesitas ser moderno. Tú necesitas un teléfono celular. Cuando tu estás lejos y la Abuelita necesita tu ayuda, ella puede llamarte no importa donde estés.

    What does Rodolfo suggest that his grandfather get? (2)

Listening Comprehension Answers:
For all chapters, the answers are indicated in parentheses following each question. (See questions 1-10 on the previous pages.)

Reading Comprehension answers:

3a (8%) 11. __1__ 12. __3__ 13. __4__ 14. __3__

3b (12%) 15. __1__ 16. __4__ 17. __2__ 18. __4__

PUBLIC AND PRIVATE SERVICES 3

Nombre ______________________________ Fecha ______________________________

EXAMINATION

Part 1 SPEAKING (30%)
Part 2 LISTENING (30%)

Part 2a Directions: For each question, you will hear some background information in English. Then you will hear a passage in Spanish twice, followed by a question in English. Listen carefully. After you have heard the question, read the question and the four suggested answers. Choose the best answer and write its number in the appropriate space on your answer sheet (9%).

1. What can be found on the tables in this restaurant?

   1. a telephone
   2. a flag .
   3. a newspaper.
   4. flowers

2. What does this hotel guest want to do?

   1. make a phone call
   2. buy some souvenirs
   3. buy post cards
   4. mail a letter

3. What is missing on the envelope?

   1. the name of the city
   2. a stamp
   3. the zip code
   4. the addressee´s name

Part 2b Directions: For each question, you will hear some background information in English. Then you will hear a passage in Spanish twice, followed by a question in Spanish. Listen carefully. After you have heard the question, read the question and the four suggested answers. Choose the best answer and write its number in the appropriate space on your answer sheet (9%).

4. ¿Qué está enseñando la profesora?

   1. las fórmulas químicas
   2. como escribir una carta personal
   3. como usar la computadora
   4. el proceso de hacer el papel

5. ¿Qué tienes que dar a la bibliotecaria ?

   1. un pasaporte
   2. dinero
   3. un libro
   4. un disco compacto

6. ¿Cuánto pesa el paquete?

1. treinta libras
2. veinte libras
3. diez libras
4. dos libras

Part 2c Directions: For each question, you will hear some background information in English. Then you will hear a passage in Spanish twice, followed by a question in English. Listen carefully. After you have heard the question, read the question and look at the 4 pictures on your test. Choose the picture that best answers the question and write its number in the appropriate space on your answer sheet. (12%)

7. What is your host father buying?

1. 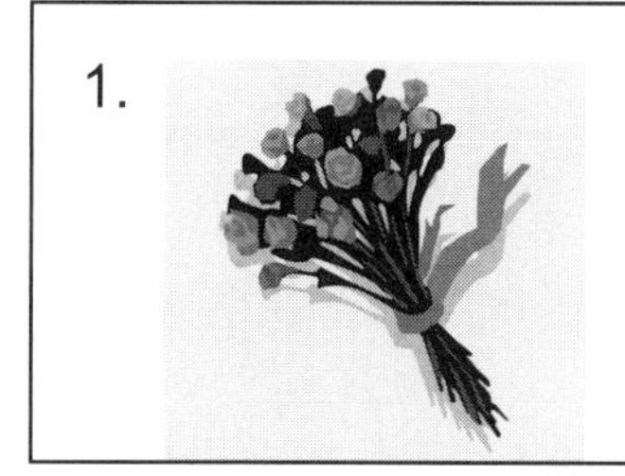	2. 	3. 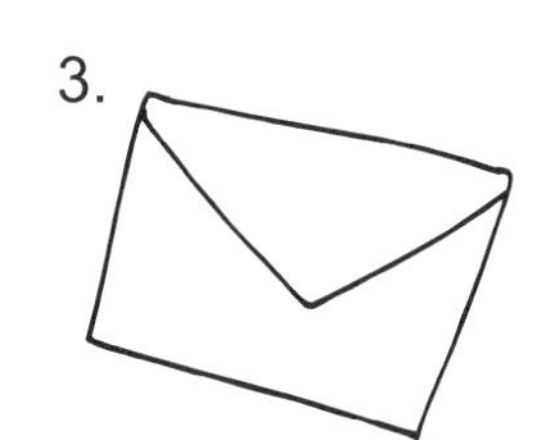	4 

8. What is the person at the door delivering?

1. 	2. 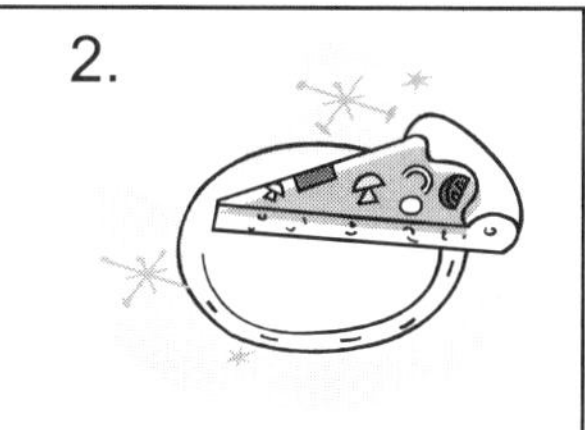	3 	4. 

9. Who is the visitor?

1. 	2. 	3. 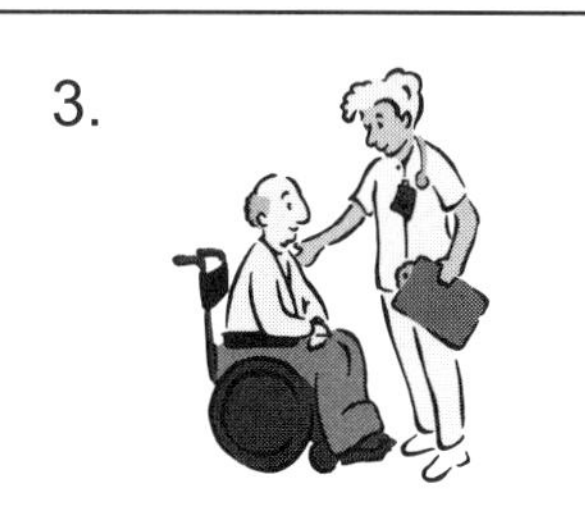	4. 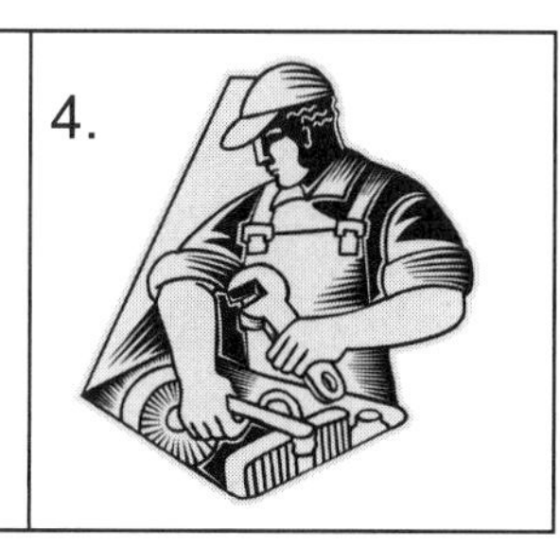

10. What does Rudolfo suggest that his grandfather get?

1. 	2. 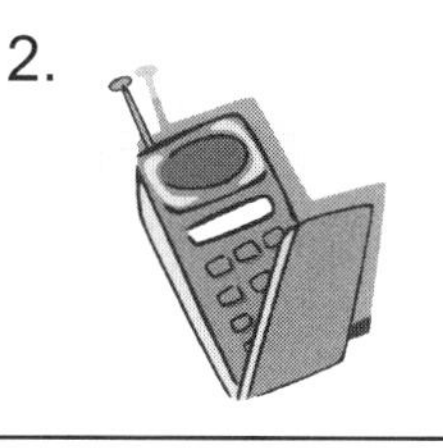	3. 	4. 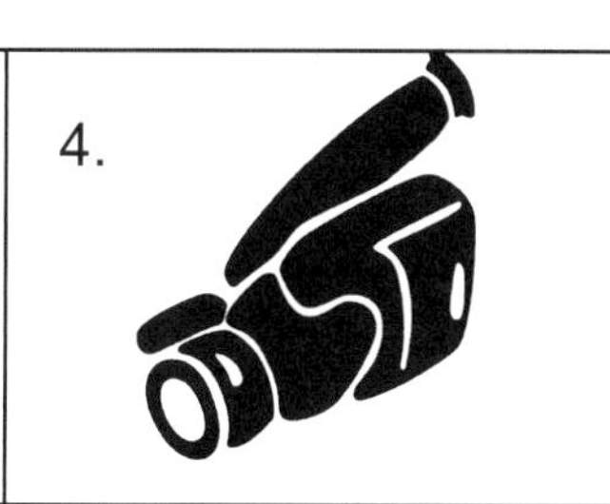

Part 3 READING (20%)

Part 3a Directions: Answer the question in English based on the reading selection in Spanish. Choose the best answer to each question. Base your choice on the content of the reading selection. Write the number of your answer in the appropriate space on your answer sheet (8%).

Comida Sobre Ruedas es un programa de servicio público para la gente incapacitada. Es para la gente que no puede salir de casa, no puede ni cocinar ni ir de compras. Este programa es también para personas que tienen más de 75 años y viven solas. **Comida Sobre Ruedas** entrega tres comidas nutriciosas todos los días a la casa de las personas necesitadas. Para más información sobre **Comidas Sobre Ruedas** llame el 555-8961.

11. What does this community service provide?

1. transportation for the elderly
2. a daily meal
2. a regular visit by a nurse
3. physical therapy

Un Mundo Sin Dinero

Desde hace tiempo, el país de Japón ha introducido "las tarjetas inteligentes" con microchips que permiten a la gente pagarlo todo electrónicamente, desde los sellos hasta el almuerzo en un restaurante elegante. ¿Cómo lo hacen? ¡Con un teléfono celular!
Sí, con un teléfono celular simple. Imagine un mundo donde no se paga nunca en efectivo. Este verano se venden en Japón, teléfonos celulares con una chip de computadora integrada que Usted puede llenar de dinero electrónico. ¡No más billetes y monedas! ¡No más billeteras!

12. According to this article...

1. Japan is the leading producer of "smart cards."
2. Cellular phones will eventually be the size of a stamp
3. The use of paper bills and coins will gradually become extinct
4. Japan will no longer permit leather wallets to be sold in the country

Directorio de Sitios Web

Arte y cultura Poesía, Pinturas, Literatura...	Familia y sociedad Comida, Salud, Casa...
Diversiones Juegos, Teatro, Deportes ...	Internet y tecnología Correo, Chat, Antivirus ...
Economía y negocios Empleo, Tiendas, Finanzas...	Noticias Periódicos, Revistas, Radio, TV...
Educación y formación Escuelas, Ciencias, Idiomas...	Política y gobierno Países, Historia, Mapas...

13. Which web site would you access if you were looking for a job?

1. Familia y sociedad
2. Arte y cultura
3. Política y gobierno
4. Economía y negocios

DIRECTORIO DE SERVICIOS POSTALES

	Ventanilla
Entrega especial	7
Filatelia / Sellos comemorativos	21
Giro postal	7 - 8
Información	20
Paquetes	9
Pasaportes	22
Sellos	1 - 8

14. Which services are offered at Window 7?

1. parcel post and passports
2. passports and stamps
3. stamps, special delivery and money orders
4. philately and parcel post

Part 3b Directions: Answer the question in Spanish based on the reading selection in Spanish. Choose the best answer to each question. Base your choice on the content of the reading selection. Write the number of your answer in the appropriate space on your answer sheet. (12%)

MUNICIPIO DE RÍO BLANCO

	Nos. de teléfono
Oficinas del Gobierno / Alcalde	66.87.90
Corte de Justicia	66.87.82
Oficina de Impuestos	66.87.91
Parques / Recreo / Piscina	64.33.07
Comisión Municipal de Saneamiento	76.41.08
Riciclaje	76.41.05
Biblioteca Municipal	68.99.34
Bomberos (emergencia)	911
Estación Central	68.93.06
Estación de Calle Martí	63.07.07
Policía	911
Estación de Calle Sydney	66.77.00

15. ¿Por qué llamaría el 76.41.08?

1. para obtener información sobre la colección de la basura
2. para hablar con el alcalde
3. para obtener información sobre lecciones de natación
4. para hablar con un detective

16. Para saber cuando se puede usar el campo de basquétbol, Ud. tiene que marcar

1. el 63.07.07
2. el 66.77.00
3. el 66.87.82
4. el 64.33.07

UNIÓN PAN-LATINA www.unionpanlatina.com

Para enviar dinero a México y Guatemala Fecha __6/8____
Indique Servicio
___Dinero en minutos / ___ Dinero Día Siguiente / ___ Dinero a Domicilio

Cantidad de dinero con letra cuatro cientos $ 400	No. de operador 7125
Destinatario Pepe Martinez	Hora de envio 10
Teléfono 358 33 55	Tipo de identificación pasaporte
Dirección 10 Avenida Alameda	Fecha de nacimiento
Ciudad San Antonio, Texas	No. Seguro Social 501 72 6643
Remitente Juana Martinez	No. de controlo 645
Teléfono 254 430 2154	Cantidad $ 400.
Dirección 265 Los Brasos	Cargo $
Ciudad Waco	Impuesto $ 10
Pregunta secreta (Mensaje)	Cantidad total $ 410

17. ¿Dónde vive la persona que recibe el dinero?

1. Lima, Perú
2. San Antonio, Texas
3. Guatemala
4. Veracruz, México

18. ¿Cuánto dinero fue mandato al destinario?

1. $300
2. $317
3. $310
4. $400

Part 4 WRITING (20%)

Part 4 Directions: Choose two of the three writing tasks provided below. Your answer to each of the two questions should be written entirely in Spanish and should contain a minimum of **30 words**.

Place names and brand names written in Spanish count as one word. Contractions are counted as one word. Salutations, closing, and commonly used abbreviations are included in the word count. Numbers, unless written as words, and names of people do not count as words.

Be sure that you have satisfied the purpose of the task. The sentence structure and-or expressions used should be connected logically and demonstrate a wide range of vocabulary with minimal repetition.

4a. You are writing a letter to your Spanish-speaking pen pal about a public service that your community has introduced. In your letter you may wish to include:

- The name of this public service program
- For which group this program was created (youth. elderly, mothers, immigrants, etc.)
- A description of this public service program
- Whether you feel it is beneficial
- If you will participate in it

4b. You would like to compliment an immigrant from a Spanish-speaking country who is in the public service field (postal worker, politician, visiting nurse, teacher etc.). You have decided to write to the local Spanish newspaper about this person. In your letter to the editor you may wish to include:

- The name of this person and the country of his or her origin
- Mention of some personal facts about him or her.
- Indicate what field this person works in
- State what this person has done to deserve a noteworthy mention in the paper

4c. One of the public services that your community provides is a conservation program. You work for this program after school and you have been asked to write a memorandum for the Spanish-speaking population on both the conservation and recycling programs. In the memorandum you may wish to include:

- A list of items that need to be recycled
- Indicate how these items will be collected
- How the community can conserve water and/or electricity
- How the community can reduce air and/or water pollution

PUBLIC AND PRIVATE SERVICES 3

Nombre y Apellido ________________________________ Fecha _______________

Part I **Speaking** __________ (30%)
Part 2 **Listening (30%)**

2a.	2b.	2c.
1._____	4._____	7._____
2._____	5._____	8._____
3._____	6._____	9._____
		10._____

PART 3: READING (20%)

3a.(8%)	3b.(12%)
11._____	15._____
12._____	16._____
13._____	17._____
14._____	18._____

Part 4 **Writing (20%) 20 words** **Write 2 paragraphs** **4a , 4b or 4c**

1 ____

____

____

____

____

____

____

____

____

2 ____

____

____

____

____

____

____

____

____

____

TRAVEL

TRAVEL 3

TEACHER'S SCRIPT FOR THE EXAM, PART II (Listening, 30%)

Part 2a Directions: For each question, you will hear some background information in English. Then you will hear a passage in Spanish twice, followed by a question in English. Listen carefully. After you have heard the question, read the question and the four suggested answers. Choose the best answer and write its number in the appropriate space on your answer sheet (9%).

1. Your family is in Spain on vacation. You stop to ask the hotel desk clerk for information. You ask:

   Vamos a Barcelona mañana por tren. ¿Tiene Ud. un horario de la estación de ferrocarril de Madrid? Quiero saber a que hora sale el último tren antes del mediodía.

   What kind of information do you want to know? (3)

   1. the location of a pharmacy
   2. what time the post office closes
   3. the train schedule
   4. the price of an airmail stamp

2. Your friend Yolanda tells you how she gets to work. She says:

   Generalmente, voy al trabajo en carro. Pero, mi carro está en la estación de servicio para reparaciones. Para ir al trabajo hoy, fui en bicicleta. No me cuesta nada. Al mismo tiempo hago ejercicio.

   How is Yolanda getting to work today? (2)

3. You call your friend by cell phone. You say to her:

   Voy a Puerto Rico por una semana de vacaciones. Estoy haciendo mi maleta ahora, pero mi maleta no es grande. No tengo bastante espacio para mis zapatos y mis faldas. Tienes una maleta que me puedes puedo prestar?

   What is your friend doing? (2)

TRAVEL 3

Part 2b Directions: For each question, you will hear some background information in English. Then you will hear a passage in Spanish twice, followed by a question in Spanish. Listen carefully. After you have heard the question, read the question and the four suggested answers. Choose the best answer and write its number in the appropriate space on your answer sheet (9%).

4. You are talking to your friend about an upcoming trip to Mexico. You say:

   El mes próximo mi familia va a México. Vamos en carro. Mi madre no quiere ir por avíon. Tiene miedo de volar. El viaje por carrova a durar dos semanas.

   ¿Cómo va a viajar tu familia en México? (4)

5. You are in a waiting room when you hear this announcement.

   El vuelo número trescientos veinte de las Lineas Aereas de Chile para Santiago sale por la Puerta número diecidocho. Queremos que los pasajeros tengan listo el pasaporte.

   ¿Dónde estás tú? (1)

6. You are at a travel agency. You overhear a gentleman speaking to the travel agent at the next desk. This man says

   Quiero hacer una reservación para una habitación con cama sensilla. Me gusta mucho nadar y tomar el sol. Prefiero una habitacion en la planta baja que da al océano. Quiero la cama para este fin de semana.

   ¿Adónde va este señor de vacaciones? (4)

Part 2c Directions: For each question, you will hear some background information in English. Then you will hear a passage in Spanish twice, followed by a question in English. Listen carefully. After you heard the question, read the question and look at the 4 pictures on your test. Choose the picture that best answers the question and write its number in the appropriate space on your answer sheet. (12%)

7. Your host father is getting ready to leave the house. He says to your host brother:

   Está lloviendo y tu madre tiene el coche ahora. Tengo prisa. El autobús es muy lento. Tengo que estar en la oficina en media hora. Llamame un taxi por favor.

   How will your host father get to work today? (2)

8. Graciela, an exchange student from Honduras is speaking to the class about her father. She says:

   Mi padre trabaja para una compañía de aviación en mi país. Es piloto y él viaja entre Honduras y el continente de Europa. Es una carrera muy interesante y yo espero ser piloto un día también.

   What vehicle does Graciela´s father use in his line of work? (3)

9. Your Spanish teacher is talking about his childhood. He says:

   De niño yo vivía en un pueblo muy pequeño que estaba en un desierto en el estado de Nevada. Durante el verano hacía un calor terrible. En el mes de julio mi familia fue de vacaciones a las montañas porque allí hacía muy fresco. Teníamos una casa allí.

   Where did your teacher spend the month of July as a child? (1)

10. Your family is on vacation in Venezuela. Your older brother says:

   Yo quiero ir al correo. Quiero comprar algunas estampillas para mi amigo Pablo. A él le gusta colleccionar estampillas de los países sudamericanos. Tú tienes que ver su álbum. ¡Qué colección!

   What does your brother want to buy for his friend? (1)

Listening Comprehension Answers:
For all chapters, the answers are indicated in parenthesis following each question. (See questions 1-10 on the previous pages.)

Reading Comprehension answers:

3a. (8%)	11. __1__	12. __3__	13. __3__	14. __2__
3b (12%)	15. __3__	16. __ 1__	17. __ 2__	18. __4__

TRAVEL 3

Nombre _________________________ Fecha _______________

EXAMINATION

Part 1 SPEAKING (30%)
Part 2 LISTENING (30%)

Part 2a Directions: For each question, you will hear some background information in English. Then you will hear a passage in Spanish twice, followed by a question in English. Listen carefully. After you have heard the question, read the question and the four suggested answers. Choose the best answer and write its number in the appropriate space on your answer sheet (9%).

1. What kind of information do you want to know?

   1. the location of a pharmacy
   2. what time the post office closes
   3. the train schedule
   4. the price of an airmail stamp

2. How is Yolanda getting to work today?

   1. on foot
   2. by bicycle
   3. by bus
   4. by taxi

3. What is your friend doing?

   1. She is shining her shoes
   2. She is packing a suitcase
   3. She is shopping for clothes
   4. She is boarding a plane

Part 2b Directions: For each question, you will hear some background information in English. Then you will hear a passage in Spanish twice, followed by a question in Spanish. Listen carefully. After you have heard the question, read the question and the four suggested answers. Choose the best answer and write its number in the appropriate space on your answer sheet (9%).

4. ¿Cómo va a viajar tu familia en México?

   1. en avión
   2. en tren
   3. en autobús
   4. en auto

5. ¿Dónde estás tú?

   1. en un aeropuerto
   2. en una clínica médica
   3. en la estación de ferrocarril
   4. en una terminal de autobús

6. ¿Adónde va este señor de vacaciones?

   1. a las montañas
   2. a la tienda de muebles
   3. al bosque
   4. al mar

Part 2c Directions: For each question, you will hear some background information in English. Then you will hear a passage in Spanish twice, followed by a question in English. Listen carefully. After you heard the question, read the question and look at the 4 pictures on your test. Choose the picture that best answers the question and write its number in the appropriate space on your answer sheet. (12%)

7. How will your host father get to work today?

8. What vehicle does Graciela's father use in his line of work?

1.	2.	3.	4.
			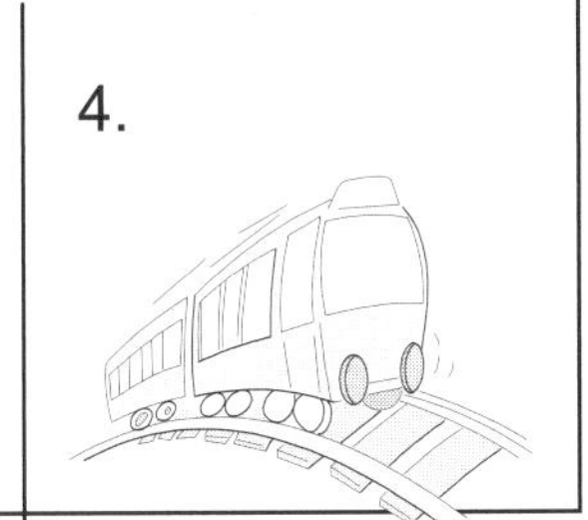

9. Where did your teacher spend the month of July as a child?

1	2	3	4

10. What does your brother want to buy for his friend?

1.	2.	3.	4.
			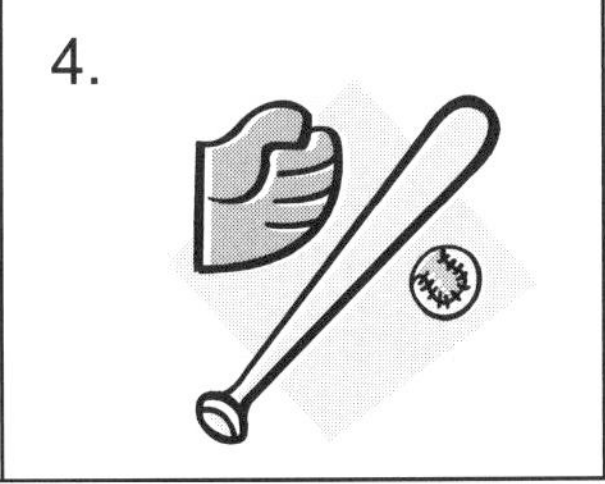

Part 3 READING (20%)
Part 3a Directions: Answer the questions in English based on the reading selections in Spanish. Choose the best answer to each question. Base your choice on the content of the reading selection. Write the number of your answer in the appropriate space on your answer sheet (8%).

Viaje a Macchu Picchu y al Valle Sagrado de los Incas

Nuestro servicio incluye:

Transporte en avión Lima - Cuzco - Lima
Traslado en la ciudad de Cuzco y al Valle Sagrado (en autobús turístico).
Boleto de tren hacia la ciudad de Aguas Calientes
Alojamiento en los Hoteles Inca
Alimentación (desayuno y cena en el hotel)
Boleto Turístico para visitar Macchu Picchu.
Guía Profesional.
Itinerario : 4 días/3 noches

11. How many means of transportation are included in this itinerary?

1. three - airplane, bus and train
2. two - tourist bus and train
3. two – airplane and boat
4. three - airplane, train and mule

12. What is **not** included in this package?

1. a professional guide
2. hotel lodging
3. lunch
4. a tour of Macchu Picchu

Los Subterraneos de Nueva York

El transporte público dentro la ciudad de Nueva York es la mejor manera de moverse en los cinco condados. Los subterráneos son rápidos. En el verano éstos tienen aire acondicionado, y en el invierno tienen la calefacción. El único método para pagar el boleto es comprar la tarjeta MetroCard en las estaciones del subterranéo en efectivo o con tarjeta de credito. El precio de la MetroCard es $2.00. Hay también tres otras opciones de las tarjetas
Metrocard :

La tarjeta ilimitada por un día cuesta $ 7
La tarjeta ilimitada por una semana cuesta: $ 21
La tarjeta ilimitada por 30 días cuesta: $ 70

Se pueden usar estas tarjetas ilimitadas tanto en subterráneos como en buses todas las veces que usted quiera.

13. In this article, one learns ...

 1. about the history of the subway system
 2. how to identify the various subway lines
 3. how to pay for a MetroCard
 4. what to do in an emergency situation

14. Which statement is **false** according to the article?

 1. The trains have air conditioning
 2. One can only buy a Metrocard with cash
 3. A Metrocard for 7 days costs $21.
 4. An unlimited Metrocard can be used on both the subway and the buses

Part 3b Directions: Answer the question in Spanish based on the reading selection in Spanish. Choose the best answer to each question. Base your choice on the content of the reading selection. Write the number of your answer in the appropriate space on your answer sheet. (12%)

ESTACION DE FERROCARRIL

LLEGADAS

hora	vía	
11:30	7	BARCELONA
11:45	8	LEON
11:55	10	CORDOBA
12:05	6	VALENCIA
12:40	4	MALAGA
13:15	6	LISBOA

SALIDAS

hora	vía	
11:40	6	GRANADA
12:00	7	PARIS
13:00	6	SALAMANCA
13:30	5	MURCIA
14:39	9	TOLEDO
14:05	6	AMSTERDAM

15. ¿A qué hora llega el tren de León?

 1. a la una y cuarto de la tarde
 2. a las dos y cuarto
 3. a las once y cuarenta y cinco de la mañana
 4. a las once y cincuenta y cinco

16. ¿Adónde va el tren a mediodía?
 1. a Paris
 2. a Salamanca
 3. a Valencia
 4. a Lisboa

AEROLINEAS MOCTEZUMA	Tarjeta de embarque 7B5649Z
NOMBRE ***VARGAS FRANCISCO***	VUELO ***670***
DE ***VERACRUZ*** . A ***TIA JUANA*** .	
ASIENTO ***12E*** PUERTA ***7*** HORA ***16:30***	
FECHA ***EL 3 DE MARZO*** CLASE ***PRIMERA***	

17. ¿Qué es?

1. un pasaporte
2. una tarjeta de embarque
3. una sala de espera
4. un agente de viajes

18. ¿Cómo se llama el pasajero?

1. Moctezuma
2. Veracruz
3. Juana
4. Vargas

PART 4 WRITING (30%)

Part 4 Directions: Choose two of the three writing tasks provided below. Your answer to each of the two questions should be written entirely in Spanish and should contain a minimum of **30 words**.

Place names and brand names written in Spanish count as one word. Contractions are counted as one word. Salutations, closings and commonly used abbreviations are included in the word count. Numbers, unless written as words, and names of people do not count as words.

Be sure that you have satisfied the purpose of the task. The sentence structure and /or expressions used should be connected logically and demonstrate a wide range of vocabulary with minimal repetition.

4a. An organization to which you belong is sponsoring a trip. You have been asked to write as description for a flyer. In your description you may wish to include::

- The name of the organization (e.g. the Scouts, the "Y") which is sponsoring the trip.
- To where your organization is going
- What means of transportation will be used
- How long this trip will be
- What will be the cost of the trip and what the price will include
- What will be done on this trip

4b. Your school is sending you to an International Youth Conference to a Spanish-speaking country. You are making arrangements by e-mail with a limousine service to pick you up at the airport. In your message you may wish to include:

- Your name
- The date and time of your arrival
- The name of the airline and the flight number
- A brief physical description of yourself
- A description of what you will be wearing
- Whether you will be alone or with someone
- Where you want the limousine service to bring you

4c. During a recent trip to another country, you used the public transportation system in a large city. Unfortunately you left an item on the vehicle. You are required to write a letter to the Lost and Found Office. In your letter you may wish to include:

- The means of transportation you were using when you lost the item
- Where you boarded this vehicle and where you got off
- The time of day you were on this vehicle
- What item you lost
- A description of this item

TRAVEL 3

Nombre y Apellido ______________________________ Fecha _____________

Part I **Speaking** __________ (30%)

Part 2 **Listening (30%)**

2a.	2b.	2c.
1._____	4._____	7._____
2._____	5._____	8._____
3._____	6._____	9._____
		10._____

PART 3: READING (20%)

3a.(8%)	3b.(12%)
11._____	15._____
12._____	16._____
13._____	17._____
14._____	18._____

Part 4 **Writing (20%) 20 words** **Write 2 paragraphs** **4a , 4b or 4c**

1____

2____